# MUIRHEAD LIBRARY OF PHILOSOPHY

AN admirable statement of the aims of the Library of Philosophy was provided by the first editor, the late Professor J. H. Muirhead, in his description of the original programme printed in Erdmann's *History of Philosophy* under the date 1890. This was slightly modified in subsequent volumes to take the form of the following statement:

'The Muirhead Library of Philosophy was designed as a contribution to the History of Modern Philosophy under the heads: first of Different Schools of Thought—Sensationalist, Realist, Idealist, Intuitivist; secondly of different Subjects—Psychology, Ethics, Political Philosophy, Theology. While much had been done in England in tracing the course of evolution in nature, history, economics, morals and religion, little had been done in tracing the development of thought on these subjects. Yet "the evolution of opinion is part of the whole evolution".

'By the co-operation of different writers in carrying out this plan it was hoped that a thoroughness and completeness of treatment, otherwise unattainable, might be secured. It was believed also that from writers mainly British and American fuller consideration of English Philosophy than it had hitherto received might be looked for. In the earlier series of books containing, among others, Bosanquet's *History of Aesthetic*, Pfleiderer's *Rational Theology since Kant*, Albee's *History of English Utilitarianism*, Bonar's *Philosophy and Political Economy*, Brett's *History of Psychology*, Ritchie's *Natural Rights*, these objects were to a large extent effected.

'In the meantime original work of a high order was being produced both in England and America by such writers as Bradley, Stout, Bertrand Russell, Baldwin, Urban, Montague, and others, and a new interest in foreign works, German, French and Italian, which had either become classical or were attracting public attention, had developed. The scope of the Library thus became extended into something more international, and it is entering on the fifth decade of its existence in the hope that it may contribute to that mutual understanding between countries which is so pressing a need of the present time.'

The need which Professor Muirhead stressed is no less pressing to-day, and few will deny that philosophy has much to do with enabling us to meet it, although no one, least of all Muirhead himself, would regard that as the sole, or even the main, object of philosophy. As

Professor Muirhead continues to lend the distinction of his name to the Library of Philosophy it seemed not inappropriate to allow him to recall us to these aims in his own words. The emphasis on the history of thought also seemed to me very timely; and the number of important works promised for the Library in the very near future augur well for the continued fulfilment, in this and other ways, of the expectations of the original editor.

H. D. LEWIS

# MUIRHEAD LIBRARY OF PHILOSOPHY

## General Editor: H. D. Lewis

*Professor of History and Philosophy of Religion in the University of London*

*The Analysis of Mind* by BERTRAND RUSSELL 8th impression
*Clarity is Not Enough* by H. D. LEWIS
*Coleridge as Philosopher* by J. H. MUIRHEAD 3rd impression
*The Commonplace Book of G. E. Moore* edited by C. LEWY
*Contemporary American Philosophy* edited by G. P. ADAMS and W. P. MONTAGUE 2nd impression
*Contemporary British Philosophy* First and second series edited by J. H. MUIRHEAD 2nd impression
*Contemporary British Philosophy* third series edited by H. D. LEWIS 2nd impression
*Contemporary Indian Philosophy* edited by RADHAKRISHNAN and J. H. MUIRHEAD 2nd edition
*Ethics* by NICOLAI HARTMANN translated by STANTON COIT 3 vols
*Freedom and History* by H. D. LEWIS
*The Good Will: A Study in the Coherence Theory of Goodness* by H. J. PATON
*Hegel: A Re-Examination* by J. N. FINDLAY
*Hegel's Science of Logic* translated by W. H. JOHNSTON and L. G. STRUTHERS 2 vols 3rd impression
*History of Æsthetic* by B. BOSANQUET 2nd edition 5th impression .
*History of English Utilitarianism* by E. ALBEE 2nd impression
*History of Psychology* by G. S. BRETT edited by R. S. PETERS abridged one-volume edition 2nd edition
*Human Knowledge* by BERTRAND RUSSELL 4th impression
*A Hundred Years of British Philosophy* by RUDOLF METZ translated by J. H. HARVEY, T. E. JESSOP, HENRY STURT 2nd impression
*Ideas: A General Introduction to Pure Phenomenology* by EDMUND HUSSERL translated by W. R. BOYCE GIBSON 3rd impression
*Imagination* by E. J. FURLONG
*Indian Philosophy* by RADHAKRISHNAN 2 vols revised 2nd edition
*Introduction to Mathematical Philosophy* by BERTRAND RUSSELL 2nd edition 10th impression
*Kant's First Critique* by H. W. CASSIRER
*Kant's Metaphysic of Experience* by H. J. PATON 3rd impression
*Know Thyself* by BERNADINO VARISCO translated by GUGLIELMO SALVADORI
*Language and Reality* by WILBUR MARSHALL URBAN 3rd impression
*Matter and Memory* by HENRI BERGSON translated by N. M. PAUL and W. S. PALMER 7th impression
*The Modern Predicament* by H. J. PATON 3rd impression
*Natural Rights* by D. G. RITCHIE 3rd edition 5th impression

𝔐uirhead 𝔏ibrary of ℙhilosophy
EDITED BY H. D. LEWIS

# PHILOSOPHY AND RELIGION

AXEL HÄGERSTRÖM

# PHILOSOPHY
# AND
# RELIGION

BY

AXEL HÄGERSTRÖM

TRANSLATED BY

ROBERT T. SANDIN

LONDON: GEORGE ALLEN & UNWIN LTD

PRINTED IN GREAT BRITAIN
*in 11 on 12 point Imprint type*
BY UNWIN BROTHERS LIMITED
WOKING AND LONDON

# TRANSLATOR'S PREFACE

In the recent history of Swedish philosophy, two movements were original enough to be regarded as distinctively Swedish. One of these was Boströmianism, that form of personal idealism which dominated Swedish thought in the latter half of the nineteenth century, much as Hegelianism dominated German thought. The other was the so-called Uppsala philosophy, which represented a reaction against Boströmian idealism and, indeed, against all forms of metaphysics.

It may be accepted that the founder of the Uppsala school was Axel Hägerström (1868–1939), although the development of the distinctive ideas of the movement was the composite achievement of a number of extremely capable philosophers, not the least of whom was Adolf Phalén (1884–1931). The present volume makes some of Hägerström's most important writings available to English readers. At the same time, because of Hägerström's influence, it should contribute to an increased awareness of the nature of Swedish philosophical reflection in the twentieth century.

The essay, *A Summary of My Philosophy*, was published in 1929 in the series *Die Philosophie der Gegenwart in Selbstdarstellung*, Leipzig, Felix Meiner (Vol. 7). *On the Truth of Moral Propositions* was Hägerström's inaugural lecture as professor of practical philosophy at Uppsala University in 1911 (published as *Om moraliska föreställningars sanning*, Stockholm, Bonnier, 1911). The essay entitled *On the Idea of Duty* is a selection from a larger work, *Till frågan om den gällande rättens begrepp. I*, Uppsala, Almqvist and Wiksell, 1917, This essay was translated by Prof. C. D. Broad and was published in the volume, *Inquiries into the Nature of Law and Morals*, Uppsala, Almqvist and Wiksell, 1953. This treatment of the idea of duty (pp. 116–201 in the English volume) is re-printed here (in Prof. Broad's translation) because of its fundamental importance in Hägerström's moral philosophy.

The essays on religion were originally lectures prepared and delivered by Hägerström at Uppsala. They are among the papers edited and published after Hägerström's death in the volume, *Religionsfilosofi*, Stockholm, Natur och Kultur, 1949. The editor, Dr. Martin Fries, has also prepared a large number of other previously unpublished manuscripts for posthumous publication and has thus made a tremendous contribution to the study of Hägerström. The essay *Metaphysical Religiosity* was a series of lectures delivered in 1923. The *Lectures on So-called Spiritual Religion* were delivered in 1926. An English translation by Prof. Broad appeared in *Theoria*, Vol. 14, 1948, pp. 28–67, although the translator was not identified. I have prepared an entirely new translation for this volume. The essay on *The Truth-value of Christian Dogmatics* is selected from a large manuscript which Fries has entitled *Vår tids religiösa problem* (*The Religious Problem of Our Time*). The lectures were delivered in 1920 and in a somewhat different form in 1929. The portion translated here is taken from *Religionsfilosofi*, pp. 154–168, 219–250.

My translation has been approved and authorized by the Hägerström committee, two of whose members, Dr. Martin Fries and Prof. Bjorn Collinder, closely examined the entire manuscript, comparing it with the original. To them I owe an immense debt of gratitude. Thanks also are due to the third member of the committee, Prof. Karl Olivecrona, for kind encouragement and advice. Prof. H. D. Lewis, the editor of the Muirhead Library of Philosophy, helped immeasurably with his encouragement and his close scrutiny of the manuscript. He offered a number of suggestions which greatly improved the translation. Prof. Burnham Terrell and Mr. John Trentman, both of the University of Minnesota, did me the service of comparing parts of the translation with the original. They also helped me correct certain errors.

Despite this excellent assitance, I am sure that the translation still has its limitations. Readers who know the difficulty of Hägerström's style no doubt will be understanding. Even the best translation of Hägerström's works would place unusual demands on the reader. I hope, however, that my translation is adequate to the demands of the careful study which Hägerström's thought deserves.

I wish to thank Prof. C. D. Broad and the *Kungliga humanistiska vetenskapssamfundet i Uppsala* for their permission to re-publish the selection from *Inquiries into the Nature of Law and Morals*. The reader will add his thanks to Prof. Broad for the delightful introduction he has prepared for this volume.

ROBERT T. SANDIN

# CONTENTS

# CONTENTS

# MEMOIR OF AXEL HÄGERSTRÖM

## C. D. BROAD

Axel Anders Hägerström was born in 1868 at the parsonage of Vireda, near Jönköping, in the province of Småland, and died in 1939 (shortly before the outbreak of the Second World War) in Uppsala. A most interesting, and in places very moving, book of reminiscences, based largely on family letters, has been written by the younger of his two daughters, Mrs. Margit Waller, and was published in 1961 by the firm *Natur och Kultur*, under the title *Axel Hägerström, människan som få kände* ('Axel Hägerström, the man whom few knew'). In what follows I am immensely indebted to that book.

Hägerström's paternal ancestry had been clerical for several generations back. His father, Karl Frederik Theodor (1834–1906) was pastor in the Swedish state-church, first in Vireda, and later in Örberga, near Vadstena in the province of Östergötland. His paternal grandfather, Carl Peter (1798–1863) had been pastor in Östra Tollstad in the see of Linköping. Both of them had been students at Uppsala university. Hägerström's father married twice, and Axel Anders was the first child of the second marriage. The first wife died in 1865, shortly after the birth of her second child. The two children of the first marriage, Reinhold (b. 1863) and Gustaf (b. 1865), were treated by the second wife as her own children. Axel in his earlier years was intimate with and much influenced by his two slightly older half-brothers, of whom Reinhold became postmaster at Åtvidaberg in Östergötland, and Gustaf a lawyer in Jönköping.

Hägerström's mother, Augusta Maria Skarin (1840–1933), was the second of the children of Johan Skarin (1804–1864) and Charlotte Björk (1814–1903). The Björks were originally Swedish Finlanders, and Charlotte, Hägerström's maternal grandmother, was born in Finland. Her elder sisters, Marie and Emilie, were in their later days landowners, living on their estate of Spexhult, near Nässjö in Småland. Johan Skarin, Hägerström's maternal grandfather, had been *kronofogde*, an office, which no longer exists, concerned with the collection of taxes and crown-dues in an administrative district.

Karl Frederik Theodor Hägerström and Augusta Maria Skarin

had four more children in the ten years after Axel's birth: a son who died in infancy, then two daughters Emilia and Bertha, and finally a son David. So the family in which Axel grew up consisted of two slightly older half-brothers, two slightly younger sisters, and a brother younger by just ten years. Axel's home life, for his first twelve years at his father's parsonage at Vireda and thereafter in that of Örberga, was that of a typical Swedish 'son of the manse' at that period. For the parents it was a life of strenuous parochial duty, with much practical beneficence to the poor on an income which, with care and self-denial, provided a decent sufficiency but permitted of few, if any, luxuries. For the children it was one of strict discipline and unquestioning obedience in things temporal and spiritual; but tempered by parental affection, and with many opportunities for meeting neighbours and for acquiring health and hardihood by running, swimming, skating, etc., in beautiful rural surroundings.

Both Axel's parents were in their several ways striking personalities, and each had a profound influence on him. The father was an orthodox 'church-and-state' Lutheran, with no great interest in theological theory, but an unquestioning faith in the dogmas which he had been taught in early life. They included, as a prominent ingredient, the doctrine of hell-fire and of the eternal damnation of the impenitent sinner; and he was wont to enlarge on this theme in his sermons, and no doubt in the home. This aspect of Christian doctrine made a deep impression on Axel. One day, in his early childhood, as he sat with his mother beside the fireplace, he thrust his hand into the flames, in order to experience for a brief moment in this life a foretaste of what he might have to bear unendingly in the life to come. Luckily, his hand, though painfully burned, was not permanently injured.

Axel's mother was a deeply religious woman of a very different school. While living with her mother's sisters, Marie and Emilie Björk at Spexhult, she had come under the influence of an evangelical revivalist movement in the Swedish church, originating in the work of Carl Olof Rosenius, which laid great stress on conviction of sin, experience of conversion, and thereafter a confident trust in ultimate salvation through Christ. Christianity was for her a deep and abiding personal experience, which she evoked and sustained in her children, and particularly in Axel and his elder half-brother Reinhold.

Another member of the family who had much to do with Axel in his childhood and early manhood was his maternal grandmother, Charlotte Skarin (*née* Björk), a cultivated and spirited old lady who died in 1903 at the age of eighty-nine. She took up her abode in the Hägerströms' parsonage at Örberga when Axel was twenty years old and spent her last fifteen years there. But she had already begun to play an important part in his life considerably earlier. When he first left home at the age of eleven, to attend the high-school for boys at Jönköping, she was living in that town. Axel, together with his two half-brothers, lodged and boarded with her during term-time, and she mothered the young boy. Later, when she moved from Jönköping, Axel lodged with other elderly ladies who eked out their incomes by taking in high-school boys as paying-guests.

Axel was at school in Jönköping from 1879 to 1886. He was a boy of outstanding ability, he worked hard, and he gained a very thorough knowledge of Latin, Greek, and mathematics. He had set his mind on taking the 'student-examination' in 1885 at the age of seventeen, a year before the usual age. He had made all preparations for doing so, and there is no doubt that he would have succeeded, if he had sat for the examination. The story of how he came to give up this cherished ambition at the last moment is a moving one, and it throws great light on his character and on his state of mind at the time. It is told in contemporary letters to his half-brother Gustaf, then a student at Uppsala, and to his home. The essential facts are as follows.

Evangelical revivalism was very strongly represented in Jönköping in those days, and a prominent clergyman in the town, J. A. E. Sundelin, was its most notable clerical representative. He was a man of genuine piety, a most powerful and moving preacher, and he was in close touch with the High School in the capacity of its '*Inspektor*'. The Hägerström boys came from home with the seeds of Christian devotion already sown and nurtured by their mother, and, under Sundelin's influence, an intense and anxious evangelical piety grew up in Axel and in Reinhold, the elder of his two half-brothers. Reinhold, who had by then taken his 'student-examination' and left Jönköping, knew of Axel's intention to enter, a year before the normal age, for that examination. He disapproved on moral and religious grounds, holding that Axel was moved by un-Christian motives of personal ambition and desire to show off his intellectual superiority. He wrote to his half-brother a strongly dissuasive letter, in which evidently there was no lack of plain speaking, and Axel received this just as he was about to make the final arrangements for entering for the examination.

Axel had set his heart on this; and, whether or not the personal ambition and the desire to figure as a youthful prodigy were sinful, these had certainly been among his strongest motives. He passed rapidly through a strong emotional crisis, in which very natural feelings of rebellious obstinacy and of anger with Reinhold were at first predominant. He managed to repress these initial reactions and to give himself time for reflection and self-examination. As a result he had to admit Reinhold's account of his motives, to agree that these should find no place in the heart of a converted Christian, to write to Reinhold without rancour, and (though with bitter disappointment) to forgo a project for which he had been preparing himself with intense application and in which he would almost certainly have been successful.

The ground-swell left by this emotional storm is very visible in the moving letter which Axel wrote at the end of March 1885 to his other half-brother, Gustaf, in Uppsala. He eventually took the examination, with complete success, at the then usual age of eighteen in May 1886. In the autumn of that year he entered Uppsala University as a freshman, becoming, like his father and his paternal grandfather, a member of Östgöta Nation. Gustaf was by then in his second year at Uppsala, studying law.

At that time Axel fully intended to study theology and to follow his father and his forefathers as a clergyman of the state-church. He had a taste for preaching, and he had already 'wagged his pow' in the paternal pulpit at Örberga in the vacation during the absence of the curate through illness. His parents took for granted that he would become a clergyman. In May 1887 he took and passed the so-called 'theologico-philosophical' examination, which was a necessary preliminary to admission to the theological faculty. His teacher in philosophy for this was Erik Olof Burman, at that time docent in Uppsala in what the Swedes call 'theoretical philosophy', and later professor there in what they call 'practical' (and we should call 'moral') philosophy.

Axel quickly became passionately interested in philosophy, and by the middle of 1887 had decided that he could not be a theologian and would not be a clergyman. He wrote to his father, accordingly, a very frank and firm, though respectful and affectionate, letter. He states in it that he does not doubt Christianity; but he dislikes dogmatic theology, and he is not willing to take upon himself that function of *public representative* of Christian belief and practice which is an essential part of a clergyman's office.

This must have been an extremely hard decision to make, to announce, and to maintain. He knew that it would bitterly disappoint both his parents, whom he loved and respected, and who had made and were making considerable sacrifices for him and their other children. And both he and they were well aware that it must defer for years, and perhaps for ever, the attainment of a decently remunerated position in life. A painful situation arose, but Axel was adamant once he had made up his mind on what he ought to do. He felt that it was best for all parties that he should for a time not return home during the vacations. His mother fairly soon became reconciled to her son's choice, but it was not until Axel had taken his doctorate in philosophy that his father fully acquiesced in it.

Meanwhile Hägerström worked assiduously at philosophy. He passed his Fil. Kand. examination in December 1888, and on September 6, 1893, he was awarded his doctorate on a thesis on Aristotle's basic ethical concepts and their theoretical presuppositions. Shortly afterwards, at the express wish of C. Y. Sahlin, the then professor of practical philosophy in Uppsala, who had been one of his teachers and also one of his examiners, he was made docent in that subject. That carried no salary with it; but it gave him a certain academic status, entitled him to give lectures, and helped him to obtain private pupils.

Such coaching work was Hägerström's main source of livelihood at the time and for the next twenty-five years. He had had considerable teaching experience from very early in life. It began in his schooldays in Jönköping with informal and unpaid help to certain other boys in his then favourite subject of mathematics. During school holidays and university vacations he had on several occasions acted as resident tutor to the children of some of his maternal relatives who lived in the country. There are several accounts by distinguished former Uppsala students of their experiences with him as a coach in philosophy. From all these it is plain that he was a most stimulating, illuminating, and conscientious teacher, who took infinite pains with his pupils and evoked a corresponding effort in many of them. He was very shy at that period, and it is recorded that the tuitions would be conducted with Hägerström in an inner room, out of sight of his class in the adjoining room, communication being made between the two through the half-open door.

His own philosophical work had to be carried on in the vacations and in those times of the day or night in term-time not occupied by actual teaching or by his most conscientious preparations for it. He plainly overworked himself continuously for many years, taking the very minimum of sleep and of food, and living a most ascetic life. His only two indulgences were strong coffee and his pipe. He was a man of strong feeling, by nature readily aroused to anger by opposition, and he took himself, human life in general, and philosophy in particular with deadly earnestness. Life, under the conditions in which he was living in Uppsala, imposed great strains on him, and he must have exerted an iron discipline on himself. A rather serious crisis was developing throughout 1895 and culminated and subsided during 1896. The circumstances were as follows.

In 1895 the professorship of practical philosophy in Uppsala fell vacant through Sahlin's retirement. Hägerström decided to apply, and set to work to write two elaborate dissertations to submit to the experts who had been appointed to report on the qualifications of the candidates. One dissertation was an investigation of the possibility of an empiricist ethics, with special reference to the main contemporary forms of that doctrine. The other (which was a continuation of this) was on the notion, as occurring in the main contemporary forms of idealism, of moral feelings and impulses as rational. Hägerström, at the early age of twenty-eight and with Burman as a competitor, had no expectation of being the successful candidate. But the Swedish system of selection (which, whatever may be its merits, seems to an Englishman, accustomed to a very different system, to be ideally fitted to produce those heart-burnings and those unedifying public *post mortem* squabbles which it not infrequently does) includes the following feature among its other peculiarities. The board of experts appointed to review the claims of the rival candidates for a chair are expected, not only to recommend the one whom they think on the whole most suitable, but also to declare publicly which of the others they consider to be 'competent' and which 'incompetent' for the office. Naturally, it is gratifying and useful to an unsuccessful candidate to be declared 'competent', and proportionately humiliating and detrimental to be declared 'incompetent' to hold the chair for which he has been applying.

Hägerström had hoped that his two dissertations would secure for him a public pronouncement of 'competence', in this technical sense, which would set the seal of expert approval on his philosophical work and might stand him in good stead in future applications for vacant professorships. But on January 1, 1896, he was privately advised to withdraw his candidature, because the committee of experts intended to declare him 'incompetent', if he should proceed with it. This advice he firmly refused to take; and early in March 1896 the committee made their public announcement, recommending Burman as successor to Sahlin and declaring Hägerström 'incompetent', in the technical sense.

The experts consisted of the retiring professor Sahlin, P. J. L. Leander (professor of practical philosophy in Lund), and Reinhold Geijer (professor of theoretical philosophy in Uppsala). None of them were unfriendly to, or unappreciative of, Hägerström. Indeed, it will be remembered that it had been on Sahlin's personal recommendation that Hägerström had been appointed docent soon after taking his doctor's degree. The only one of them who went into considerable detail in criticism of Hägerström's two dissertations was Leander. All recognized his philosophical ability and learning, but they were uncertain as to whether it would develop on what they regarded as sound lines.

As the background of all this was the fact that there was a certain system of philosophy which had for years been predominant in Swedish academic circles and had become a kind of accepted orthodoxy. This was the form of idealism developed by C. J. Boström, Sahlin's immediate predecessor in the chair of practical philosophy in Uppsala. This atmosphere of Boströmian orthodoxy seems to have been as pervasive in Sweden, and in the end as deadening, as the Absolute Idealism which was academically predominant in British and American universities at much the same period. Hägerström had already begun to react against it, and the three experts no doubt regarded him (much as Bosanquet might have regarded Moore and Russell when they first began to write) as a clever and promising but uppish young man, who needed a rap on the knuckles to keep him in his place.

Hägerström was furiously angry. As his contemporary letters to his parents and his fiancée show, he was for a while in that dangerous emotional state where wounded self-esteem and a high-minded desire to vindicate a general principle mingle, in unknowable proportions, to make one desire to hit out in public, and where (to quote from *The Importance of being Earnest*) 'plain speaking ceases to be a duty and becomes a positive pleasure'. He seriously contemplated publishing an attack on the 'competence' of those who had pronounced him 'incompetent'; a course of action which would hardly have been decent, and would certainly have been extremely detrimental to all hopes of future academic preferment.

Most fortunately, he had no officious friends to aggravate the situation by rushing into print in the newspapers with attacks on the experts and the successful candidate—a by no means unknown sequel to professorial appointments in Sweden. He was fundamentally a wise, though passionate, man; accustomed to self-examination and capable of rigid self-control. His personal resentment gradually subsided, and he set about writing a purely impersonal reply to the detailed criticisms which Leander had published on his two theses. This was in print by the end of May 1896; but he delayed publication until the July of the following year, when it appeared as a pamphlet, the Swedish title of which may be translated: 'On Empirical Ethics and Moral Feeling—Answer to Criticisms'.

During this difficult period Hägerström was in frequent correspondence with the lady who later became his wife, and her understanding and loyalty must have been a great source of strength and consolation to him. She was Esther Nyander (1872–1957), daughter of a clergyman who was a contemporary and a friend of long standing of Hägerström's father. Axel had first met her in 1892, when he was at home, and she, with her parents and her younger brother, was on a visit there. Her father, Nils Johan Nyander (1840–1929) had been since 1889 vicar of Östra Harg, a parish in Östergötland. Like his friend, Axel's father, he was a churchman of the authoritative and active, rather than the meditative or devotional, kind. The Nyanders were better endowed than the Hägerströms with this world's goods. Nils Johan had married Anna Sophia Rehnström, daughter and sole heiress of a landed proprietor of Sjutorp in Småland. The shrewdness with which he managed his worldly affairs, combined with the devotion with which he performed his priestly and parochial duties, furnish one more illustration of the truth of Samuel Butler's commentary on the text *You cannot serve God and Mammon:*—'It's difficult, no doubt; but so is everything that's worth doing'.

Esther paid a second visit to the parsonage at Örberga in the summer of 1894, and Axel and she came to know each other well. They parted with an understanding that they would marry, if and when Axel's circumstances should permit; but there was no formal engagement. In January 1896, at the height of the crisis about the declaration of 'incompetence', Axel wrote a most moving letter to Esther, stating his position and his irrevocable intention of replying publicly to the criticisms of the experts. He pointed out the probable economic consequences of such action, and gave her the choice of release from her tacit engagement to him. Esther then, as always, 'behaved like a brick'. She decided, on the day on which she received this letter, to stick to Axel through thick and thin, and she at once wrote to him accordingly.

In June 1896, at Esther's suggestion, the engagement was publicly announced. It had the full approval of the parents of both parties. The Hägerströms had already come to regard Esther as a daughter; and the Nyanders, whilst aware that Axel had his angularities and that his worldly prospects were not of the brightest, liked and respected him and knew that he was the right man for Esther.

By April 1899 Hägerström's financial circumstances had so far improved that he was able to announce to Esther that he had rented a small house, with three rooms and a kitchen at 450 kr. *per annum* (equivalent to about £22 10s 0d) at the then value of the £.

He thought this dear. Their wedding took place, with considerable rural pomp and ceremony, in Östra Harg church on June 28th; and the honeymoon was spent at Sjutorp, which had now come into possession of Esther's mother. They returned to Uppsala, and took up residence at this house (No. 6, *Skolgatan*). Early in 1900 Hägerström was allotted a stipend of 1500 kr. *per annum* as docent, and he had already in 1897 been awarded 500 kr. *per annum* out of an endowment administered by the university. So he now had the equivalent of about £100 a year, in the currency of those days, over and above what he could earn by coaching. Two years later the Hägerström's moved to a larger house, No. 12, *Trädgårdsgatan*, which was to be their home for the next twenty-two years.

It was an extremely happy marriage, in which the storm-tossed spirit of Hägerström found understanding and a measure of tranquillity. He and his wife had two children, both daughters. The younger of them, Margit, who became Mrs. Waller, relates an amusing story of a professor of theology in Uppsala, who, whilst heartily disapproving of Hägerström's subversive theories of the nature of legal and of moral obligation and of theology, felt obliged in justice to concede: 'and yet, for all that, he is said to be kind to his wife and children!'

During his engagement and the first years of his married life Hägerström had been working on a critical and historical account of Kant's ethics. This occupied him for five years. It appeared in 1902. Like some others of his major works, it was in German, which of course secured for it a much wider circle of instructed readers than it would have had if written in Swedish. Hägerström lacked the gift of compression, and this work occupies 850 printed pages. The aim of it is to provide and to justify a version of Kant's ethical doctrines which shall be free from what Hägerström regarded as Boströmian misinterpretations current in Sweden.

He now began to occupy himself with what was to be one of the main tasks of his life, viz. the philosophy of law. In 1904 a vacancy occurred in the chair of practical philosophy at Lund. Hägerström applied for it, and submitted an essay on this topic entitled *Stat och rätt* ('State and Law'). It was highly commended by the appointed experts, both of whom were philosophical jurists; but the chair was eventually given to E. Liljeqvist, a Boströmian. Hägerström took this with equanimity. He was happy in Uppsala, and was beginning to be generally recognized there as an original and seminal thinker and teacher.

Burman, the successor to Sahlin in the chair of practical philosphy at Uppsala, suffered from frequent spells of serious ill-health, and Hägerström acted as his deputy when he was thus in-capacitated. The first occasion was in 1903-4. When Burman finally retired in 1910 Hägerström had deputized for him for an aggregate period of eleven terms. He had thus become, *caeteris paribus*, the obvious successor to Burman. He had, moreover, greatly strengthened his claims to the chair of practical philosophy by courses of lectures which he had been giving. These were at once topical in their subject-matter, and completely objective in their treatment of it.

The period was one of great political and social ferment in Sweden. In 1905, after years of growing tension which very nearly culminated in a fratricidal war, Norway broke away from the union with Sweden, which had been imposed under the Treaty of Kiel in 1814 as a reward to Bernadotte and as a consolation to Sweden for the loss of Finland to Russia under the Treaty of Frederikshamn five years earlier. In 1909 there occurred a long and bitter general strike in Sweden. Many who were to be the founders of the present highly successful Swedish 'welfare state' were then young and enthusiastic adherents of socialism in general and of Marxian theories in particular.

Hägerström viewed all this with understanding and with sympathy, but with a philosophic desire to analyse, to explain, and to 'know the causes of things', rather than to admonish or to take part in political controversy. In 1907 he gave a course of lectures in the university on 'The Driving Forces of the Social Movement', and in 1908–1909 he was lecturing on the history of socialistic ideas. The substance of the former course was published in 1909 under the title *Social teleologi i marxism*. The lectures in the latter course were first published posthumously in 1946. One can well imagine the interest, and the lively discussion among intelligent students, which these courses aroused at the time.

In November 1910, when it was known that Burman would be retiring, Geijer, his colleague in the chair of theoretical philosophy at Uppsala, proposed that Hägerström should be *invited* to succeed Burman. It will be remembered that Geijer had been one of the experts who had declared Hägerström 'incompetent' for the chair in 1896. So this action was not only a high compliment to Hägerström, but also a graceful burial of a now rusty hatchet. The question was referred to three experts, Geijer himself, Burman (the retiring professor), and Vitalis Norström (professor in Göteborg). They advised unanimously that Hägerström should be invited. He was installed on March 18, 1911. His inaugural lecture, *Om moraliska föreställningars sanning* ('On the Truth of Moral Ideas'), insisted on the point (which may seem obvious here and now, but was far from generally accepted there and then) that the business of moral philosophy is not to decide *what* is right or *what* is wrong, still less to admonish us to do the former and eschew the latter, but is to *analyse* the notions of 'right' and 'wrong', 'morally good' and 'morally evil', and to ascertain the functions which they fulfil in human life.

Hägerström held the professorship from 1911 until his retirement in 1933 on reaching the pensionable age of sixty-five. These were years of intensely hard work in reading, thinking, writing, and teaching, and of ever-growing influence in philosophy and in jurisprudence in Sweden and the other Scandinavian lands. He was making an extremely thorough study of the history of Roman legal institutions and of their social and religious background, and was immersing himself in the vast literature, particularly in German, written by jurists and philosophers of law, on the concepts and principles of legal obligation. Outstanding products of this study, and of his reflexions upon it, were the following famous and highly influential published papers:— (1) *Är gällande rätt uttrych av vilja?* ('Is Positive Law an Expression of Will?'), which appeared in 1916 in a *Festschrift* for Vitalis Norström; (2) *Till frågan om den objektiva rättens begrepp* ('On the Question of the Nation of Objective Right'), published in 1917; and (3) *Das magistratische Ius*, written in German and published in 1929 in a *Festschrift* issued by the Law Faculty of Uppsala in celebration of the 300th anniversary of its first doctor's promotion.

All this while Hägerström was at work on his immense treatise (in German) entitled *Der römische Obligationsbegriff im Lichte der allgemeinen römischen Rechtsanschauung*. The first volume of this appeared in 1927. It seems, like Hume's *Treatise on Human Nature*, to have 'fallen still-born from the press'; though presumably with a heavier bump, since it runs to some 630 pages of close print. The second part, on which Hägerström continued to work for the rest of his life, was published posthumously in 1941. It is no less voluminous.

The immense influence which Hägerström has had on legal philosophy (and perhaps on legal practice) in Scandinavia has been exerted at least as much indirectly, through the outstanding converts whom he made and pupils whom he trained, as directly through his published writings. To confine oneself to those no longer living, one may mention Professor Vilhelm Lundstedt (1882–1955). Lundstedt had had a distinguished academic career in jurisprudence at his own university of Lund, when in 1914 he became professor in Uppsala in Roman and Civil Law. He was not at that time specially sympathetic to Hägerström's views. The two men were introduced to each other by Arthur Engberg, a friend and former pupil of Hägerström's. They became firm friends, and in course of time Hägerström converted Lundstedt to his own views on the nature of law and of obligation. Lundstedt was a stimulating teacher, and a fertile and influential writer, and he did much to spread Hägerström's ideas among those who were to become prominent either as academic or as practising lawyers in Sweden. Shortly before his own death Lundstedt held a public lecture in Uppsala on Jurisprudence as a science, and in this he paid an eloquent tribute to Hägerström and his influence.

Another distinguished Swedish thinker, no longer living, who was greatly influenced by Hägerström (more especially by the latter's epistemological doctrines) was Adolf Phalén. He became Professor of Theoretical Philosophy in Uppsala in 1916 at the early age of thirty-two, and he died, still a comparatively young man, in 1931, leaving a deep impression on his contemporaries and his juniors.

As Hägerström's circumstances grew easier, and as recognition of himself and his work steadily spread, the inner tension in him relaxed. He mellowed, and became more 'human' and approachable in his relations with those outside the circle of his family, his intimate friends, and his pupils. As a young man he had been too poor, too shy, and too much engrossed in his work to take any part in the social life of Östgöta Nation. At the age of 57, however, he was invited to become its 'Inspektor', and he accepted. A Nation in Uppsala always has as its honorary chief officer one of its members who is a highly distinguished senior member of the university, generally (perhaps always) an eminent professor. He is entitled 'Inspektor', and, once appointed, he holds office continuously for a considerable period; whilst the elected officers, of whom the chief is 'First Kurator', being students, come and go.

Hägerström was Inspektor of Östgöta Nation for eight years on end. It is needless to say that he performed the administrative duties of his office efficiently and conscientiously. What is of more interest is that he entered into, and came thoroughly to enjoy, the social and festive life of the Nation; made excellent and witty speeches on appropriate occasions; and became highly popular with members of all ages. In this connection he once said of himself: 'I was old when I was young, so I may take leave to be young now that I am growing old'. A very interesting portrait in oils of Hägerström at the age of sixty, painted by another Östgöte, David Wallin, was presented to the Nation and unveiled at a dinner in 1929. It now hangs, along with the portraits of many other famous members of Östgöta Nation, in their nation-house at Uppsala.

After his retirement in 1933 Hägerström had a further six years of life, filled with vigorous philosophical activity. He managed to complete the second volume of *Der römische Obligationsbegriff* . . ., though this was not published until two years after his death.

From his school-days he had loved mathematics, and he was a quite competent non-professional mathematician. He now became deeply interested in Einstein's theory of relativity, which was much in the news at that time; and he devoted much critical thought to the philosophical incoherencies which, as it seemed to him, underlay the theory as expounded by its author and other eminent physicists who were writing popular expositions for the layman. In this, as in other instances, scientists wisely went on with their work, undeterred by the often annihilating criticisms of philosophers on the palpable nonsense which (if their statements were interpreted literally) they so often talked and wrote.

In the summer of 1939 Hägerström was stricken with a sudden heart-attack, from which he never recovered. Three weeks later, on July 7th of that year, he died, *felix opportuniate mortis*, before the then imminent catastrophe of the Second World War had been precipitated.

Hägerström's writings do not make easy reading, even for those who are familiar with the languages in which he wrote, whether they be in German or in that Germanized version of his native tongue which he was wont to use in expressing his philosophic thoughts. And, although decently educated English and American students of philosophy may fairly be expected to tackle works in German on their own subject, they are unlikely to be able to read even much simpler Swedish than Hägerström wrote. For this reason, in the main, the work of Hägerström and his disciples has remained almost without influence on Anglo-Saxon jurists, moral philosophers, and epistemologists. Conversely, though Hägerström (like every educated Swede) had an excellent working knowledge of English, he seems to have been very little influenced by contemporary English or American philosophers.

As a result, the damaging attacks upon a prevalent system of Absolute Idealism that had degenerated into an academic ortho-doxy, which were launched almost simultaneously early in the present century by Hägerström and his followers in Uppsala and by Moore and Russell in Cambridge, occurred in complete isola-tion from each other. Again, the development of various forms of what I will call 'non-predicative' analysis of deontic and evalua-tory sentences in the indicative, which began in England and the USA between the First and the Second World War and has been pursued with such energy by so many able writers ever since, was initiated and has continued in complete ignorance of Hägerström's somewhat earlier and extremely thorough version of the same type of theory. Lastly, the 'anti-metaphysical' evangelicism, which may perhaps now be described as the last word but two in much Anglo-Saxon philosophy, was anticipated, unknown to its English and American protagonists, by Hägerström in the slogan '*praeterea censeo metaphysicam delendam esse*'.

For these reasons it is most desirable that Hägerström's main writings should be available, as they now are, in translation to English-speaking readers. There remains another reason, which I will add by way of conclusion. Hägerström was throughout his life essentially a highly religious and a highly dutiful man. He arrived, indeed, at what many would regard as a 'nihilistic' analysis of morality and of religion. But, unlike many 'analytic' philosophers, he had at any rate first-hand religious experience and first-hand experience of moral conflict and of acting from a sense of duty in face of serious obstacles, as the factual basis for his analyses. And, in spite of his 'nihilistic' theories, he continued to the end to value genuine religion and genuine morality as springing from the deepest roots in human nature and bearing the finest flowers in human life.

ONE

A SUMMARY OF MY PHILOSOPHY

## PRAETEREA CENSEO METAPHYSICAM ESSE DELENDAM

I was born in the year 1868. Towards the end of my school years, strong religious influences at home and the interests in dogma which my teachers in religion aroused in me prompted me to devote myself earnestly to studies in dogmatic theology. In the year 1886 I became a university student. First I passed the so-called theological-philosophical examination. The philosophical studies connected with this examination led me to break with my earlier dogmatic interests, and I decided to devote myself to philosophical studies. In the year 1887 a book by the Uppsala philosopher E. O. Burman, *Kant's Theory of Knowledge*,[1] introduced me to Kant's *Critique of Pure Reason*, which opened to me a new world.

What especially captured my attention was 'the paralogisms of rational psychology' and above all the theory of the unity of self-consciousness as the ultimate ground of the objectivity of knowledge. I took as my point of departure what was for me the self-evident proposition, that consciousness can know something only of its own determinations, or that consciousness cannot go out beyond itself. It seemed to me to be a necessary consequence of this, that only the consciousness within us which is elevated above the limits of individuality can supply a knowledge of something objective—of something which is projected beyond the states of consciousness of the individual subject. I believed that Kant had found this in the unity of the pure self-consciousness. For if this consciousness—the thought, 'I think'—as present in every thought of a reality, cannot itself be made an object of thought and consequently cannot be regarded as *one* consciousness among others but is rather the logical condition of the thought of a reality, then it is in and of itself universal and necessary. As the innermost element of every consciousness, it is also itself accessible to the limited consciousness. Knowledge of an object by the individual subject, which always presupposes an intuition by which something is determined as an object, must be, then, a cognition of the intuitive content possessed by this original consciousness itself,

[1] E. O. Burman, *Kants kunskapslära*, Uppsala, 1884.

B

bound up with it by the unity of consciousness; i.e. it must be a cognition of the transcendental synthesis of all possible intuitions through the unity. That is, the original knowledge is this self-consciousness's own synthesis out of intuitional elements which are given in it. And human knowledge is a knowledge of this Ur-knowledge, which is itself immediately accessible, because pure self-consciousness is the completely inward. The content of intuition, by contrast, is foreign to pure self-consciousness; it is apprehended in the forms of sensibility, space and time. For this reason knowledge is never knowledge of the purely rational, but rather holds for phenomena only.

Yet I came very soon to regard Kant's theory of phenomena as incorrect. I was strengthened in this opinion by my study of the development of the Kantian line of thought in Fichte and Hegel. In a book which I published two years after my appointment as *Privatdocent* at Uppsala University (1893), *Concerning Moral Feeling and Moral Impulse as Rational Phenomena in the Main Forms of Modern Rationalism*,[1] I sought to show the following: Kant, and the philosophical movement which went out from him, regarded the sensibly given, the object, as standing in opposition to the independence of the transcendental self-consciousness and as limiting it. On such a view, however, it necessarily becomes impossible to determine the sensible by means of the same consciousness. Because it is in opposition to this consciousness, it cannot be conceived as to its content. As a result all knowledge becomes impossible, even the knowledge of the identity of the object with itself. The reason for the latter is that pure self-consciousness, as the inner unity of thought, is supposed to confer on the object of thought its identity with itself. This consciousness is indeed limited or annulled in relation to a sensible object. A pure rational intuition, through which a reality is determined without sensible aspects, is impossible. I sought in particular to demonstrate that moral and religious consciousness, in opposition to the view of the Kantian movement, cannot constitute the material for non-sensible knowledge. Knowledge of that sort cannot include any passivity within itself. If it were apprehended in a passive consciousness, the non-sensible would itself be determined by the form of the finite consciousness and therefore would not be itself

---

[1] *Om den moraliska känslan och den moraliska driften sasom förnuftiga fenomen i den moderna rationalismens huvudformer*, Uppsala, 1895.

non-sensible. The content of the moral and religious consciousness, however, is given in feeling and impulse, which by their very nature are essentially passive.

I sought with all my might, however, to work my way out of the nihilism into which I had fallen. The problem concerned the possibility of any objectivity in knowledge, assuming that only consciousness itself is immediately given—assuming, that is, that it is impossible to know anything except consciousness's own determinations. This assumption seems to lead to pure solipsism—if it even leads that far. (The consciousness in which I apprehend myself cannot be identical with the 'I' which I apprehend. Here too, therefore, consciousness seems to go out beyond itself.) But it was clear to me that in any case the problem had to be solved in the way which Kant had indicated. Every attempt, of whatever particular form, to solve the problem of the objectivity of knowledge through a psychological investigation of the nature of human consciousness, seemed to me to be based on an incredible confusion of thought. Indeed, such an investigation presupposes the possibility of the very knowledge, which is to be explained. In order to explain the possibility of this knowlege, it makes use of an object which is already presupposed as known. It takes its departure, in fact, from the existence of a reality in time and space, supposedly capable of being known. 'Man' is the concept of a *psycho-physical* reality.

I turned back to Kant, therefore, in order to discover the real error in his argument—still holding fast to the principle of the transcendental consciousness as the only universal and necessary consciousness and as that which is absolutely accessible, and to his assumption that objectivity in knowledge is always given through the knowledge of this consciousness's original synthesis of what is sensibly present. In a larger work, *Kant's Ethics in Relation to his Epistemological Presuppositions*,[1] I wished, without criticizing him in the least, to set forth my view of what he had really meant. I was of the opinion that it was a complete misunderstanding to conceive of the transcendental consciousness 'psychologistically,' as a formal determination of the human consciousness. It is for him much more a consciousness whose uniqueness consists in the fact that what is thought in it is identical with the thought itself.

[1] *Kants Ethik im Verhältnis zu seinen erkenntnistheoretischen Grundgedanken*, Uppsala, 1902.

It exists only for itself and therefore cannot be thought of as a determination of an objective reality, nor, for that reason, as a determination of the psychical subject.

I next sought to resolve the above-mentioned difficulty (i.e. that of conceiving of consciousness as that which is immediately given in all knowledge and as the principle of the objectivity of knowledge) in the following way. I sought to determine the 'self-constitution' (*sich-setzen*) of the pure consciousness in relation to its inner act of setting up an object over against itself. Pure consciousness is not the identity of subject and object in the sense of thought and being. For being is by its very nature distinct from consciousness. *Pure* consciousness is consciousness itself as a unity comprised within itself. Since pure consciousness is essentially a unity within itself, the apprehension of the object in pure consciousness in no way involves a destruction or limitation of the unity itself. In its unity the sensible reality can be apprehended in so far as in itself it is determined only in one manner. But it is actually determined only in one manner. The sensible relation of exclusion by no means implies that the being of the one is excluded by the being of the other. That is, it implies no logical opposition. In pure consciousness the sensible reality is also apprehended. For pure consciousness does not exist as consciousness apart from setting up an object within itself. This belongs to the concept of consciousness. Therefore knowledge is possible on the supposition that consciousness can know only its own determinations. It is possible as knowledge of that which is innermost in all consciousness. This innermost something is an absolutely universal or objective consciousness. Knowledge is possible as knowledge of this transcendental consciousness, which apprehends in itself the sensible reality only in one manner in time and space.

However I soon perceived that through this line of thought the fundamental proviso of the transcendentalist view had been lost. The proposition, which is regarded as self-evident in the history of philosophy as well as in general, viz. that consciousness itself is the only immediately given, is false. Every consciousness refers to something other than itself. The objectivity of knowledge cannot lie in its character of being a consciousness of its own inner objective unity of consciousness. The objectivity of knowledge must lie in the very nature of what is apprehended, in the very nature of the object. The object is by no means something which limits the independence of consciousness and as a consequence something external to consciousness, which, as such, cannot be immediately apprehended in its reality—as idealists and realists alike have taken it, irrespective of how different their views of the reality of things in themselves may have been.

My new view I expressed in the book, *The Principle of Science, I. Reality*.[1] The general motif of this work appears also in a popularly written dialogue, *The Botanist and the Philosopher; on the Necessity of Epistemology*[2] (lectures delivered in the fall of 1909), and also, as it concerns the critique of subjectivism, in the essay, *Critical Points in the Psychology of Value*, [3]and in a work which was published, although not generally distributed, *Towards an Analysis of the Empirical Self-Consciousness*.[4] *The Principle of Science* has occasioned peculiar misunderstandings concerning my actual intentions. For in the first place, in order to adapt myself to the current fashion of thought and in this way to find a basis for understanding, I had to make use, at the beginning, of familiar, but really misleading definitions, which were, however, already refuted by the treatise itself. And in the second place, I was not able to avoid being influenced by the transcendental view, by which I had been completely dominated earlier. Nevertheless, I regard it as my most important book, and until now I have found no cause to abandon the fundamental propositions which I have affirmed in it.

The book has three purposes, which are closely related to one another, namely, (1) to refute subjectivism (Schopenhauer's *pons asinorum*); (2) to maintain the completely logical character of sensible reality, i.e. to repudiate the conception of a logical form and a non-logical matter in the knowledge of the sensible; (3) to show the impossibility of metaphysics as a doctrine of the Absolute (in the sense of that which in itself is real, as the ground of 'relative reality'), and this respecting both an objective reality and consciousness or the 'I' itself.

I should like to set forth here the major contentions of this work.

[1] *Das Prinzip der Wissenschaft, I. Die Realität*, Uppsala, 1908.
[2] *Botanisten och filosofen. Om kunskapsfilosofiens nödvändighet*, Stockholm, 1910.
[3] 'Kritiska punkter i värdepsykologien', published in *Festskrift tillägnad E. O. Burman*, Uppsala, 1910.
[4] *Till analysen av det empiriska självmedvetandet. En psykologisk och filosofisk undersökning*, Uppsala, 1910.

In this connection, however, I shall also mention certain consequences of these contentions which are not explicitly stated in the book but which I have conveyed in my university teaching. Here I pass over certain statements in the treatise, the obscurity of which I soon perceived for myself. These statements, indeed, became clearer in the course of scientific discussions concerning epistemological and other related questions, which were to some extent inspired by the book and by my educational work at Uppsala with various scholars, but especially with Phalén.[1] These discussions have also provided me with a greater clarity concerning certain implications of my view. For the rest, I have not been significantly influenced by contemporary philosophy, on account of what is, in my opinion, its uncritical point of departure.

## I. THE CRITIQUE OF SUBJECTIVISM

Subjectivism I refuted by showing that in no consciousness can the consciousness itself be given. That which is apprehended is always something other than the apprehension. For this reason it is altogether impossible to regard consciousness itself as 'immediately' given for itself and thus as the ultimate ground of knowledge, as Descartes, Hume, and Kant have done, to say nothing of the general trend of modern epistemology. In fact, a *criterium veri* which pertains especially to the consciousness of some state of affairs becomes an impossibility. For the existence of that which constitutes such a criterion—whether it is 'evidence' or 'clarity and distinctness' or universal 'validity'—can be established only through a cognition of an object. 'Evidence', 'clarity and distinctness', etc., can be determined as real only in an apprehension which has these appearances as objects. Moreover, there is no bridge which leads over from consciousness to the objects, which are necessarily distinguished from it.

Thus epistemological idealism, which regards being as only the determination of consciousness, is untenable. But it is to be observed that epistemological realism, on the other hand, is just as impossible. Epistemological realism belongs, in point of fact, to the ordinary consciousness. If I apprehend this table as real, it appears

---

[1] Although subsequently Phalén has taken up a different standpoint regarding various fundamental questions, even his later writings have been of great value to me.

to me if I had gone out beyond the table which I apprehended and which was thus an image in me, and as if I had arrived at something else—at the *real* table. The real table, indeed, has the same properties as the table which I apprehend, while yet not being identical with it. The table in my apprehension—the table-image—is not identical with the real table. However the 'reality' of the table cannot be determined in any other way than by means of the assertion that there is something which is not the same as that which is given in my apprehension. That reality, which, according to the ordinary view, is not apprehended in the awareness of the table but is something beyond that which is apprehended, itself lacks any properties of its own by which it can be distinguished from the given. Consequently it actually becomes, by its very nature, the completely unintelligible, the 'thing in itself,' which nevertheless is regarded, inconsistently, as accessible to the apprehension. One supposes that it presses in upon consciousness from without, that it is reproduced in it as an image and is thereby apprehended. The image resembles the thing in itself, the completely unintelligible.

The basis of this view is obviously to be sought, above all, in the subjectivism of the ordinary consciousness. According to this interpretation, the table which I apprehend is only an image; that is, the apprehension in which it is given to me belongs to it as a property. And the contradiction is complete. The realist view also has another basis which we shall see later. In short, epistemological idealism, according to which the existent is only consciousness's own determination, and epistemological realism, according to which the existent is the 'thing in itself.' while it is yet determined by consciousness, are both equally untenable.

Only an investigation of the nature of the judgment, on the one hand, and of reality as such, on the other, can lead us out of this dilemma. The first proposition which I affirmed was that in every judgment the reality of something is presupposed. Every judgment is an apprehension of some state of affairs as real. If I think that 'The horse is running,' I mean, naturally, that the running itself, as a state of the horse, actually is present and is therefore not merely something which I imagine. 'The sum of the angles of a triangle is 180 degrees' signifies that the 180-degree sum-of-the-angles is something real and not merely an apprehension. It *is* so. If I think that I should be honest, I presuppose obligatoriness as something which belongs to honesty as something real, and not merely an apprehension. Indeed, even if I make a judgment about something which I know exists only in my imagination, e.g. an animal which is half horse and half dog, and if I assert that what is given in the image is in form both a horse and a dog, what I mean is that this thing given in the image *actually* has partly the appearance of a horse and partly the appearance of a dog. It is indifferent whether or not I myself, who have this image, actually distinguish these formal concepts when the image arises. They are present in any case.

Accordingly I renounced every attempt to define the judgment without taking into consideration the reality judged about. It has been said, for example, that the judgment is an apperceptive combination of concepts. But such a combination is in no way a consciousness of anything, even if as a result of it a unique concept should arise, which was neither the one nor the other of the combined concepts. Only in this unique concept would one be able to discover a judgment. The combination of concepts can only be an occasion for a judgment to arise; it cannot be the judgment itself.

Further, an attempt has been made to define the judgment as the avowal or disavowal of a specific concept. But it is obvious that anyone who defines the judgment in this way presupposes the actual existence of this very avowal or disavowal—presupposes, that is, that it itself, not just the apprehension of it, exists. But it is out of the question that in the judgment concerning the avowal or disavowal of the concept one should have in mind (as far as the reality of the matter is concerned) something other than what he has in the judgment, 'The horse is running'. As a matter of fact, this avowal or disavowal of a concept is only the result of an already existing judgment as a consciousness of the reality of something, or it is the ground on the basis of which we apprehend something as real.

There has also been an attempt, particularly in modern epistemology, to define the judgment as the idea of the value of a certain way of apprehending (an object). But such a definition, naturally, presupposes that one thinks of the value in question as really present. It is likewise presupposed that one is thinking of conscious beings, for whom the value holds. And one cannot maintain, without arguing in a circle, that the reality of these beings signifies only that it is of value to conceive them.

Especially at the present time there is an inclination to regard the judgment as the idea of the 'validity' of that which is comprehended in the judgment. However, in all 'validity' one presupposes the reality of a thinking being, for whom the content of the judgment is valid. This latter view of the nature of the judgment is universally applicable especially to judgments about mathematical and logical relationships and to laws of natural phenomena (natural laws). In the case of these judgments, so it is thought, the content of the judgment may not refer to *reality*. It seems to be assumed that reality pertains to individual things, which present themselves in perception, whereas the contents of judgments of the sort we have mentioned are a product of thought, existing, therefore, only in thought. Consequently such judgments may not be concerned with reality. A geometrical straight line, for example, cannot be perceived. It is utterly impossible to understand, however, why only perceptions should be granted access to reality and why, conversely, the circumstance that a geometrical straight line, for example, is apprehended in thought, and thus is not itself the cause of the apprehension, should exclude it from reality.

## 2. THE CONCEPT OF REALITY

When the nature of the judgment has been established in the manner indicated, the question presses itself upon us, What is to be understood by reality? In the first instance, I have tried to show that reality itself cannot be derived through an analysis of the essence of something which is real. This means that it cannot be a property, alongside other properties, of that which is real. If this were the case, the other properties of that which is real would not themselves be real. But special difficulties are added to this one, especially as they relate to the real thing, from which one proceeds in determining reality itself as an abstraction from this real thing. If one proceeds from something particular, for example, from God or from Thought (*das Denken*) as the specific real thing to which reality belongs as a property, then reality must be absent from every other thing—anything else would have to become a relative reality. But while lacking reality on this view, the relativity of reality must be determined as actually existing—a flagrant self-contradiction. On the other hand, if one proceeds from the collective apprehension of all that is real and views reality as the most universal characteristic of these real things, then one has to take into consideration the fact that the separate realities exclude one another in the degree that they exist alongside one another. But in that case reality as present in the one is excluded from reality as present in the other. As a result of this, each separate reality would be limited. This limitation of reality, however, must itself be completely real.

## The Law of Contradiction as a Law of Reality

In order to achieve clarity concerning this question of what reality in itself means, I have taken the law of contradiction as my starting point in the work mentioned above. This principle is generally taken to be a law of thought, in the sense either of a law of nature or of a normative law. This conception does not get to the heart of the matter. According to my view, the heart of the matter concerns reality itself. The law of contradiction declares, in fact, what reality in itself is—although it is not a consequence of this that it makes any declarations about what is real.

The law of contradiction is ordinarily formulated as follows: Two judgments, one of which denies what the other affirms, cannot both be true. What does it mean to say that a judgment denies something, e.g. that man breathes with gills? The denial seems to concern reality itself. But it appears impossible that a judgment, in which the reality of something is always declared, should deny the reality of that which is judged about. Concerning pure nothing, nothing at all can be judged. But what is it the reality of which is declared in a negative judgment? Here it can only be a question of the conception of that, the reality of which is apparently denied, e.g. the conception of man as breathing with gills. Such a conception must be apprehended as present in the negative judgment. One finds that the content of this conception is real, inasmuch as one distinguishes it within the conception as a whole; but at the same time he finds that the complex, to which the conception, together with its content, belongs, has a different character from that of the content of the conception. The phrase 'not real' is only a negative expression for the positive character of that which is real *in toto*.

Conversely the affirmation of something in a judgment implies that one is conscious that, in that which is apprehended as real *in toto*, the content of the conception appears not only in the conception, but also in the complex to which the conception belongs.

From this it follows that two judgments, one of which denies what the other affirms, must have for their contents different worlds, which do not cohere with one another. The judgment that both of these judgments cannot be true must therefore have these different worlds for its content. But in this judgment both of these worlds are regarded as constituting the respective contents of different judgments, which themselves belong to a single coherent unity. And the judgment that they cannot both be true involves a denial of the possibility of actually conceiving these worlds as common members of that coherent unity to which the judgments themselves belong.

But this denial of a possibility of thought appears to be of a different sort from the denial involved in negative judgment, of which it is said that it cannot be true together with the affirmative judgment. In the latter, reality is ascribed to an idea, which has as its content what the former denied. But in claiming that a contradiction exists, what is denied is the possibility of thinking both judgments true. Here also, however, we have an idea whose content, as existing only in the conception, is determined as real. This is the idea of the words in which the two judgments are said to be simultaneously true, of these words as expressing a unitary idea. But the subjectivity of the content of the idea, which is asserted when one confirms the occurrence of a self-contradiction is unique in so far as it is revealed through a direct consideration of the different worlds given in the judgments. *To the apprehension of these worlds as together real, through their belonging to different judgments which are together real, belongs the apprehension of the subjectivity of the aforementioned idea.* The actual impossibility of a self-contradiction, therefore, signifies only that that which I have before me in establishing [the occurrence of] a self-contradiction is a coherent unity, or, more simply, a determinate object of thought. Since the self-contradiction must *be* impossible in so far as it is supposed to have any meaning at all, reality must be included in the coherent unity or in the determinateness.

Against this explanation of the significance of the negative judgment, it can be objected, however, that the reality of the idea of a physical object, A, cannot imply the reality of this object itself. For how can this idea have the physical object, A, as a determination? But that the idea of the physical object, A, has this object as a determination is out of the question only under the absurd subjectivist presupposition. On this presupposition that which is conceived in the idea acquires through the conception a quality which is essential to its reality, the quality, namely, of being conceived, so that we should be able to conceive only our own ideas. This subjectivist presupposition, to be sure, is a natural consequence of the natural idea of the 'I' (more on this later), but it is nevertheless false. It appears in its deceptive naturalness in the expression, 'consciousness of something', where it is applied that in the idea as a whole only the consciousness and nothing else is present.

In truth, the idea of the physical object, A, could not be determined simply through the attribute of consciousness, if this meant that the idea was not also the object, A. For then it would be implied in this attribute that the idea is nothing but consciousness, without anything further. The situation is different if the attribute of consciousness does not rule out the possibility that the whole is also the physical object, A. (Then the following sentence, although a possible one, would be a *petitio principii*: Consciousness *in abstracto* has no meaning, because in the concept of consciousness one always thinks of something of which one is conscious. The sentence would contain the assertion that in a consciousness of something the act of being conscious and that of which one is conscious could not be distinguished from one another. With equal justice one could say that consciousness has no independent meaning, because it cannot be thought of apart from the organism in which it is present.)

If in the idea of a physical object, A, the object itself could not be distinguished, but was there only as an idea, then every idea together with its content would be a simple determinateness. For the idea as such, which would be the only thing that was real, is necessarily simple. Then, too, every difference in content would yield different ideas. That is, one could not say that the idea of the physical object, A, was the idea o*f a physical object*. For the physical object *in abstracto* is something different from the physical object, A. This consequence, however, is an absurdity, for, of course, objectivity belongs to the object, A. (This is not to say that in every idea of the physical object, A, its objectivity *in abstracto* is distinguished.)

However, if both the consciousness and the physical object, A, can be distinguished within the whole which is characterized as an idea of this object, then must they not indeed stand in a relation to one another? But the form of the relation can be no other than consciousness itself, and so the one member of the relation becomes the relation itself, and thus becomes the whole. This is just the meaningless view of subjectivism.

I shall show shortly that the concept of relation is a metaphysical concept, which depends upon the confused pair of concepts, 'reality in itself' and 'reality through some other thing'. If we employ this concept (of relation), as, for example, in the spatial relation, there is present, in truth, a whole in which two parts can be distinguished (the phenomena which stand in the 'relation'). There is no third something which is common to the two as the relation itself. The relation under consideration, in fact, is, as such, the whole itself as a logical unity. In the case of an equilateral triangle, the relation between the equilateralness and the triangularity is not a third something, but is rather the whole itself as logical unity. Concerning the relation of space, I shall show later that 'being outside of' can by no means be conceived as a property of the physical object. The judgment which asserts the reality of a positional relation between A and B has for its content a perceptible whole, which is given to the senses. In this whole, of course, A and B can be distinguished, but by no means can there be distinguished a relation of 'outside of A' or 'outside of B'. Therefore the fact that, in respect to the idea, we cannot distinguish a third something which stands for the relation between consciousness and object, naturally does not at all prevent these parts of the whole from being distinguished. What this distinction (between consciousness and object) involves will now be examined more closely.

There is just one thing to be added first. Suppose we do look on the physical object, A, itself as determining the idea as the whole. Suppose further that (in the context to which the idea itself belongs) the physical object, A, belongs to a larger whole, which cannot be distinguished as a part of the idea of the physical object, A, e.g. its position next to physical object, B. This does not mean that this latter relationship of belonging [to the larger whole] can be conferred on the idea. *Only* what can really be distinguished within the content of the idea belongs to the idea as the whole.

Connected with the question of self-contradiction is the question of what is called 'real possibility'. What does it mean that A is a real possibility, that it can be included within the context to which its idea belongs but may also not be included? Since every judgment is a consciousness of reality, there must be a consciousness of reality present here too. This can only be the consciousness of two distinct ideas of A with reference to its relation to objective reality. Thus one is conscious of two distinct worlds, which belong to different ideas, and at the same time of the impossibility of an idea in which they would be real at the very same time. However, one also knows something more, namely that as far as *given facts* are concerned, it is not possible to fit the different relationships into the sum-total of reality *except* by reference to the ideas in question. Any assertion which went further would be meaningless under the existing circumstances. One speaks here of a *lack* of knowledge, an expression the actual meaning of which will be explained later. In every case the consciousness of possibility is a positive consciousness of reality. (On the positive meaning of the phrase, 'the meaninglessness of an assertion', see above.)

## Consciousness and its Object

Now to the question of the meaning of this distinction between consciousness and its object. If AB is given as objectively real, it is meaningless to deny the objective reality of B. That is, I see B, which appears in the objectively given AB, as itself objectively real, and in connection therewith I understand the meaninglessness of denying its reality. But if AB is given as only subjectively real, in such a way that its objectivity is at least indeterminate—a mere possibility—then I see B as real in the idea to which AB belongs, and at the same time I understand the meaninglessness of denying this. In a hypothetical argument such as the following: 'If gold is soluble and this substance is gold, then this substance is soluble', I have before me as something real the idea of the solubility of gold and the idea of this substance as possessing the quality of gold, and I affirm the solubility of this substance as belonging to the same idea, just as I affirm the meaninglessness of denying this. This is the meaning of '*ergo*' in an argument which is considered to be formally correct. That the argument is hypothetical implies merely that only the idea of what is thought in the premises is actually given and is the object for the analysis. It is clear, then, that there is a differentiation of aspects in a whole given as real, so that these parts themselves must be determined as real within the whole.

On the other hand, it is just as obvious that separate objects of thought cannot be determined as real in an idea without there being a whole to which they belong as members. But how, then, is the differentiation of parts possible? If the objects can be determined as real only as aspects of the whole, then is not the whole itself the only thing that is real? How can the objects in themselves be determined as real? I apprehend my work-room *and* the garden it faces as both real, but I can do this only because they present themselves in the same complex of space. But then is not this complex the only thing that is real? The work-room as such surely lacks any spatial connection with the garden. How, then, can it be apprehended in its isolation as real?

There is a surreptitious logical mistake here. Even if the garden is actually present in consciousness at the same time as the room, the room in its isolation signifies nothing but its reality. The fact that the room *as such* is not connected with the garden implies only that its *reality* does not face the garden. And this is certainly true, for the reality of a matter of fact cannot itself be limited. I see the room as real as well as in its relation to the garden, but this would not imply that its reality faced the garden. The difficulty arises here only if one does not distinguish between the reality and what is real, but rather takes reality to be a part of the real. Then what is real becomes something in itself and something separated from the other, since the concept of reality cannot be determined through any other thing.

This way of thinking is manifested in the traditional understanding of one of the elements of a judgment as the logical subject. The logical subject is that which is independent in relation to the predicate, and for this reason the predicate must belong to it as a part. But it is impossible that the logical subject should be determined by a predicate which is distinct from it. That is, this kind of understanding, which in the last analysis is derived from animism and which has left its mark on the form of language, implies the denial of the possibility of what we call a synthetic judgment.

The same confusion of reality with that which is real is found in the idea of relation. What stands in a relation to something must be independent of that to which it stands related. But on the other hand, the relation itself, of course, means a dependence on this other thing. If now the work-room is apprehended as real without thinking of the garden, then one can say that the room in its isolation is real for me. If I then think of its connection with the garden, its *reality* is still not changed in any way thereby. The thing which is real is only seen in a larger connection. In my book, *The Principle of Science*, I have expressed this view as follows: The determinateness of the concept of a genus—its reality—is not increased through thinking of it through its species. A has its own determinateness just as before, even if it is thought through AB. But AB, which has its own determinateness, is more, of course, than merely A.

In the same work I have, in connection with the foregoing, defined the distinction between differentiation in judgment ('thought' —*das Denken*) and differentiation in mere idea in the following way. The judgment takes each simple element as real in itself, and this understanding is possible in such a way that one has before him a whole, in which aspects are differentiated as determinate unities. In logical differentiation a plural number has an entirely different meaning from what it has in counting. A number as such signifies a sensibly given difference, where the conceptual, real difference does not play any role. But in logical differentiation the apprehension of the difference contains a larger totality with a unique characteristic, in which each aspect is distinguished in itself with real determinateness. In pure conception (apart from judgment) difference signifies only that one sees phenomena next to, in, or after one another. Therefore a pure conception does not yield any knowledge of distinct realities and is to that extent only subjective. But pure conception is certainly not to be regarded as illogical for this reason, so that its content could not be determined in a judgment as real. For spatial and temporal difference by no means signifies that the reality of the one excludes the reality of the other, and this is the only thing that would make the content of the idea illogical. (More on this directly.)

It is of special importance here to establish the meaning of an expression which we use for the sake of brevity, viz. 'subjective reality'. In the idea of the physical object, A, taken as a whole, I can distinguish this object as real. I see it at the same time as represented and as real. This is not to say that the reality of the object is itself that which is represented, any more than the reality of my work-room lies next to the garden simply because the room itself does. But what is the situation when the idea of the physical object, A, is a judgment concerning its reality? In that case cannot the reality of the thing be distinguished in connection with the idea as well as it can in connection with the whole? No. For the reality of a matter of fact cannot itself be determined as real; that would be meaningless. But if the judgment concerning the reality of the object is itself thought of as real, then, of course, in this judgment as an idea of the object the object is apprehended at the same time as real and as represented. But mark well: if the object must be represented at the same time that a judgment concerning its reality is being uttered, then in this latter judgment (i.e. the judgment concerning the reality of the object) nothing at all is judged concerning the object as represented in the judgment. This would imply that the idea of a judgment would be a judgment of itself, which is meaningless. But if in a new judgment something is judged concerning the reality of the judgment itself, then naturally the object which is the content of the judgment as an idea of the object is determined as real. But this does not exclude the possibility that this same object is at the same time reckoned as belonging to the spatial complex to which the idea itself belongs. The judgment about which a judgment is made is then described as true. Conversely, if this complex is determined as possessing a different character with regard to the physical object, A, then the judgment is described as false. But in itself it is not false. For even if when I make a 'false' judgment I think of the thing as belonging together with another real thing, not merely through the idea of the thing which is given to me, still it is only an illusion that I make a judgment opposed to the judgment in which my own judgment is determined as false. The idea of the thing which belongs to a judgment is not apprehended in that judgment itself. Therefore declaring that a judgment is false, of course, implies a reference to a new aspect, not contained in the content of this judgment, namely to this judgment itself as a determinate idea of a thing. (Naturally, of course, in judgments concerning matters of fact new facts which were not taken into consideration by the one who judged falsely must come into view.)

For this reason declaring that a judgment is false always implies that that whose reality is declared in the false judgment is placed in a wider connection. This has nothing at all to do with the question of reality. As a matter of fact, in every determination of a judgment as false, this judgment is made by the very person who declares it to be false. For as long as he sees its real content as only represented, he ascribes reality to it, without making this reality in any way dependent on the idea to which that which is real belongs. Reality itself cannot be determined through any other thing. He who declares a judgment to be false therefore has a consciousness of the reality of the very same thing as that which is determined in the false judgment as real. But it is self-evident that he cannot disregard the new factors and therefore that he cannot fail to place that which is determined as real in a wider connection.

In itself every judgment is true. For reality itself, which is apprehended, cannot be distinguished as one except in the apprehension and so cannot be determined as subjective. This would presuppose that reality itself could be determined as real. 'Subjective reality' is, strictly speaking, a *contradictio in adiecto*, even though, naturally, what is determined as real can belong to what is *in toto* given as real only as the totality is represented. And naturally we are speaking here of 'subjective reality,' as contrasted with objective reality, only in the previously mentioned sense which we introduced for the sake of brevity. In general it is meaningless to ask whether the reality of a thing determined in a judgment is itself real.

The standpoint here adopted is the necessary consequence of rejecting the view 1) that reality means something different from what is apprehended, with which the apprehension may be compared, and 2) that reality is consciousness or a determinate form of consciousness, e.g. thought as valid through itself or lively 'impressions'. Both of the latter alternatives lead ineluctably to the conclusion that knowledge has itself for its object.

## Reality, Self-identity, and Determinateness

What has been suggested here about the content of the concept of reality I have expressed in my aforementioned book in the following ways: Reality as self-identity (more concerning these expressions presently) is the only thing which is *immediately given*; or, it is *knowledge (das Wissen)*—in contradistinction to mere factual certainty; or, it is the *absolute*; or, it is the *concept, valid (gültig) in itself*. All these expressions are borrowed from the terminology of subjectivism and metaphysics. This is to be explained on the ground that my intention in writing this work was primarily that of *refuting* subjectivism and metaphysics. It was natural, in order to make myself understandable, that I should make use of the terminology belonging to these points of view. Nevertheless this dependence on these philosophical views (even if it was only of a negative character) led to the result that I was not entirely aware that my use of this terminology could produce misunderstanding.

It was customary, indeed, to represent subjectivism as the view that consciousness itself is the immediately given and that knowledge of objects is mediated through this immediately given—that the object is merely an abstraction from the latter. *Against* this view, I maintained that reality as self-identity is the very validity of all knowledge and in this sense the immediately given. Conversely, knowledge of reality is mediated by determinate phenomena, in so far as the validity of knowledge is nothing but the reality of the thing as a self-identity. Contrariwise, I have maintained most emphatically that knowledge is not mediated through the concept of reality in such a way that something could be deduced from this concept. *The* sense in which *all* knowledge is immediate is that in knowledge something determinate is always *given* as real. That reality as self-identity is the concept which is valid in itself implies only that it is validity itself. It is in *the same* sense that reality is characterized as the *absolute*. If reality is defined as knowledge itself, there is not the least thought of self-consciousness. What is expressed is only that it is the intuitively given reality of the *object*, which transforms apprehension into *cognition*, so that more than merely a factual representation, tied up with *subjective* certainty, is present. Every other explanation of this terminology—which has itself been defined more concisely through the debate over these points—would be an unfair misrepresentation of my view, even though I did not at the time recognize its inappropriateness nor realize completely the implications of my view.

In my book, however, I took as my point of departure the principle that *reality* and *self-identity* are *correlates*. (The second expression is determined by the terminology of transcendental philosophy; here I use the more satisfactory term, 'determinateness'. This view (that the two terms are *correlates*) I have since given up, and I now construe them as different expressions for one and the same thing. This is only a clarification, however, and is not a basic change in the view.)

Above, in discussing the law of contradiction, we attempted to show that determinateness or coherence implies reality. But the matter needs to be investigated more closely, with special reference to the nature of *empirical knowledge*. Before we turn to this investigation, however, a common error concerning the nature of *determinateness* should be mentioned. Some people have thought that the logical unity of the object—its determinateness—is inconsistent with the plurality of aspects in its content, and have thus been led to the view that such a plurality is something irrational. Thus it is often thought that explaining or conceiving a thing through its cause is the same as reducing different things to their identity. In that case there would be in fact no causal relationship since this would presuppose different things, and nothing would be conceived. Actually, explaining a phenomenon means placing it in a larger context and hence involves a transition to a larger, not a lesser domain of content. In metaphysics also 'true being' is regarded, on the same grounds, as pure unity or identity —determinateness without anything that is determinate. To believe this is to believe that the sensible relation of exclusion—the sensibly given plurality—involves a logical relation of exclusion, so that the reality of the one could not exist along with the reality of the other. But it has been shown that *this latter* relation of exclusion implies the meaninglessness of an assertion. But the sensible relation of exclusion has in itself a complete clarity or determinateness. Kant undoubtedly intends the same thing by the '*amphiboly* of reflexive concepts', but he was nevertheless caught in the prejudice of the illogical character of the sensible. Indeed, he regarded the pure self-consciousness—the identity of object and subject—as the logical unity. Thus any plurality of the object came into conflict with the unity of thought itself.

We turn now to the question, whether or not determinateness in itself can be reality. We begin by asking the question, What would be implied if there should be a special knowledge of reality which did not simply presuppose the determinateness of the object? This would imply that the special character of either the object or the consciousness of the object determined the object's character as real. The first possibility would imply that reality itself would be a quality belonging to the observable character of a determinate object, which is absurd. The second possibility refers to a special feeling of certainty, which is connected with certain ideas. This feeling would then establish the idea as an apprehension of reality. But the certainty itself, which is connected with an idea, presupposes that the object has already been apprehended as real. Certainty in connection with the apprehension of reality qualifies the natural expressions, 'This is so' or 'This is surely so'. Consequently certainty has different degrees. One says also, 'This is probably so'. But reality itself has no degrees. It seems to be impossible, therefore, that a special part of the content of consciousness should be represented as real. Neither the special character of the object nor that of the apprehension can be the factor which defines the apprehension of reality.

But if, on the other hand, all content of consciousness, as something determinate, is real, then the dividing line between that which is merely thinkable and that which is real is obliterated, which appears to be meaningless. An illusion is involved here, however. Is it really the case that anything we like is thinkable, if only it is in itself an internally coherent whole? It is clear that one can think of whatever different wholes one chooses and can compare them with one another, but not unconditionally. If they were given to consciousness immediately together, one would not have before one a unified object since they do not stand in a mutual connection with one another. That is, one would not apprehend anything at all.

But how, then, could different wholes be compared? This could be done through their being referred to different ideas in which they appear in themselves but apart from each other. But this would not be possible unless the ideas themselves were taken as belonging to a whole, in addition to which none other is conceivable. For if in connection with the ideas more wholes should present themselves to consciousness, one would again have before one's mind, of course, different worlds, which could be unified only through a reference to other different ideas in a consciousness. If now the same holds of these ideas, and so on *in infinitum*, then it would be utterly impossible through referring to different ideas to place different wholes together in relation to one another. If it is actually possible to place different logical possibilities together in relation to one another through their being referred to different ideas, then these ideas must be assigned to a whole in addition to which none other presents itself to consciousness, so that an assertion concerning another whole appears as meaningless.

The same point can be expressed more objectively as follows: Every possible determinate thing must belong to a comprehensive whole, besides which none other can be discovered. Otherwise the individual moments could not be determined in their unity with one another. And then the fact that they belong to different wholes would imply that the one object, taken together with the other, would not be anything determinate, because the whole itself would have no determinateness.

It is clear now that without a presupposed continuum besides which none other presents itself as conceivable, the demonstration that something is self-contradictory, and thereby a proof, a simple conclusion or a judgment, i.e. *thought* in the proper sense, would be impossible. For the demonstration that something is self-contradictory includes a thought of different worlds through their being referred to different ideas. But it is also clear that the one and only continuum which is presupposed by all thought in the proper sense is the real. This is true, however, only in virtue of the fact that it is determined as the one and only continuum and that every object of thought must be regarded as determinate, and therefore as real, by reference to this continuum. That is, reality means the same thing as determinateness. Only an untenable, if indeed natural, subjectivist point of view, under which the idea consists simply in being an idea, makes it necessary to exclude certain objects of thought, given in the idea, from that which is real. The twin brother of subjectivism, dogmatic realism, which regards that which is real as something other than the content of consciousness (since the content of consciousness can only be a picture of the real), defines the real so broadly that—nothing is left over. But there are also practical grounds which are responsible for the ordinary, confused concept of reality. When it comes to calculating the consequences of our actions, only objective reality has meaning. Consequently a qualified character of reality has been ascribed to this objective reality.

### Space-and-Time as the Only Conceivable Continuum for the Real

We must now consider the question, What is the only continuum, besides which none other is conceivable, which is presupposed by all thought in the proper sense? One may proceed here from Descartes' proposition that one cannot doubt one's own existence as a conscious being. This is correct, in the sense that a conscious being cannot conceive his own existence, with the ideas belonging to it, as a mere idea in himself or in another such being.

Nothing prevents one from *saying* such a thing, of course, but then there is no real concept standing behind such words.

The question arises, however, What differentiates this conscious being from others? Descartes thinks that the conscious being is itself given in immediate self-consciousness as a simple *res cogitans*. But this simple *res*, which is determinable only as the substance which is conscious, possesses, on account of its simplicity, no determinate character which differentiates it from other *res cogitantes*. There must therefore be another principle of differentiation. This can be none other than the place in space and the point in time for the existence of the particular conscious being. But time and space have a meaning only if they are in some way determined. Empty extension is a mere word, for in it all determinateness of position is absent. In the same way, an empty before-and-after is only a word. But determinate space and determinate time are what we call the world of experience in space and time. Now if this world alone differentiates the one conscious being from another, while this being cannot, in its thought of itself, be conceived as a mere idea, then also no one can conceive his own world of experience as a mere idea. From this, then, it follows, inversely, that so far as other continua are thought of together with the continuum of experience, they may constitute a unified object for consciousness only on the condition that these other appearances are related to ideas in individual conscious beings which belong to the world of experience. Thus the continuum of experience becomes the whole, and other continua, which are *prima facie* separate from it and are therefore not conceivable in immediate connection with it, must be arranged within the continuum of experience if they are to be thought of together.

The reverse procedure is impossible. Consequently a spiritual reality is a *contradictio in adiecto*. Either such a reality must be conceived as being alongside the world of experience and must thus become a 'finer matter,' or else the world of experience must itself become a mere idea of the spirit—which we can *say* well enough, but cannot conceive, because we cannot conceive the existence of ourselves, differentiated from other persons through space and time, as a mere idea.

It is customary to say that consciousness itself has neither length, nor breadth, nor weight, and consequently could not be in space. And naturally the first part of this statement is correct, if one regards the quality of consciousness, in abstraction from the visual and tactile space in which it is located, as belonging to a determinate conscious being. But this holds in general for every quality which determines space. And for all that, qualities are also necessary for every determination of mere extension in order that the concepts of length, breadth, and weight may have meaning. The detachment of consciousness from space in such a way that it becomes a reality in and for itself is only the counterpart of the view which makes the spatial world a mere modification of space, excluding all sensible qualities (i.e. mechanistic materialism). It will be shown later that this theory uses mere being, instead of the sensible qualities, as the principle of differentiation of matter, in contrast to empty space, and that it is only a metaphysical play with words, behind which no thought stands.

For every individual, his world of experience, given in every case, is *the* continuum. Even the world of dreams can serve as *the* continuum. But if in the course of new experiences what was initially given becomes subjective in certain respects and thus becomes a mere moment in a more comprehensive continuum, then this new continuum is itself only a new form of spatial and temporal reality. And further, relative *subjectification* does not imply that, under the *existing* circumstances (i.e. where the point of departure is taken from previously given contents of consciousness) the world of experience which was given at that time is not *the* continuum. Relative subjectification implies only that *this* continuum is placed in a larger one through one's considering new contents of consciousness.

That the scientific world-picture is the true one, in comparison with the unscientific, implies only that the former construes the latter, with regard to new contents of consciousness, as merely a member of a more comprehensive continuum. By no means is the latter thereby made void. Only the metaphysical 'world-view' must be determined as void, on account of the complex of feelings and representations which lies at its foundation. For in this view, under the influence of this complex, one constructs meaningless combinations of words and yet believes that the words have a meaning.

The world of experience is more precisely determined through perceptions and through inductions from perceptions in association with conclusions drawn from the assumed continuum. An apprehension which is associated with certainty and a unique (indescribable) feeling of constraint is designated as a perception. In such an apprehension the content is located, apart from any conclusion, in the spatial complex to which it itself belongs. (This is not to say, by any means, that its content, as distinguished from other contents of ideas, immediately appears as *real*. That would mean that reality was a quality of the content.) Induction is an apprehension, associated with certainty (without the feeling of constraint mentioned above), which has as its content that which is common to the preceding perceptions. Therefore, it has as its content a universal combination of concepts, which have individually occurred together in the previously given perceptions, and it is just as immediately determinative for the world of experience as are perceptions. That is, in the apprehension of the concept its conceptual content is immediately placed in the same spatial and temporal complex with the concept itself. And this implies that future perceptions are understood as possessing a content which coheres with the content of this concept. The fact that induction only yields what is called probability implies that in *reflection* about the conception, which the inductive generalization itself is, there seems to be a real possibility that future perceptions will yield a different result. (That the consciousness of possibility is itself a consciousness of reality has already been shown.) However, it also implies something else. In reflection about the inductive generalization there is always present a consciousness of reality which goes beyond mere possibility and is necessary for the idea of probability. This is the consciousness of the fact that future perceptions will contradict the inductive generalization the less, the wider is the basis of perception and the more 'exact' is the observation. (It is this which is meant, though expressed less correctly, when it is said that in induction one presupposes the uniformity of reality.)

But in all the more precise determinations of the world of experience through perceptions and inductions, an already determined objective world is presupposed, to which the perceptions and the inductive representations are ascribed. Especially is a determinate causal continuum presupposed, i.e. laws of what occurs or sequences of concepts which determine what occurs. This appears, for example, in the demand for 'exactness of perception'. This demand presupposes the assumption of certain causal laws by which it can be determined whether or not, in a particular case, what is perceived as an objective moment in the world of experience is the cause of the content of perception as a subjective pheno- menon and is thus of determining significance for the character of the subjective phenomena. The assumed causal laws continue to hold as objective, so long as new facts can be conceived and also predicted within the framework of these laws.

From what has been said it follows that every attempt to base the character of the world of experience as the continuum either on the inner validity of a presupposed thought or on particular percep- tions, leads to mere combinations of words. Thought itself pre- supposes for its own possibility an already given world of experi- ence in space and time as the continuum, besides which none other appears as conceivable. Perceptions themselves cannot be conceived apart from conscious beings which are differentiated by the determinate space and the determinate time which are the world of experience itself.

It might be objected that the proof that the world of experience in time and space has this character of being *the* indispensable continuum really moves in a circle, for it takes its point of depar- ture in the idea of conscious beings who themselves belong to the world of experience. But whenever any epistemological question is raised at all, the reality of the idea the truth of which is being inquired into is presupposed. Otherwise one would be asking about nothing. But this means that the reality of a conscious being who has the idea is presupposed. And this consciousness of reality presupposes the very world of experience, in order that the presupposed conscious beings may be differentiated. This is to say, indeed, that the reality of the world of experience, in the sense mentioned, does not admit of being proved, since in every attempt to prove the truth of an idea, the reality of the world of experience is presupposed. What does admit of being proved is only that the person who, himself belonging to the world of experience, deter- mines the world of experience as in principle a mere illusion, heaps up words without meaning. But does one need to know any more in this regard?

It might be objected further that if reality itself cannot be regarded as something real or if determinateness cannot be regarded as something determinate, then it is also meaningless to make judgments concerning reality or determinateness *in abstracto*, as here appears to be done. Regarded abstractly, these concepts appear to be mere words. Now it is clear, however, that everyone knows which actual idea is to be designated as an apprehension of reality or of determinateness. That is, the denotation of the words appears to be given, but not their abstract connotation. On the other hand, the words must possess real meaning if it is to be possible to determine something as real or determinate, in contrast to that whose determination as real or as determinate appears to be a mere collection of words.

The solution of this problem can be found only in the fact that the words acquire meaning in the actual ideas which lie within their denotation. But if the denotation of the words—that which is designated by the words—can be determined, then there must be something universal which determines this denotation. But if this universal something cannot be the content of a universal idea attached to the words, then that which determines the denotation must lie in a general, determinable feeling, for which the words, immediately regarded, are the expression. If this same feeling is associated with an idea, then on account of this association the idea comes to be designated by means of such words. But since the words function as designations of such ideas, they acquire a real meaning. That is, the ideas so designated are actually different ideas from those which, though having the same character otherwise, cannot be so designated.

If this is the case, then the abstract use of the words 'reality' and 'determinateness' as expressions of feeling evokes ideas which are associated with the corresponding feeling, and in this way they acquire meaning. With reference to the word 'reality', it can only be the feeling of certainty which is determinative for the denotation of the word. The word 'reality' is basically nothing but the expression of the feeling of certainty. The corresponding feeling, for which the word 'determinateness', i.e. 'to be in one mode', is the immediate expression, can only be the logical feeling of evidence. If ideas which are associated with the feelings mentioned now arise, the words acquire meaning. What is expressed by the general sentence, 'Reality and determinateness mean the same thing', then, is that the meaning which these words have acquired, through ideas associated with such feelings, is the same. The distinction between the meanings of the words has to do only with the fact that the ideas, which have the meaning in question, are associated once with the feeling of certainty, another time with the logical feeling of evidence, and one is led by these different foundations of feeling to distinguish as well between the meanings of the words in these ideas which are associated with the feelings. But the abstract sentence itself naturally loses all significance if one does not actually have ideas associated with the feeling of certainty or the feeling of evidence. For then one has no material by which to verify the correctness of the sentence. Only if one has the actual knowledge do such words as 'the world of experience', 'the impossibility of the self-contradictory as a mere collection of words', 'judgment' acquire a real meaning. The same is to be said regarding the words 'perception' and 'induction'.

### 3. THE REJECTION OF METAPHYSICS

*Metaphysics dominates not only in philosophy, but in science generally. But it is nothing but a series of combinations of words, concerning whose character the metaphysician knows nothing.* To make this situation clear is the main tendency of the book which I am here discussing and of my later works.

We should designate as metaphysics every view which makes something real out of reality itself—reality in itself (*an sich*)—whether one speaks simply of pure being, as if one had thereby represented something real, or whether one takes some particular real thing and regards its reality as one property along with others. In the idea of true being one thinks of something which includes reality within itself, so that this property may be abstracted out of the very thing which is thought of: *id cuius essentia* (that which is thought of in the situation) *involvit existentiam.* It is clear that true being is the more determinate reality itself. The disastrous consequences of a metaphysical view have already been pointed out. What is supposed to be true being, if it is something simple, excludes everything else from reality. That which is relative lacks reality, while yet this deficiency is supposed to be entirely real. If true being consists of a plurality of realities, these mutually limit one another, and thus they also limit one another's reality. Their connection with one another itself becomes something unreal, etc.

### The Two Roots of Metaphysics

But metaphysics is firmly rooted in the ordinary consciousness and consequently spreads out like a smoke screen of thought not only over philosophy but generally over everything called science. Two roots of metaphysics in the ordinary consciousness are especially to be considered here.

(1) The *one* is the alleged knowledge that there is something which goes beyond that of which one has knowledge, but which may not be determined except in that it is something. Here we seem to presuppose the reality of the one and only—reality. For where the unknown is concerned, in so far as it is unknown, we are given nothing except simply the condition that it is real. With regard to the unknown we operate with nothing but abstract determinateness, without anything standing before us which possesses the determinateness. Now since this has no meaning, we must be concerned here with an entirely different form of knowledge. But we designate this for ourselves by means of misleading words.

The *actual* knowledge which each person has who recognizes his own lack of knowledge may now also be revealed. One is left with a certain mere possibility, e.g. the possibility that perhaps gold is soluble. What does this mean, assuming the correctness of what we have been saying? It means that the solubility of the gold, of course, is present in the idea of the gold and to that extent belongs to the universal continuum of experience. But one assertion or another, which goes farther, is meaningless *with regard to given facts*—the idea that to the words there corresponds a unified idea is subjective. Or one has different mere possibilities in mind. One knows, for example, that there are stars beyond the Milky Way, but one regards an assertion regarding their number as meaningless with regard to the given continuum of experience. In either case it is a matter of positive knowledge, even if one says of this knowledge that it comprises a knowledge of a deficiency of knowledge. This designation need not lead to the belief that the non-existence of a determinate knowledge could actually be an object of knowledge. If the content of a cognition is itself not known, then the knowledge itself is not determinate, and in that case, of course, it cannot, as *this* knowledge, be determined as not existing. A 'deficiency' of knowledge is therefore only a negative expression for the positive knowledge referred to.

However, one also knows very well something else in a state of consciousness of this sort. One knows very well that gold is one of the two, soluble or insoluble. One also knows very well that the number of the stars is actually determinate. That we cannot determine the matter is something else. It appears, therefore, as if one can actually have a knowledge of pure reality—without anything which is real.

But what does this proposition mean, 'The gold is either soluble or insoluble'? The proposition becomes clear through the recognition of the absolute (in the sense of independent of present experience) meaninglessness of certain assertions. It is absolutely meaningless to say that gold is both soluble and insoluble, and it is absolutely meaningless to say that it is *neither* soluble nor insoluble. In the case of these assertions, both the idea of the solubility of the gold and the idea of the subjectivity of this idea are subjective. The very same result is reached through an investigation of the proposition, 'The number of the stars referred to is actually determinate, even if it is not here a question of a determinate possibility'. One can think that it is impossible for there to be both a thousand and more than a thousand or less than a thousand, and yet at the same time think that their number is determined by none of these possibilities. But naturally one can think of meaninglessness in this respect in many other ways. What one is thinking of with these words cannot be stated. But it is certain that if one does not chatter, but thinks—some kind of thought must be present.

But what is the reason that it seems natural to assert that a reality can be determined as existing if there is nothing given which is determined as real? This question is the same as that concerning the apparent naturalness of the proposition that I can have knowledge of my lack of a certain piece of knowledge. If this were a proposition with a meaning, I could also meaningfully say that a reality can be determined as existing even if nothing is given to be determined as real. But the basis of the apparent naturalness of the second proposition is easy to discover. It lies in the fact that I confuse the *absence of knowledge* with the uncertainty which arises when I recognize my inability, in regard to the given experience, to assert anything with real meaning about the determinateness of the state of affairs in relation to that which is real *in toto*. This uncertainty, which is a *feeling* attached to the questionable knowledge, is so intimately associated with the idea in question that the whole appears as a particular consciousness with its own particular object, although this object can only be determined through the expression of the existing feeling-situation. For example, I know that I cannot determine the colour of my neighbour's new dog. With this knowledge the feeling of uncertainty is intimately associated. I say that I am uncertain *what* colour the dog is. This phrase, '*what* colour', which is an expression of feeling, appears as the object of the uncertainty. Thus it appears to be the object of the knowledge which I do not have. So the knowledge which is lacking seems to have an object, namely the phrase, 'what colour'. And it becomes natural to say that this is the very knowledge which is lacking. Thereby the field is opened for natural, although meaningless, formations of words, which one believes to have a meaning. The reality which one does not know has no other determination for consciousness than this—to be real. It is therefore a reality in itself.

However, the state of affairs we have just described is one of the roots of the acceptance of epistemological realism, viz. that in knowledge a reality in itself appears. The dependence of epistemological realism on mere words, concerning whose character one hangs suspended in ignorance, reaches the ridiculous when one hears doubt expressed as to whether this reality, which is real in itself, is in agreement with the conditions of experience which are given to us, e.g. with the law of contradiction.

(2) The other root of metaphysics which I wish to mention here is the consciousness of the 'I'. I appear to myself as the completely inward. My reality seems to me to be intimately connected with my self-consciousness. My reality appears to be my own consciousness of it. I am for myself, as it were, a world enclosed within itself. Since, now, all my ideas lie within myself, so also, it appears, the entire reality which is thought of lies only in this world enclosed within itself. Here we have epistemological idealism in its inception. And yet no one can avoid regarding himself as a reality alongside other realities. On the other hand, I become for myself only an insignificant part of the world which is supposed to be given in me. Thus we move in a continual contradiction. However, the contradiction is already present in the foundation of idealistic thought; this foundation is purely metaphysical. My *reality* is supposed to be identical with my consciousness of it. Thus reality itself becomes only a part, discoverable by means of analysis, of an original, pure unity of consciousness and being. It becomes in itself a particular real thing alongside other

things; and I myself *in toto*, in whom the unity of reality is only a moment, cannot be conceived as real.

The contradiction in question acquires an especially important form in the case of the consciousness of will. In this consciousness I conceive myself as active and therefore as the cause of something else, yet in such a way that the effect to which I am related as the cause is included within myself. I am in a world which is enclosed within itself, and yet I stand in relation to something else, which nevertheless has its reality in me.

The contradiction in question, like every other contradiction, can only be a collection of words without meaning, even if one does not know that one is only operating with words. The basis of the fact that this collection of words is constructed so much as a matter of course and seems so natural lies in an entirely inseparable association between the individual psycho-physical organism's consciousness of its continuing existence in space and time and a continuing life-feeling of the same organism. The content of feeling is found both in the feeling itself and in the idea of the organism, inasmuch as it is located in the organism. Indeed, on account of the constancy of the feeling, the content of the feeling is located in the organism not momentarily, but permanently: the content of feeling persists as long as the psycho-physical organism exists. Hence the inseparable association. Therefore the word 'I', whereby the psycho-physical organism designates itself, is the expression both of this life-feeling and of the idea of the organism.

The contents of other feelings are also objectified through being located in the organism. I experience fear. This is by no means a consciousness of an object. But I also have *knowledge* of fear in that I locate this condition in myself and thus in the organism. But because these other feelings are accidental, the organism is not permanently qualified through their contents, and consequently there is no inseparable association between them and the idea of the organism in its continuing existence. Hence also they are not, in conjunction with the idea of the organism, of determinative significance for the 'I'. Rather their contents are located in a psycho-physical organism which has already acquired its character of 'I' in such a way that 'I' expresses the above-mentioned inseparable association. That is, the contents of these other feelings are introjected into an already given 'I'. I feel happy or sad. 'I' is therefore the natural expression not for a unified consciousness, but rather for an inseparable combination of feeling and conception.

This must lead, when we reflect about the 'I', to self-contradictory propositions, if we also presuppose, as a result of this fundamental though unperceived inseparable association, that behind the word there lies a unified consciousness. The 'I' becomes for the organism in question a spiritual or inward reality. The 'I' is *real*, because thereby a continually living psycho-physical organism in space and time is designated. The 'I' is something *spiritual* or *inward*, because by this word a feeling is expressed, whose content can be neither localized nor temporalized nor find its character of reality in the feeling itself, even if that content is located in a particular idea in the organism. (Pain, for example, is indeed a consciousness—an experience—with its own particular content, but in itself it is by no means a consciousness of an object in time and space. Only the consciousness of the reality of the pain has this character.) When one reflects about himself, one passes— because of the original association between the feeling and the idea of the psycho-physical organism, which is actually empirical knowledge—from the thought of the feeling over to the thought of such a cognition. And since one cannot find any localization or temporalization in feeling, the 'I' appears as a spiritual or inward reality, given in experience. And this is so in spite of the fact that the consciousness belonging to self-consciousness which is, properly speaking, *knowledge*, is only an apprehension of the psycho-physical organism.

There is no unified idea behind the assertion that I am a spiritual reality, given in experience. But one does not recognize this, on account of the transfer of thought, which depends upon this association and which finds expression in the words. And there is another point. One passes over from the thought of the feeling to the thought of the cognition; but the content of the feeling, which, as such, is characterized by a lack of localization and temporalization, is conceivable as real only as a content of the feeling. Hence the feeling is determined as a cognition of itself—an immediate self-consciousness: the identity of consciousness and the reality of which it is the consciousness. Now, however, when at the same time the 'I' is conceived as a reality independent of consciousness and existing apart from it, namely as the psycho-physical organism to which the consciousness of the 'I' pertains as a consciousness of

C

reality and in which the feeling of the 'I' itself is located, then the contradiction appears as a flagrant one.

Suppose that the 'I' actually is to be thought of as given in an absolute knowledge, which therefore is identical with the reality of which it is the knowledge. Then if one is to avoid the flagrant contradiction mentioned above, he must think of the 'I' as given in the feeling of the 'I', apart from any idea of a psycho-physical organism, with which the 'I' is otherwise connected. Nor may the feeling of the 'I' itself be localized and temporalized in a psycho-physical organism. If this were done, it would be impossible to hold to the belief that the combination of words, 'pure ("pure" in the sense of separated from every idea of a psycho-physical organism) self-consciousness' has some kind of meaning. For if one thinks of the feeling of the 'I' as itself belonging to the context of experience, it is impossible to conceive it as a consciousness which is its own reality. Indeed, it is then determined through something else.

Therefore the feeling of the 'I' must be so understood that the world of experience, as an object of reflection, is entirely eliminated. For in the world of experience it is immediately necessary to refer the feeling to the psycho-physical organism. That is, if one is to think of the 'I' as given in an absolute knowledge, then if the flagrant contradiction mentioned above is not to arise, one must be immersed in the contemplation of the feeling of the 'I', in complete disregard of every reflection concerning the world of experience which crops up. But now inasmuch as even the thought of the absolute self-consciousness as real must permit the thought of the world of experience to crop up, it follows that if one is to really think of this self-consciousness, one must be immersed in the feeling of the 'I' itself, without there being any consciousness of reality present—a condition which is, indeed, scarcely attainable except in ecstasy, in which, of course, one hardly *thinks* at all. What is held by Kant and his successors, however, would be entirely inconceivable, viz.: The 'I' as given in pure self-consciousness, purified from every idea of a *res cogitans*, invests knowledge with its universal validity. Finally this consciousness becomes one with true being!

The opposite extreme from this view, pure sensationalism, depends upon a similar mystification, which also originates through the influence of the consciousness of the 'I' upon thought. If the

'I' is self-consciousness as the identity of subject and object, then also every particular idea in me is a form of self-consciousness, i.e. it is in the last analysis a consciousness of the idea itself. But since actual empirical knowledge appears as dependent on perceptions, one reaches the result that all knowledge consists in perceptions, each with its particular content, and therefore does not consist in pure consciousness without any particular content. But since the perception must still, at the same time, be given immediately for itself, its different contents must be merely a determination of the consciousness which belongs to the perception. Since, however, the consciousness of something, regarded as consciousness, is simple, the content which determines the consciousness must itself be simple. Consequently the perception, with its complicated spatial and temporal content, must consist of a plurality of consciousness, each with its own absolutely simple content, as elements, and these are designated as sensations. The apprehension of a space determined by different qualities is then understood either as a secondary construction out of original sensations or as a combination of sensations which enter into the life of the individual and of a particular innate (!) intuition of simple, abstract extension without any determination. These elementary sensations, which yield knowledge apart from any apprehension of a space to which the quality of the sensation belongs, are supposed to be, first of all, sensations of touch, of colour, and of form. But one can calmly assert that there are no such sensations, nor have there ever been any, at least not for any man whose consciousness can be investigated, and that on the view described knowledge is made to depend upon a mystification as fabulous as the Kantian pure apperception, which cannot be an object of thought. Now since sensationalism cannot assume the possibility of another knowledge than that of the sensations themselves—since, indeed, sensation is to be a knowledge of itself—these nothingnesses become—the whole concrete reality itself.

In short, the two roots of metaphysics in the ordinary consciousness which have here been cited constitute the foundation, on the one hand, of epistemological realism and, on the other hand, of epistemological idealism, the two fundamental forms of metaphysics. And no particular form of metaphysics can ever become anything other than a more or less ingenious play with words. Taking one's departure from the meaningless identification of separate things—namely the identification, on the one hand, of 'being' *in abstracto* (whose psychological foundation is the pure feeling of certainty without anything determinate which one knows) with that which is real, and the identification, on the other other hand, of consciousness with that of which one is conscious—one argues in approximately the following manner: The elephant is a dog, therefore, he does not have a trunk; hence the conceived-of elephant, which has a trunk, is not the real elephant . . .

## Metaphysics in Some of the Sciences[1]

I now leave the question of the penetration of metaphysics into the pure theoretical sciences and pass on to the situation in the area of so-called practical knowledge or knowledge of value and the alleged theoretical knowledge which is connected with it. Here metaphysics does not *enter in*, but rather everything *is* metaphysics, i.e. in reality there is for consciousness nothing but words, whose meaninglessness from a conceptual standpoint one does not see clearly, no matter how much these words may express feelings or wishes or, inversely, may influence the life of feeling or of will.

(1) *Moral Philosophy:* I have devoted the latter period of my authorship to the consideration of the actual nature of value judgments and, in connection therewith, to the consideration of law. In the work which introduced this series, *Critial Points in the Psychology of Value*,[2] I tried to show, on the one hand, that one must ascribe to a valuation the content of an intellectual moment, if values are to be compared or are to be brought into a mutual dependence, e.g. as means to end. On the other hand, value itself means nothing, except as there is present in the person who values something a certain feeling of pleasure or displeasure or a desire, which is connected with the object designated as good or bad. For an observer who stood indifferently before everything (except knowledge itself), the objects of which he possessed knowledge would lack every character of value.

[1] A rather long and difficult discussion of some metaphysical implications which Hägerström saw in certain concepts of the natural sciences, e.g. 'thing' and 'motion', has been omitted here. In Appendix A, I have given a translation of a briefer and perhaps less obscure treatment of the same questions, which is to be found in an earlier manuscript of the *Selbstdarstellung* (in Swedish). (Tr.)

[2] 'Kritiska punkter i värdepsykologien' published in *Festskrift tillägnad E. O. Burman*, Uppsala, 1910.

Suppose, as often happens, that one thinks in the following way: 'The original experience of value is a feeling or a desire. Hence an object comes to be determined as actually good or bad, according as the idea of its reality arouses in mankind generally a feeling of pleasure or displeasure or a feeling of desire or aversion.' This is nothing but a conceptual confusion. If one should actually establish that an object possessed the character in question, this conception of the object would be entirely independent of the feeling or the desire to possess it, which is associated with the idea which he has formed of the situation. Hence on the view assumed, this idea would not be a consiousness of value. For on this view value itself may be present only for feeling or desire. Modern so-called value-psychology is therefore completely mistaken, in so far as it believes it possible to determine what value is in the manner suggested. It is not noticed that the word is being used ambiguously. In the book referred to I arrived finally at the conclusion that 'valuation', as a feeling or a desire, is to be defined as the adoption of an attitude which enters into the idea of the state of affairs in such a way as to give that idea its meaning.

In my inaugural lecture, *On the Truth of Moral Propositions*,[1] published as a pamphlet, I drew from this the natural conclusion: The value-judgment, which determines value, as actually valid, whether it is for me or for man generally, cannot possibly be true. For in every apprehension of a thing as characterized in this way or that, the thing is so determined that it possesses in reality a certain character and is thus independent of the apprehension itself. But the consciousness of value is characterized outright by the fact that the object—value—depends upon the feeling or desire which belongs to it. Naturally the same holds if one says that the valuation itself is a feeling or a desire, but this view declares that it is possible to determine feelings or wishes as correct or incorrect. This determination, indeed, is itself only a value-judgment, which has valuations as its object, and consequently, from the point of view of truth, it must be subjected to the same criticism.

In a later writing, *On the Question of the Concept of Objective Law*,[2] however, I first drew from my earlier investigations the full

[1] *Om moraliska föreställningars sanning*, Stockholm, 1911.

[2] *Till frågan om den objektiva rättens begrepp*, Uppsala, 1917 (Eng. tr. by C. D. Broad in *Inquiries into the Nature of Law and Morals*, Uppsala, 1953).

conclusion: The 'value-judgment' itself is only an illusion in so far as in it a judgment is made as to the value of something's belonging to reality. Now I discerned for the first time that the whole idea of value, which is supposed to belong to the reality of the valued object, was impossible. If feeling or desire is itself an experience of value, then the word 'value' is only an expression for a feeling or a desire and not an expression for a thought.

If one says, 'It is good to possess a barrel of potatoes', this is the same, in so far as 'good' actually has a valuational significance, as 'How good it is, indeed, to be in possession of a barrel of potatoes!' or 'Oh, if one only had something like that!' Thus it is manifestly an expression of feeling. But now since an expression of feeling can also become a declarative proposition, in virtue of its connection with a certain idea, one believes that 'value' is an actual determination of the state of affairs, i.e. one does not notice the meaninglessness of the words from the point of view of thought. In order to determine the assumed thing, one passes over in thought to something else, which actually may then be traced back to the object itself, e.g. 'The possession of a barrel of potatoes guarantees the possibility of satisfying the need for food'. Of course, this is something altogether different from the assertion that the object is valuable.

One must not forget here, however, that the so-called value-judgment, in the above sense, also gets its meaning from a close association between expressions of feeling or of will and the idea of the reality of a state of affairs. Consider such propositions as the following: 'From the point of view of value, it is on the whole prudent in life to keep in mind the principle of the greatest possible satisfaction', or 'The greatest conceivable welfare of all is the highest good', or finally 'It is right to develop one's natural abilities and to suppress the desire for ease'. Such propositions are by no means expressions for the actual condition of feeling or of desire. Rather they are expressions for a close association between the word 'good', or a similar word, and the idea of the actualization of that which one designates as good. Such an association has a suggestive effect on the life of feeling or of will, because the designations, 'good', 'bad', etc., are in themselves expressions of feeling or of will. Just as the feeling expresses itself in a reflexive manner, so also these expressions work back upon the life of feeling. The military march itself is a natural expression of warlike feeling, and, inversely, it awakens the same feeling in the hearer.

The development of these associations of words among men is in fact a condition of the progressive domination of mankind and of the individual over external and internal nature. But these associations themselves, naturally, do not serve as a basis for distinguishing between true and false judgments. We express them, however, in the form of declarative propositions. And then we believe that it is a question here of an actual thought with the character of truth. As a result of our ignorance of its proper character, we attribute to the proposition the significance of an idea, though a distorted one, of reality. In obligation as objective, for example, we conceive that another action (than the obligatory one) must lead unconditionally to the ruin of the individual.

Accordingly we must distinguish between 'value-judgments' which only express actual feelings or wishes and 'value-judgments' which represent not only impulsive, but also imperative moments. In reality they easily pass into one another. In any case, what is apprehended in consciousness by these judgments is nothing but combinations of words of the ordinary metaphysical variety, inasmuch as one does not pass over to ideas of reality. The *reality* of a state of affairs is determined by means of the predicate 'value'. Reality itself becomes a member of the whole which is determined as something real. If we fail to discern that we have only words before us in thought, we arrive at all kinds of meaningless propositions—for example, the proposition that there are two realities, *one* which is *reality* in itself and *another* which is the world of *values*.

It must be added, however, that the 'value-judgments' which are here treated as metaphysical are only those judgments about the value of this thing's or that thing's becoming real. To this group, therefore, aesthetic value-judgments do not belong. I have not made a special investigation of aesthetic value-judgments, but naturally, with regard to the question of their objectivity, they are subject to the general criticism which is based on the dependence of value upon feeling or desire.

One may now ask, 'Does not this insight into the actual state of affairs lead to a dissolution of morality?' But let the questioner keep the following in view: Why should the universal, social feeling-reaction against the anti-social individual and anti-social

behaviour, which in everyone is directed primarily against others
and secondarily against himself, disappear just because one ceases
to believe that the repulsiveness is a predicate of the person or of
the behaviour? Should the 'Fie!' become impossible just because
one knows that 'Fie' is not a property? When we understand what
significance the matter has for the society in which we live and
before which we simply cannot stand indifferent, why should we
not wish to take part in the hammering together of a close association between the words, 'Thou shalt not!' and particular kinds of
action, like theft, murder, and fraud, even if we do not assume that
there is a practical law which declares what we 'must' do in an
objectively valid manner, on the basis of a recognition of a real
Right? Why should not the individual, who is conscious of the
consequences of unbridled passion and is horrified thereby, want
in all circumstances both to forbid himself to engage in certain
kinds of behaviour and to show respect for the prohibitions of his
neighbours? In the moment of temptation the practical 'No!'
inseparably connected with the idea of a certain action, curbs the
passions through its power of suggestion to the will, in case passion
itself has enervated both one's clear discernment of the consequences and one's horror of them when one thinks of them.

(2) *Philosophy of Law:* But as I have said, it is in the sphere of
the philosophy of law above all that I have applied the principle
that there is no practical knowledge as alleged. My most important
writings in this connection are *Is Objective Law an Expression of
Will?*[1] and *On the Question of the Concept of Objective Law.*[2] From
time immemorial men have assumed a law, valid for society,
which grants rights to and imposes obligations upon the individual,
both in the external relations of the individual and in the relation
of society to the individual. The actual character of the 'idea' of
objective obligations has already been pointed out. Concerning
the idea of right, I have sought in my teaching to show that one
believes oneself to have an idea of a power, in relation to things or
persons, which is exalted above every natural power. My property-
right is independent of my *natural* power over the thing.

In a large work, *The Roman Concept of Obligation in the Light*

---

[1] 'Är gällande rätt uttryck av vilja?' published in *Festskrift tillägnad
Vitalis Norström*, Goteborg, 1916.
[2] *Till frågan om den objektiva rättens begrepp*, Uppsala, 1917. (Eng. tr.
by C. D. Broad in *Inquiries into the Nature of Law and Morals.*)

*of the General Roman Interpretation of Law*,[1] I have shown that in Roman law civil rights involved special mystical powers of the Roman citizen over things and persons. Originally these powers were ascribed to the soul (*animus*) of the citizen and were conceived animistically as the master of the inner being of the thing or the person represented. I have sought to show in this writing that the modern science of law has arrived at completely confused ideas of the 'state', due, on the one hand, to its dependence on inherited ideas of actually existing rights and duties, and, on the other, to its tendency to maintain the positive character of all law. It is as though the state, by its will, gave objectively existing rights and duties in the traditional sense. But the state cannot determine whether an obligation weighs upon me or whether I actually possess an inner power to rule over things or persons. Besides, what is the 'state', which is supposed to give the law, except a multitude of men who are connected with a certain locality and are organized simply through the law, that is, in reality through particular rules of conduct which have an actual power over people? In the modern concept of the state the old animism comes strongly into play. The state becomes a will.

Furthermore, I have sought to show in my teaching that 'consciousness of right' is by no means independent. Since the reality thought of when one represents this consciousness to oneself is purely fictitious, no actual experience lies at the basis of it. Material interests determine the content of the taboo, which is secretly presupposed in the consciousness of right. On the one hand, there are the universal interests in the conditions of life and the requirements of material and spiritual culture. Thus, for example, without the principle, 'Contracts must be kept', the whole productive enterprise of the society would fall apart. Consequently this principle is assumed by the consciousness of right. On the other hand, in the class struggle the interests of the individual classes determine *their* consciousness of right. From this it follows that the view, in jurisprudence, which regards propositions about rights as if they were in principle determined by the consciousness of right, is false.

In Uppsala Wilhelm Lundstedt, Professor of Civil Law, defends my views in the philosophy of law. He has also given me

[1] *Der römische obligationsbegriff im Lichte der allgemeinen römischen Rechtsanschauung*, Uppsala (I) 1927, (II) 1941.

c*

much stimulation. At present a vehement scientific debate is going on in Sweden between Lundstedt and other jurists, who, as though fighting *pro ara et focis*, are defending their inherited methods of natural law.

(3) *Philosophy of Religion:* Finally it should be mentioned, in connection with the philosophy of religion, that in my teaching I have advocated the view that the supposed idea of the divine as a spiritual reality depends, on the one hand, upon traditional materialistic ideas of 'spirits'—in so far, that is, as one actually represents anything by the word—and on the other hand, on religious feelings of a peculiar kind, which are connected with the idea of an objective spiritual being and whose content is transferred to the object. Thus these feelings associate themselves so firmly with the idea that the word, which expresses the objectively conceived spiritual being, is at the same time an expression of feeling. Since the content in the feeling itself is neither localized nor temporalized, it is natural, when one reflects about the meaning of the word, for the 'spirit', which was represented as objective, to be determined as elevated at least above space. The feeling, whose content can only be designated as actually spiritual, on account of the lack of localization and temporalization, is itself regarded, exactly as in the case of the consciousness of the 'I', as a knowledge of a spiritual reality. This is so to the extreme in mysticism.

## CONCLUSION

In general, all that is called *Geisteswissenschaft*—whether it con cerns the I, society, the state, morality, or religion—is only an intellectual play with expressions of feeling, as if something real were designated thereby. In assuming the possibility of such a science, one presupposes that feeling itself could include knowledge within itself.

The motto which I have placed at the head of this essay, *Praeterea censeo metaphysicam esse delendam*,[1] is not simply an unfavourable evaluation of metaphysics. It is a declaration of the opinion that we must destroy metaphysics, if we ever wish to pierce through the mist of words which has arisen out of feelings and associations and to proceed 'from sounds to things'.

[1] 'Moreover I propose that metaphysics must be destroyed.'

# TWO

# MORAL PHILOSOPHY

# I

# ON THE TRUTH OF MORAL PROPOSITIONS

## I. THE PROBLEM OF CONFLICTING MORAL VALUATIONS

Herodotus relates that the Persian king, Darius, put the following question to some Greeks, who were visiting in his court: 'For what price would you be willing to eat the dead bodies of your fathers?' 'Not for anything in the world', came the answer. Whereupon Darius called in some representatives of an Indian tribe, among whom that which was abhorrent to the Greeks was the custom, and he asked them for what price they would be willing to burn the dead bodies of their fathers. They vigorously repudiated every thought of anything so horrible. The author applied this in the following way: If one showed all possible customs to men and asked them to choose out the best, each one would select those which he himself happened to follow. A similar proposition among the Greeks, which undoubtedly originated in the time just preceding the Sophists, is the following: If one allowed men to cast into a pile the customs which they regarded as good and noble, and afterwards permitted each one to choose out of the pile those which seemed to him to be base and outrageous, nothing would be left over, but everything would have been distributed among them all.[1]

For us, children of a more recent time, who have access to a richer material, the variations in the contents of moral values are even more unmistakable. We may omit any reference to the views of primitive peoples and limit ourselves to such views as have grown up on civilized ground. For example, let us set the famous representative of Hellenistic culture, Aristotle, over against Christian morality or the morality influenced by Christianity. To live for the sake of another person (other than one's friend) is unworthy of the free man, says the philosopher. Self-sacrifice without regard for a relationship of friendship is the highest virtue, it is emphatically maintained from the other side. For Aristotle moderate retaliation for injury is a part of virtue. But in the original documents of Christianity, it is declared, 'If anyone

[1] See Gomperz, *Griechische Denker*, I, p. 325.

strikes you on the right cheek, turn to him the left one also'. According to Aristotle, 'barbarians' or non-Greeks, and also all those who practise a trade, are utterly lacking, for different reasons, in the ability fully to realize the ideal: viz. that intellectual, aesthetic, and ethical cultivation which is the highest good. For this reason it often happens that such people are mentioned in a certain contemptible tone of voice. In contrast to this, it is the view of Christian morality, where the emphasis is on the disposition of the mind, that no one is excluded from the possibility of attaining the highest. When Aristotle glorifies justice in social relations, this is not done out of consideration for some justice or worthiness in men, as in the morality of a more recent time, influenced as it is by Stoicism and Christianity. Rather for Aristotle the decisive thing is properly the aesthetic value of a certain system, as it relates to the distribution of the means of satisfying needs.

Thus a conflict of principle appears between these separate spheres. What is outrageous for one view is precisely what is just for the other. An even more obvious cleavage exists between, on the one hand, the morality of unrestrained sensuality, often defended during the Renaissance and developed into the superman morality of Nietzsche, and, on the other hand, the Christian, more or less ascetic, type of view.

But we can leave aside all historical examples and confine ourselves only to our own contemporary society. Immediately we see the conflict between, one can almost say, the moral points of view of different social classes. In the present bitter strife between capital and labour, as they are called, it is maintained, from the one side, that the individual has the right to provide for himself by lawful agreements with other persons whom he finds suitable, and also that he has an unconditional responsibility to abide by lawful contracts into which he has entered. Violations of such rights and obligations are viewed as outrageous. But from the other side it is maintained that the individual has an unconditional obligation to provide for the interests of the class with which he is united. All rights and obligations which are in conflict with such a duty are chimerical. And a weakening of the principle of class-solidarity is here the real and the only moral outrage.

Or consider the conflict which exists concerning the question of the moral quality of the right of property. On the one hand, the

individual is regarded as morally justified in possessing that which
he has acquired within the limits of the law, regardless of whether
or not it is the product of this own labour. On the other hand, it is
maintained that income acquired apart from one's own labour
involves a violation of the working-man's right to the entire
value of the product of his labour, and so on.

But once again, if the individual attempts to penetrate through
to his own set of moral valuations, he will easily discover different
strata which are out of harmony with one another. We carry
within us the conflict between an altruistic and a vengeful morality.
We repudiate vengeance as such. But in moral indignation vengeance against 'the sinner' comes into play, born of our concern
for the right, and is not restrained by the fact that we have repudiated vengeance in principle. If our indignation is inspired
only by our moral concern, we find it altogether proper and give
unrestrained play to our retaliatory instincts. In order to cover the
abyss we say, perhaps, that we hate not the sinner but the sin. But
the psychological impossibility of such a hair-fine distinction is
quickly recognized by an unprejudiced mind.

## 2. SOME ACCOUNTS OF THE OBJECTIVE GROUNDS
### OF MORAL VALUATIONS

Confronted with such conflicts of moral valuations, we are led
unavoidably to the question, Which is the right one? What is the
standard by which we may measure the correctness of different
views? It is evident that we may not use for this purpose our own
moral consciousness, as that which is closest at hand. Indeed, it is
not itself unambiguous. There are, in particular, two kinds of
standards which seem to be practicable and which, indeed, are
actually used. The one is *evolution*. The other is *unobservable
realities* which may be viewed as manifesting themselves with
greater or less completeness in moral demands.

First, concerning evolution, we must remark that this word is
ambiguous. It can signify progress towards the realization of an
objective purpose, lying within the thing itself. But in order to
decide whether in any given case we have a progression or a retro-
gression in man's moral concepts, we would have to determine
what man's moral purpose is, and this is just what we are seeking.

Now, however, the word 'evolution' can also signify something else, namely, merely the developing adaptation of a thing to the requirements of life. Since in the struggle for existence only the best-adapted survive, progress in this respect is necessary. Judged by such a standard, the morally higher becomes that which expresses the greater adaptation and thus also the greater possibility for the preservation of the individual and of society. But in such a view life itself becomes the highest principle of value. The rules of conduct which are required by life are, as such, the correct ones. At this point, however, we have the moral problem all over again, in the form: How can one maintain that mere life is the ultimate goal, as against, on the one hand, the inclination to deny life, which runs like a mighty stream through the history of morals, and, on the other hand, those movements for which only a life qualified in a certain way, not just any life, is worth living?

So let us examine the second standard, namely, the supernatural reality which is supposed to manifest itself in the consciousness of obligation. One says with Kant: Since obligation appears as an absolute demand upon us, this demonstrates itself therein as demanding something. Now since this will in every individual is universal, as absolute, it must possess the supernatural wills in all the others as its determinations. That is to say, they must all constitute a community. From this can be derived the principle that all moral beings ought to be determined by one another. Each one ought to be treated, as it is said, never only as a means, but always likewise as an end. According to the degree to which it realizes this principle, a system of morality is the higher.

But if the above-mentioned supernatural will in us is actually to be our own will, as it must be if it is to possess direct significance for us, the question arises how its supernaturalness can be maintained. That is, it must stand, to that extent, in relation to the natural order to which we belong. But in so far as it is encumbered with natural determinations, it can no longer be said to be exalted above nature. It is said that it turns only one side towards the world of natural existence, but has another side which is separate therefrom. But then the question arises how the side which is separate from nature can be combined with the side which is naturally determined, so as to constitute a unified will. In point of fact the supernatural side necessarily becomes determined by nature, on account of the unity of the whole.

But furthermore how could such a supernatural will be conceived in its individuality without ascribing to it precisely the content of the moral consciousness? Only as demanding some action or attitude which belongs to the observable world does a supernatural will acquire any individual significance for us. That is to say, it is precisely our actual moral interests, attached to our natural life, which alone give meaning to the idea. Take away these natural elements, and the whole is lost in the dim distance.

In point of fact, the above-mentioned supernatural will in us, which is supposed to manifest itself in obligation, is actually as little lifted up above natural determinateness as are the gods of the religions. In either case, that which is conceived acquires its meaning for us only through properties which signify something in our natural life, whether it is vengeance or justice or mercy or providence. What would mercy be apart from a relationship to another being, in need of help, on whom one has compassion? But such a relationship belongs essentially to our natural world. The idea of mercy loses all meaning when it is transferred to an absolute being, who can feel no compassion. What would justice be apart from a relationship to another person, whose sphere of rights one respects? But how shall an absolute being be able to stand in such a relationship towards other persons, with their own sphere of rights?

Often an attempt is made to relieve the difficulties here by introducing the idea of a purely symbolical way of apprehending the supernatural. On account of our finiteness, it is said, we can perceptibly grasp the supernatural only through the use of natural determinations. Thus it becomes a determinate reality for us only through being related to the senses. But in this way, so it is thought, we are presented with something which is really supernatural but which is symbolized in our finite apprehension according to historical relationships. But if it cannot be grasped as something determinate unless it is related to the senses, then the idea of the thing as a certain reality, exalted above the sensible world is meaningless. One is required to disregard the sensible elements which are necessary in order for the concepton to acquire any meaning—and still a meaning is supposed to remain. It is as if one said, 'God is just—but in connection with the idea of his justice, we must disregard what *we* mean by justice'.

But even if these misgivings regarding the possibility of conceiving a supernatural will in us could be removed, we would still not have obtained therein any standard for judging the correctness of moral views. It may well be that the unobservable wills of all moral beings should be thought of as constituting a community. In the unobservable world every will would be determined by every other as an end in itself, without for that reason ceasing to be its own end. But as soon as the principle which is thus afforded— viz. that one should treat himself and others as ends in themselves—is applied to wills in the observable world, difficulties arise. The natural end of one person may here come into conflict with that of another. What is the right relationship between the competing spheres of interest? In point of fact, any answer at all could be given from the standpoint of the stated principle. If he who is by nature greedy for power sacrifices his natural interests out of consideration for others, he makes himself a means for them— and according to the principle the action is unjust. Therefore he ought not so to act. So in this way any exploitation of man would be justified. But in the same way it could be said, on the other side, that if the individual satisfies his desire for power without consideration for others, he makes them the means for himself— and according to the principle he acts unjustly. Therefore he ought not so to act.

If one refers to conscience as that which affords the norms for unifying these spheres of interest, then, as seen from a purely scientific point of view, one has actually only made a declaration of bankruptcy. For our concern has been precisely to find a standard for judging the correctness of particular moral views. The fact that, nevertheless, such a way of proceeding is often employed, shows that one wishes to make science a handmaid of morality—which is by no means better than its being a handmaid of faith.

Thus the consequence seems to be that there is no objective distinction between right and wrong. But can our conceptions of right and wrong actually be only mocking appearances? Naturally, a question of truth must be answered in a scientific way. Therefore all other interests than the desire for truth must be suppressed and only objective grounds must be adduced. It will not do to view such an assumption *a priori* as absurd, simply because it may not agree with certain interests, regardless of how significant they are. *Plato amicus, veritas amicior*!

### 3. ARE MORAL PROPOSITIONS EITHER
### TRUE OR FALSE?

In this connection, however, we have to inquire first whether or not it is correct to ask about the truth or falsehood of moral judgments. If someone inquires whether gold is just or unjust, of course he would be immediately laughed out of court. The history of science, and particularly of philosophy, abounds with such improper questions, even if they are not so obviously improper. Just as gold is neither just nor unjust, so it may be that obligation or moral right is of such character that one can say neither that it actually holds nor that it does not hold for a certain mode of acting. It may be, therefore, that when we conceive a certain action as objectively right, another as objectively wrong, we combine with rightness and wrongness a concept which is altogether foreign to them. In such a case the question of the truth of moral propositions would be absurd. If, regarded in and of themselves, they do not at all represent anything as true, nor say anything at all about this or that's actually being such or such, it would be meaningless to ask about their truth.

### 4. THE DEVELOPMENT OF MORAL IDEAS

In order to carry out this inquiry, it is necessary to touch briefly on a certain aspect of the origin and development of moral ideas. In this connection I am confining myself exclusively to the progress which can be discerned in the views which belong to Western civilization.

It is often pointed out and established by a great many observations, that there is an intimate connection between primitive moral ideas and custom. I need only refer in this respect to Westermarck's famous work on *The Origin and Development of the Moral Ideas*. Custom functions among primitive peoples not only as universal habit, but also as a coercive force. Infractions of custom lead to retributions from the side of the whole society, and fear of these retaliations preserves the sanctity of custom. But another motive of a special kind attaches itself to this one, namely, the idea that it is *right* to follow custom and that the retributions which society dispenses, as the upholder of custom, are right. The individual feels constrained by many other coercive forces. But with regard to custom in particular he has the feeling that its observance is right and that the coercion is as it should be.

Herein is to be found the idea, admittedly an unclear one, that the action in question ought to be done for its own sake, and likewise that retaliations against infractions of custom are themselves good. In a word, these retaliations acquire an independent value for the individual. And indeed they positively represent a kind of value which cannot be subordinated to other values, a value which ought to be acknowledged under all circumstances. This, then, is also the specifically moral thing in the individual's relationship to custom.

There is to be found here, one may well say, a phenomenon of adaptation. One becomes reconciled to the constraint by making the prescriptions of custom and the retaliations of the power of custom into an independent supreme value. Such an acceptance of custom is rooted in the soil of its utility for the individual and for society. It is useful for the individual, because by this acceptance he is enabled to adhere more steadfastly to custom.   Infractions of custom bring him ruin. It is useful for the whole, because the whole gains coherence through the firmness of custom.

Custom functions in this way, however, through two different motives, the one, fear of a superior power, the other, the idea of a supreme value which is present here. Hence from the very outset the specifically moral motive, viz. concern for that which is conceived as the supreme value, has become intertwined with another, viz. fear of a higher power. Nor in fact does this connection with fear of punishment disappear in the course of the development of morality. Our moral consciousness, of which conscience is the supreme judge, is actuated both by direct concern for our moral task and by fear of retaliations from the side of conscience.

But if obligation or the supreme value thus holds in primitive morality only in intimate association with fear of the power of custom, then a certain tendency to combine custom and obligation with one another also becomes natural. Custom comes to appear as identical with the supreme value, the substance of right. It becomes a moral authority, sacred and venerable in itself. Obligation secures its representative in a certain reality. The connection of obligation with an authoritative reality is never lost in primitive morality. Even if obligation is more or less detached from custom, it is always attached to an existence which determines its content, which itself becomes the quintessence of it. 'This is the will of a mighty divine being', 'So the order of the world requires', or 'So a law within the conscience dictates', becomes the watchword for the more or less revolutionary morality which sets itself up against custom itself. Such a morality also finds its point of support in a norm-establishing reality. The significance of conscience, which plays a dominant role in modern morals, is to be particularly noted here. The inner summons, which we call conscience, appears to us as the moral norm. Instead of custom, divine power, or the order of the world, conscience becomes the authority which is venerable in itself—the representative of the supreme value.

But let us now look at certain tendencies which arise in moral consciousness as developments out of the association of obligation with a certain normative reality, which we have just described. Here are to be mentioned in particular the tendencies to absolutize and to internalize the norms in question. When the idea of an obligation, in the sense of a supreme value, gets established, there appears also a tendency to absolutize the reality which represents it. When a thing is raised to the level of something venerable in itself, there appears also the tendency to raise it up above all limits. How could it be sacred in itself, if it were a natural pheno-menon, dependent upon all kinds of external circumstances? In particular, it becomes necessary that the command of an authority should appear as indispensable, and that it should be uncondition-ally dangerous to transgress against it. Otherwise its inner venera-bility would be diminished. On the other hand, along with a clearer manifestation of obligation as the supreme value for the individual himself, there comes a tendency to draw the norm-establishing reality closer to man himself, to remove its external and foreign character.

These tendencies become particularly evident when moral ideas are directly associated with religious ones. In the Judaeo-Christian monotheism the unlimited reverence, the object of which is the deity, has a quality of moral authority which obviously stands in intimate association with its absolute character. One may think also in this connection of the mediaeval interpretation of evil as something unreal, a 'non-being', and of true being as one with itself, the good. In Platonism, indeed, the construction of an un-observable, absolute world of ideas has, primarily, other, more theoretical causes. But it is certain that it is their supposed absoluteness which for Plato binds them together with moral value, the good in the proper sense.

Both of these examples of a moral-religious view serve also to show how the tendency to internalize authority is operative in connection with a more determinate representation of the direct value of the moral relationship. The God of Christianity is not only to be feared, but he is also something to which a man may entrust himself, since he loves mankind. The world of ideas is for Plato not an altogether external reality for man, but it is also immanent within his reason.

But the development we are now considering reaches its proper culmination in the ideas which, in a modern, less religious consciousness, are connected with conscience. In conscience there is immediately present a feeling or a concern for a certain practical relationship as the right, or as in the highest degree valuable. But to this is also attached the idea that disobedience to the summons which is present within is absolutely ruinous for the individual and brings him into misfortune. In point of fact, there lies in the background here the idea, not always noticed, of an inner absolute power, which places demands upon us and retaliates in the severest manner against infractions. Undoubtedly religious conceptions are present here, imparted by education and the general social milieu—conceptions of a highest power, which is itself the right. It is particularly clear that this way of thinking obtains in our consciousness of guilt and responsibility. We regard ourselves as answerable to an inescapable power in our own inner being, which declares us to be deserving of punishment or else exonerates us. But when the properly moral feeling and interest step into the foreground here, and the divine power is attached to it, the religious element does not receive an independent development. The power, as the ground of the world, retires in favour of its purely moral function. Therefore we do not notice that in conscience we are fearing a god. Still that is what we are doing. One does not probe to the bottom of the matter if one seeks to understand the way in which conscience functions without considering the centuries of religious education.

Now what is of most immediate interest here is that the authoritative reality to which obligation is connected in the morality of conscience has come to be most intimately associated with man himself, while at the same time it preserves its absolute character.

It has become one with his own moral feeling and concern. The tendency to bring the authority into man has here made itself felt most decidedly.

## 5. OBLIGATION AND OBJECTIVE REALITY

What we were to investigate was the following: Is it correct to ask about the truth of moral propositions? Perhaps the claim to truth which these propositions make depends upon a connection with elements which are foreign to obligation or the supreme value itself. As a result of the foregoing investigation of the origin and development of the ideas in question, we have now been provided with an occasion for accepting such an assumption. It has been shown that, on account of the connection between obligation and custom, the former comes to be attached, even in its development, to a certain authoritative reality, whether it is the will of a god, an order of the world, or the demand of conscience. Naturally something foreign to obligation is thereby attached to it. Even if it is absolute, a reality can never include within itself a supreme value. The existence of a divine will or an inner demand can never imply, in and of itself, that we ought to follow it, that to follow it is of supreme value. Existence and value signify something entirely different. Therefore value cannot be included within existence. A moral authority or norm, as a reality which is good *in itself*, is, objectively regarded, something absurd.

But by virtue of this attachment to an element which is foreign to obligation, it becomes possible to explain how we come to think in terms of an objective distinction between right and wrong. If a certain reality is determinative for what we ought to do, then, of course, what we ought to do can be decided in an objective manner. All that is required is to reach clarity concerning which actions are in agreement with the reality in question—whether it is a question of the will of a god or our own conscience. In this way we may establish what is actually the right as against any subjective valuations which present themselves.

As a result of our description of the tendency to absolutize the normative reality in question, it is possible to understand how we come to regard a certain kind of action as right in all situations. If it is in agreement with the absolute, and therefore universal, reality, the action is right in all situations. In particular it is possible

to explain how we come to regard the very principle of right conduct as capable of being established in an unambiguous and uni-
vocal manner. The absolute reality, which is regarded as determining obligation, must be in harmony with itself. Therefore right
conduct can have only one principle, even though the particular
applications of the principle may be different on account of
differences in the situations in which it is applied. Then when we
consider the tendency to internalize authority more and more,
it becomes possible to understand how obligation comes to be
regarded not as something determined from outside, but as belonging directly to a certain way of acting.

As a matter of fact, however, it is not the case that our analysis
of these relationships provides us with only the *possibility* of
explaining the claim of moral propositions to truth. It is also a
question here of at least the most readily available *actual* ground
of explanation. For it can be shown directly that in the very
conception of an obligation, of an action as valuable in the highest
degree, there is present no consciousness of objectivity whatsoever.

Kant says in one place that duty presents itself to us only in so
far as we are acting or are thinking about acting. In this statement
there lies the idea that duty exists for us only in so far as that
which we find ourselves in duty bound to do is an actual or possible
way of acting. But in this idea, again, it is implied that the action
must arouse an interest in us. This is undoubtedly true. If we
stand as cold observers before ourselves, that is, in reality interested not in what is observed but only in the investigation of what
is observed, what can we discover? We recognize, in the midst of a
manifold of other phenomena, a feeling of duty in connection with
a judgment of value and a direct interest in a certain action. But
all this yields nothing more than a certain kind of psychological
event. That the action ought to be done is not at all a part of what
we can discover. The keenest analysis of what is present reveals
no such thing. Or in a similar way we investigate a certain action.
We can establish that the action arouses the strongest appetite or
the strongest desire or that it leads to my well-being or that of
another. We can discover—let us feign the possibility—that it is
commanded by a god or our unobservable being. But every attempt
to draw out of the situation the conclusion that it is actually in the
highest degree *of value* to undertake the action is doomed to failure.

No obligation or supreme value can be discovered in such a way, for if we are standing indifferently before ourselves and our actions, only observing, we can only establish factual situations. But in the fact that something is, it can never be implied that it ought to be. That something is better than something else is meaningless for the inbifferent observer. For him nothing is better or worse.

But turn the situation around. We are considering an action, and different motives appear. Now it becomes immediately clear to us that we ought to act in a certain way. Here we no longer stand indifferently before ourselves and our actions, but we assume a certain posture towards that which is given. In this posture a supreme value really does signify something to us.

Note that in so far as we consider that something is actually the case, i.e. that truth is present, we consider also that it is so entirely without regard for our subjective posture towards the fact, our feelings or our interests *vis-à-vis* the fact. Thus the result must be that in moral propositions as such we do not at all consider that obligatoriness actually belongs to the action. To say that it does would imply that it would hold without respect to any subjective posture regarding the fact. But that would be meaningless.

Thus when we think of an objective distinction between right and wrong, a foreign element must have been added. It is easiest to assume that, particularly in our ordinary moral ideas, this is the norm-establishing reality with which obligation is associated.

This is not to say, however, that this reality is the only foreign element which, combined with obligation, causes objectivity to be introduced there. Specifically, in certain systems of moral philosophy one believes that one can often establish an objective moral principle by starting from our actual moral valuations. Since in modern civilization these valuations always present certain common elements, because of similar life-situations, one thinks that by uncovering and systematizing them one can lay down the correct principle for judging actions. It is in this way, for example, that Spencer and Wundt proceed, each in his own way. Here moral value is connected with the actual valuations of men, which thus become the objectifying element which is foreign to value. It is clear that knowledge of actual valuations is by no means knowledge of value. To the extent that we are concerned with actual valuations, we establish only certain factual situations, and we by no means establish thereby that something is better or worse. Knowing that something is better or worse would require not only that knowledge had valuations for its object, but also that knowledge would be itself a valuation.

A similar blending or moral value and moral valuation is found in Westermarck, although he does not make use of it to build up an objective moral principle on this basis. He takes our moral concepts, and thus our concepts of the value of actions, as a consciousness of the capacity of certain actions to arouse ethical approval. Thus they become nothing but concepts of actual modes of valuation and to that extent can be determined as true or false. But in so far as they imply a consciousness of the value of actions, they do not have valuations for their objects, but are themselves valuations.

However an attempt is made in modern philosophy of value to vindicate the possibility of an objective supreme value through a new interpretation of the concept of truth itself. Truth itself is identified with the value of certain assumptions. Consequently the impossibility of talking about objective values disappears. One says, for example, 'What we call truth is only propositions which are the means for certain life-values'. Or one makes truth to be an immediate, universal value in certain judgments. Such opinions, which in our time are so widespread, fall to the ground of their own inner absurdity. For the whole theory itself depends upon the ordinary concept of truth. Every defender of such a theory must mean to assert that this *is* the way it is. 'This *is* the way it is', he must mean, 'completely independent of all valuations'. Otherwise the meaning would be that the assertions in question are themselves true only in the sense that they are the objects for certain valuations. The correctness of *this* assertion again signifies only that it is itself valued in a certain way, and so on *ad infinitum*. But then the whole theory would hang suspended in mid-air. As a matter of fact, modern philosophy of value, in so far as it has this character, only gives expression to man's deep-rooted tendency to make his own values into the true essence of reality. To possess true reality often becomes simply the same thing as to satisfy man's deepest interests. Surely the apotheosis of man can go no farther!

However one may not draw the conclusion from the foregoing that it would be impossible to delineate an obligation for other persons in any sense. It is a truth, now universally recognized and accepted, that the individual is developed intellectually as well as morally only in social associations. But this presupposes, as does the very possibility of community in the life of thought, the possibility of a set of commonly accepted moral valuations. But for this it is again required that one person can put himself not only into the other person's world of ideas, but also into his life of feeling and will. Thus on behalf of the other person, or from his standpoint, and on the basis of a certain given principle of valuation, one can express oneself as to how that person ought to act. This pronouncement acquires a special significance even for the person addressed, if through it he obtains knowledge of a certain state of affairs which is significant for his valuations, if he teaches himself to recognize the correct means for reaching a given goal or the particular means which come under an originally valued, universal rule of action. If he is really convinced of the actuality of the state of affairs in question and if this conviction enters into his valuation, then the obligation which has been placed before him comes to have significance for him also.

But it must be denied that in such a case it would be a question of an objective obligation, concerning which the person addressed could be convinced on objective grounds. If he should lack the principle of valuation which is assumed, or if he should fail to appropriate his newly-acquired knowledge of the state of affairs in arriving at his particular valuation, the obligation in question would in no way exist for him. From this point of view the only thing that can be said with reference to the claim to objectivity is that knowledge of the state of affairs, in so far as it becomes valid for valuations on the basis of a certain principle, necessarily leads these valuations in a certain direction. This can also be expressed in the following way: With greater knowledge of the character of reality and the recognition of this knowledge in valuations, there follow other special valuations.

Moreover it is to be noticed that even the fundamental moral valuation itself is influenced, of course, by knowledge of the character of reality. Greater insight into human suffering, for example, usually gives a more human colouring to the moral principle of value. So also in the realm of aesthetics, broader knowledge can open one's mind to new aesthetic values, which the valuing person may place higher than any other. However it is always the case, in this connection, that one's natural disposition, passion, class

interest, deeply ingrained habits, and such like can entirely suppress the influence of the expansion of knowledge on the fundamental moral valuation.

In any case, one may not conclude from the relationship we have
been noting that the principle of valuation itself is to be regarded
cognitively. The only thing of which one can be convinced on
objective grounds is a certain character of reality, even if a newly-
gained conviction in this respect may modify one's subjective
valuation. The attempt to convince a Caesar Borgia of the objective
rightness of a more social disposition is as preposterous as it would
be for the sheep to want to prove to the wolf that it is wrong to
bite so inconsiderately. This does not make it out of the question
that there is a duty for society to protect itself from such natures—
just as there is a duty for the shepherd to prevent the wolf from
doing harm.

We may here add the following. Let us assume that it would be
possible to lay down a certain moral valuation, belonging to all
rational beings, which would always arise if they had sufficient
knowledge of reality. Even then no objective right would be given
in any way. The knowledge imagined in this way would have as its
object actual valuations, not values. Only actual situations would
be present for it. In order for anything to become better or worse
here, the knowing subject must assume a certain posture of feeling
or of will respecting the given—but such a posture does not
belong to knowledge itself.

The final result of this investigation is that a moral proposition
as such—i.e. a proposition to the effect that a certain action represents a supreme value—cannot be said to be either true or false.
It is not at all a proposition to the effect that the action is actually
or in truth the right one. Moral propositions are sometimes thought,
nevertheless, to be objectively true or false. This is due to the
fact that obligation is associated in the ordinary moral consciousness with something which is altogether foreign to it. This foreign
element is primarily a certain supposed moral authority.

## 6. MORAL THEORY AND THE STABILITY
### OF SOCIETY

Once again we observe the universal course of the process of the
life of moral thought, and think in particular about the tendency

which appears therein to draw the absolutized, sacred, and venerable authority nearer to man himself, to internalize it. In the morality of conscience this process has reached its culmination. There the absolute authority has been internalized and has become one with our own moral interest. But notice, when this internalization is completely carried out, it leads in fact to the disappearance of the moral authority. In the degree to which it renounces its external character and becomes for us our own moral aspirations with all their obvious relativity, it is lost in the world of finiteness. For that which is worthy of being called divine, too obvious an intimacy with the human is hazardous. There remains only our moral interest itself, as an inclination towards that on which we set the supreme value.

The feeling that we stand under the demands of an absolute will lying in the background, that we are under obligation and responsible to it, must now melt away. An actually autonomous morality is within us, determined only by direct regard for what we esteem most of all. All patent or suppressed ideas that our supreme value has cosmic or objective significance disintegrate. Certainly civilized man always feels a responsibility, in *one* way, for realizing his supreme values. More than anything else, he will always be fearful of deserting his task in this regard, of failing to achieve what he can. But if such conceptions as we have just mentioned have disappeared, it will not be *punishment* which he fears. Rather his fear will be determined only by the fact that it is a matter of his supreme values, the relative realization of which alone makes his life worth living.

In this way, however, the course of the further development of morality is indicated. The character of the progress of science itself reinforces this expectation. Through the centuries science has carried on a tenacious struggle against ideas which make human interest, attired in divine costume, the central part of the universe. Inch by inch it has prepared the ground. But not even our innermost beliefs can ultimately withstand the power of knowledge.

But if the development of the world of moral ideas actually leads in a similar direction, a revolution in the outlook of western civilization is at hand, the full scope of which no one can comprehend. Undoubtedly the association of our supreme values with an absolutized reality (even if it has not always been in evidence) has been a strong force in the preservation of social as well as cultural values. The quite obviously religious popular morality, as well as the philosophical moral systems associated with it, are like towering cathedrals, in which such values have found their refuge. Only barbarians make an assault on them by casting stones.

Moral values, which in the current morality have always had social as well as cultural significance in greater or lesser degree, have found their stronghold in world powers themselves or in absolute, inescapable orders. Even if, as in the morality of conscience, this way of thinking has remained in the background, it has stimulated in men's minds a confidence in the final victory of the good. This confidence has inspired men to struggle for these values. To this is to be added the tremendous importance that this way of thinking has as a means of discipline. The idea of hell and the promptings of a bad conscience (which are actually very closely related) have been powerful taskmasters in the service of social as well as cultural values.

On the other hand, it is to be noted that the idea of one's own moral view as absolutely authoritative and thus as the only right one has led, and always will lead, to fanaticism. One feels that one's own indignation towards contrary courses of action is identical with what one quite patently assumes to be the Almighty's own condemnation of his adversaries. Or one feels that he is the administrator of the demand of a sacred world-order. His indignation becomes a holy wrath, which goes out beyond all proportions and limits. As a matter of fact, the lack of restraint in the class-hatred of our day has its roots in the fact that popular morality makes its own values absolutely authoritative. It is clear that if the consciousness of right in a society should disintegrate and each part should give to its own values an absolute sanctity, fanaticism would flourish. But in this way popular morality has come to work in an anti-social and anti-cultural direction.

All things considered, however, we who long more than anything else for the happiness and refinement of the race have no need to despair. Superstitious conceptions have often fallen away— superstitions on which, to a certain extent, the socially and culturally determined popular morality has been based. But that morality has always been raised anew, in fact rejuvenated, with a broader and a purer objective. Such a morality has a much too intimate association with society's tendency towards self-preservation to be submerged. All the evidence points to the fact that, once we have taken the final step and have left behind any patent or suppressed belief in the cosmic and thus objective significance of value, this popular morality will *not* die away. On the contrary, there is reason to suppose that, like a Phoenix-bird, it will be born anew out of the ashes of the old morality, with a more emancipated and far-sighted vision. It will also bear the stamp of a milder judgment on all human aspiration, which follows from viewing things *sub specie aeternitatis*, from the insight that everything is only a moment in an endless natural context, in which nothing is in itself higher or lower.

## 7. MORAL PHILOSOPHY AS A SCIENCE

From the foregoing it ought to have become clear what is *not* the task of moral philosophy as a science. Science has only to indicate what is true, while it is nonsense to regard the idea of an obligation as true; so no science can have it as its task to indicate how we ought to act. Systems of moral philosophy, which set up a moral principle, have combined obligation with an element which is foreign to it. They have been misled, first of all, by the claim of ordinary morality to objectivity—this because of its being attached to a norm-establishing authority. But just as a science of religion cannot be based upon a religious consciousness, so a moral science cannot have as its basis a moral consciousness. In both cases it is a question of a subjective process of thought, which itself may be an object for science, but cannot be the foundation for any science.

A moral science cannot even set up a conditional obligation. Of course, if the very principle of right conduct is assumed as given, the means for realizing the established end can be scientifically determined. But such an investigation—for example, the investigation of the means for realizing universal well-being—while significant in itself, may be of many different kinds. It may be a mixture of historical experience, sociology, physiology, and psychology. But as such it is in no way a moral science, because in itself it has nothing to do with morality. Again, as soon as one wishes to make a practical application of the result of the investigation, and says, 'Therefore you ought to act in this way or in that', he is in another sphere, where the concepts of truth and falsehood are without significance. Höffding, who otherwise maintains the subjectivity of moral standards, makes himself guilty of a confusion of concepts, when he believes that he can maintain a scientific ethic because, among other reasons, once the end has been given, the means for reaching that end can be determined scientifically. As a matter of fact his point of view leads to the concept, 'scientific expression of feeling'—a concept whose elements are so hard to combine. (Compare, for example, the following statements: 'Philosophical ethics is a systematically executed valuation', *Etik*, third edition, p. 10. 'Judgments about good and evil are expressions of feeling', p. 23.) What has been said certainly does not rule out the possibility that such an investigaton as the one under consideration may indirectly acquire perhaps a secondary significance for moral science in another way. If this or that is actually the means for the realization of a morally valued end, then he who has sufficient knowledge and accepts the end within his moral principle and also appropriates this knowledge in arriving at his particular valuation, must also morally value the means in question. But such a use of the investigation concerns only the manner in which men actually come to value things under specific conditions. In no way does it yield a conditional obligation.

Moral philosophy as a science is purely and simply a science of actual moral valuations in their historical development, based on a psychological analysis and conducted by a critical philosophical investigation of the ideas which are operative therein.

But if moral philosophy also must now stand, as must every science, on the other side of good and evil, one may not conclude from this that it teaches us that we ought to leave aside all current moral rules and only give consideration to our selfish interests. This is the standpoint of the Sophists. As a matter of fact, such a conclusion would imply that science establishes other valuations than those which are contained in our ordinary moral ideas. But science does not have to make judgments of value in this way. Just as it cannot show that given rules ought to be followed, so it cannot show that they ought not to be followed—and that other principles of conduct ought to come forward instead. Therefore the view represented here has nothing to do with the Sophist ethics, a superman morality, or such like. It maintains only that moral science may not be a teaching *in* morals, but only a teaching *about* morality.

# II

## ON THE IDEA OF DUTY

The representatives of the theories which are discussed in this essay[1] say that they maintain the view that positive law is merely a system of commands or declarations of a certain will. Law would therefore have to be regarded as an actual reality existing for a purely theoretical consciousness which merely recognizes it. We shall now examine more closely *whether they really keep to this and do not introduce something else into law in the course of presenting their theories*. But for this purpose it is necessary first to investigate more closely the psychological implications of a *command*, with particular reference to its relation to the notion of *duty*. In so doing we prepare ourselves for the transition to the main theory concerning law, which regards the latter as expressions, issuing with authority, of ideas about rights and obligations.

### 1. THE PSYCHOLOGICAL CONTENT OF COMMAND

In a command the person who issues it seeks by certain signs, especially by a certain utterance, to cause the person commanded to act in a certain positive or negative way. Let us confine our attention to an utterance, as being the commonest method of command. An utterance which has the property of being a command has a peculiar form: 'Thou shalt do so-and-so!' or 'Do so-and-so!' What kind of idea or what state of consciousness in general does the issuer of the command intend to call forth in the receiver of it?

In the first place we must insist on the difference between the content of this expression and the content of a threat, which is sometimes adjoined to a command. By using a threat one seeks merely, in order to induce a person to act in a certain positive or negative way, to arouse in him the idea that certain unfortunate

---

[1] This account of the idea of duty is extracted from the essay, *On the Question of the Notion of Law*, which has been translated by C. D. Broad and published in the volume, *Inquiries into the Nature of Law and Morals*, Uppsala, Almqvist and Wiksell, 1953. The portion reproduced here is taken from pp. 116-201 in Prof. Broad's translation. The selection is published here with the kind permission of Professor Broad and the *Kungliga humanistiska vetenskapssamfundet i Uppsala*.

D

consequences will ensue to him from the utterer of the threat unless he acts in such and such a way. A threat may possibly be
combined with a warning. The essential point about a warning is
this. He who issues it puts himself in imagination into the other
man's scheme of values, and, by reference to what is counted as a
disvalue in that scheme, strives to persuade him of the wisdom of
avoiding a certain action. But the peculiar implication of 'thou
shalt' in a command does not emerge in either a threat or a warning. As is well known, it can be uttered without any threat or warning being either openly or secretly combined with it. In that case
we have a pure command. In general it is clear that the 'thou
shalt' in every command is meant *categorically*. It is not intended
to arouse the idea of the action as something which ought to happen
merely in respect to the realization of a positive value or the
avoidance of a negative value on the part of the *person commanded*.
So a threat or a warning can only be an appendix to this 'thou
shalt', used in order to induce the person addressed to act in a
certain way by means of additional motives.[1]

But, if there is no reference in the 'thou shalt' of a command to

---

[1] Hold *v.* Ferneck (*Die Rechtswidrigkeit*, I, 1903, pp. 75 *et seq.*) assumes
that a command is meaningless without a sanction. So too Seligmann,
*Beitrage zur Lehre vom Staatsgesetz und Staatsvertrag*, p. 46. Cf. Gray
(*The Nature and Sources of the Law*, 1909, p. 25), who follows Austin.
This leads to the consequence that the only thing which is significant in a
command is the assertion that the omission of a certain action will lead
to certain unfortunate consequences for the recipient of it. On that view
it is a question either of a purely theoretical utterance, intended however
to induce to a certain action, or in addition an advice to the recipient of the
command to beware. This is also noted by Binding, *Die Normen und ihr
Übertretung*, 2. Aufl. I, 1890, p. 39. Hold *v.* Ferneck insists, however,
(loc. cit. p. 183), that a command differs from such an utterance in the fact
that it includes also an announcement of the will of the person who issues
the command. (So too in the definition of a norm, p. 79.) But such an
announcement of volition serves no purpose if the only significant thing
is a sanction. But, if the announcement of volition played no part in the
intention of the command, it would not in general occur. Now it should be
noted that, if it occurs, it does so precisely through the 'thou shalt' which
is specific for a command as distinct from a threat or a warning. In
assuming a special announcement of volition as an essential factor in a
command one is therefore assuming that the expression of a command
itself has a peculiar meaning which must be distinguished from that of a
sanction. The latter thus merely adds to the force which the mere expression of a command possesses.

any value for the recipient, it may be asked how the issuer of the command can influence the receiver of it by his mere utterance. (1) The explanation cannot lie in the utterance being intended to arouse in the recipient the idea that a certain wish or volition exists in the person who issues the command.[1] It may be that the recipient can conclude from the fact that the command is given that something of the kind exists. But that is not the same as to say that the meaning which the utterance has for one who realizes that its purpose is to convey a command consists in the arousing of such an idea in his mind. It is plain that such knowledge cannot have the least practical influence on the recipient unless he also knows that action contrary to the wish or volition of the person who issues the command will lead to unfortunate consequences for him, or on the other hand, that action in accordance therewith will bring about the realization of certain positive values for him. But, if the only intention of the person issuing the command were to operate in that way, he would need only to threaten or to issue a warning against a certain kind of action, or to promise something as a consequence of the kind of action that he wishes, or to advise in favour of it. That is to say, the 'thou shalt' in uttering a command would, on this view of its content, be quite meaningless for the purpose of the command. It should be specially noted that, if this 'thou shalt' is identical with 'I want you to' and not merely 'I wish that you would', the complete expression must be: 'I will by a certain process make you act in a certain way.' But, if the process here thought of is just that of commanding, it cannot be the same as giving utterance to such a volition: Otherwise one would be forced to the consequence that the person who issues a command expresses his volition to express a volition to express a volition . . . and so on *ad infinitum*. To this must be added that an imperative, in spite of its propositional form, cannot possibly express a judgment that something is in fact such-and-such. This is as impossible as that the 'I will' in an intention should do so. Every attempt to transform the 'thou shalt' of an imperative into something like: 'It is in fact the case that you will act in such-and-such a way' is seen at once to be a failure.[2]

[1] So Hold *v.* Ferneck, loc. cit., So too Schuppe, *Grundzüge der Ethik und Rechtsphilosophie*, 1881, p. 46.

[2] That an imperative does not express a judgment is asserted by Sigwart, *Logik*, 4. Aufl., I, 1911, p. 18, note, Bierling, *Juristische Prinzi-*

(2) It cannot be the case that the 'thou shalt' in a command is a direct expression of a personal wish or volition of the person who issues the command.[1] This too, for the reasons already given, would be meaningless for the purpose of the command. Besides, in that case the expression of the command would be either 'Would that you would act thus' (in so far as it was the expression of a wish) or: 'I shall make you act in a certain way' (in so far as it is the expression of a volition). It should further be noted that it is by no means necessary that there should be in the person who issues the command an actual volition as to his own action, in the psychological sense, which always includes a special intention. We often 'act' without any special intention. (That in such cases we talk of 'acting' and also of 'volition', 'purpose', etc., depends on the fact that the activity goes on in the same purposive way as if a special intention were present.)

(3) It cannot be a question of arousing in the recipient of the command by means of the utterance a wish to act in a certain way. Such a wish, which must always refer to some value which is to be realized by the person through the action, can be aroused indirectly through threats or promises attached to certain ways of acting. It can be aroused directly through advice in favour of a certain action, combined with promises or threats. A piece of advice is just a pointing-out the desirability, from the point of view of the person addressed, of a certain action. It therefore presupposes putting oneself in imagination into his scheme of values. It thus gives expression to a wish based upon his system of values; a wish which it is sought to awaken in him directly through giving the advice. That there can be no question here of this follows immediately from the fact that a command as such does not refer to the recipient's scheme of values.

This being so, there remains only one way of interpreting the meaning of an expression in the imperative. It can aim only at creating *directly* in the recipient of the command an intention to act in a certain way. According to the analysis of the notion of intention given in (3), this amounts to saying that, without arous-

*pienlehre*, I, 1894, p. 29, and Maier, *Psychologie des emotionalen Denkens*, 1908, pp. 679 *et seq.* Hold v. Ferneck's elaborate analysis of the command (pp. 75 *et seq.*) is spoiled by his completely overlooking this.

[1] In the same sense Kelsen, *Hauptprobleme der Staatsrechtslehre*, 1911, p. 202 and Stark, *Die Analyse des Rechts*, p. 36, cfd. with p. 91.

ing wishes as motives, it effects an association between a feeling of conative impulse and the idea of a certain action. Through the absence of motives in the person influenced, this mode of influence acquires the character of a practical suggestion. As a condition for this there must be of course special relations between the active and the passive party, e.g. a superiority in power on the part of the former which makes the latter susceptible to his influence. Often, however, the person who issues a command wishes merely by the use of 'Thou shalt' to arouse in the other party the idea of a certain action, but to do this in such a way that the idea maintains itself and represses all conflicting ideas of action and thus passes over directly into realization. In such cases the relation between the active and the passive party is such that the latter's will, in the correct sense of the word, may be paralysed. Indeed, where the order works mechanically, as when it refers to familiar military movements in accordance with fixed words of command, an idea of the action need be present only in the mind of the giver of the order. For those who receive the order the mere auditory perception of the word of command, e.g. 'Quick march!', acts without any intermediary idea of the action, and thus the reaction-time is reduced. In the latter case it is, however, natural that one seeks at the beginning of the drill to impress practically on the men the meaning of the words of command in terms of action. But the real meaning of the imperative form does not emerge even if we leave out of account the use of a mechanically operative power of command and confine ourselves to commands in which the idea of an action is effectively impressed. When no alternative is envisaged the imperative form serves merely to strengthen the suggestive force of the indication of the action and thus to repress the ideas of other possible actions. But it may happen that, although the relation between the giver and the receiver of an order is indeed such that the order might be effective, yet, in consequence of conflicting impulses which arise in the meanwhile in the mind of the recipient, the thought of other kinds of action cannot be altogether suppressed. In *that* case it is necessary to evoke a special intention in him to perform the command action, if the order is to be effective. It is here, where the whole process cannot take place in a purely ideo-motor way, that the imperative form acquires its peculiar meaning. When the idea of the action which the order arouses is prevented from predominating, because it meets with opposition in the recipient's own will, it becomes necessary to act directly upon the latter. And this takes place through emphasizing the imperative form as such, which will break down the opposition of the will. In consequence of ideas of other modes of action, which are maintained by opposing impulses, it is not enough here merely to inoculate the idea of the action commanded. In order to make that idea pass into action, it is necessary to suppress the tendency of these impulses to materialize in actual intentions, by producing through the imperative form an intention to carry out the action commanded.

We can now understand how the imperative form can function as a mere auxiliary to the power which the mention of an action has of making the idea of that action predominant. When the imperative form functions in its own characteristic way its use is to break down the resistance due to opposing impulses by arousing a direct intention to act in the way commanded. But, when nothing of this kind is needed, all that remains of the conative significance of the imperative form is the negative function of checking possible opposing conative impulses. This happens, in such cases, by paralysing all genuine willing. When this has been accomplished the field is left open for suggestion through indicating the action. The imperative form then acts in the same direction as when it exerts its characteristic function, although the latter retires into the background. In the same way the military command 'Attention!' is effective in certain circumstances, without arousing any idea of an action in those who hear it, in exactly the same way as when its meaning in terms of action is operative.

In so far as the imperative form has a characteristic meaning of its own, the following point must be emphasized about it. It is concerned with that state of consciousness (or, more correctly, that association of states of consciousness) which, according to the analysis in (3) above, is an intention. It is not concerned with the idea of an intention. If an intention is itself a state of consciousness, it would obviously be an unnecessary detour to try to impress the idea of an intention in order by that means to arouse the intention itself. Besides, it follows at once, from the fact that the imperative form baffles every attempt to reduce it to the form of a judgment that there can be no question here of evoking an idea which, if it were made clear, might become a judgment, viz. a judgment to the effect that a certain intention is really present.

But, of the two factors in consciousness of intention, viz. a feeling of conative impulse and the idea of a certain action, the imperative form as such represents by its 'Thou shalt' the former. The 'I will' of an intention represents just the conative factor in it. Thus the 'Thou shalt' of an imperative and the 'I will' of an intention are concerned with the same factor in an intention. But they are concerned with it in different ways. 'Thou shalt' in the imperative aims at directly calling forth that factor. 'I will' in the intention is an expression of that factor as already existing.

But this way of distinguishing the two needs one qualification. It is doubtless true that the 'Thou shalt' in an imperative does not express an already existing feeling of conative impulse in the giver of the command, which would be a factor in what we call an intention. It aims indeed only at arousing such a feeling in the recipient of the order. But, if the imperative form is to be really effective in arousing a consciousness of intention in the recipient of the order, it must bear the mark of being a real expression of intention. But, unless there already were in the giver of the command just that consciousness of intention which he seeks to arouse, the imperative form would not adequately express it. For this purpose what is needed is not the mere utterance of the words but in addition that they should be uttered in the way which is characteristic of the expression of an already existing volition. That very state of feeling which accompanies an actual intention colours the expression of it in a characteristic way. It is characterized especially by the feeling of energy which marks an intention. In order that this peculiar characteristic may manifest itself it is therefore necessary that the consciousness of the intention in question shall actually be present in the giver of the order. But how can a person have a consciousness of intention which refers to another's action and not his own? Note that it is not a question here of the intention to make the recipient of the order act in a certain way, though this may happen to be present in the giver of the order. *That* intention is expressed in a quite different way. However, the explanation given in (3) of consciousness of intention enables us to understand the possibility of its referring to *another* person's action. Suppose that the consciousness of what we call intention is *merely* an association of a feeling of conative impulse with the idea of a certain action of one's own. Then there is no reason why another person should not have a corresponding consciousness of intention, though of course in him the idea associated with the feeling of conative impulse would be, not an idea of 'my' action, but an idea of the other person's—of 'thy' action. The action thought of is of course exactly the same for the person who has the intention and for the one who has the consciousness of intention corresponding thereto. The feeling of conative impulse, too, which would be associated with the idea of the other man's action, may be completely analogous to the corresponding feeling in the other self. Nothing stands in the way of such a process of analogy except the assumption that a feeling of conative impulse must of its very nature be a feeling of myself as willing. But, it is impossible that a feeling of conative impulse as such should involve a consciousness of the self. For when willing is introjected into the ego the result is that an experience of willing becomes an object of perception. But a *perception* of an experience of willing cannot be the same as an experience of willing itself; the former clearly presupposes, and is distinct from the latter.

A's consciousness of intention in reference to an action of B's can be conceived as involving an idea in A of a certain intention in B. This idea can be thought to carry with it the presented conative feeling itself in association with the idea of the other person's action.

In short, we must assume that in an imperative the giver of the order has a feeling of conative impulse associated with the idea of a certain action on the part of the recipient of the order. The imperative form, just in so far as it is a reflexive expression for this association, is effective in producing in the recipient of the order a corresponding state of consciousness. So the imperative does not merely aim at producing in the recipient of the order a consciousness of intention. The state of consciousness which it aims at producing exists also in the giver of the order, though in him it does not represent a consciousness of intention in the ordinary sense of the word because it does not refer to his own action. Still it is analogous to this. Conversely, we can also say that the characteristic expression of a consciousness of intention, 'I will undertake this!', is often not merely an expression of the presence of that state of consciousness. It also often means that one wishes to strengthen the already existing association in oneself by autosuggestion. So not only can an imperative be regarded as analogous to an expression of intention, but the latter can also be regarded as analogous to the former. In the first person plural of the imperative: 'Let us!' we have an unquestionable connection between an expression of intention and an imperative.

As we have said, the suggestion in a command does not appeal to the recipient's system of values. It follows that the consciousness of intention, which it aims at producing, also does not contain any valuations along with the feeling of conative impulse. So, if the command is to be effective without the help of other means, such as threats or warnings, there must occur in the recipient an intention which is devoid of valuation. It may, however, sometimes happen that an order fulfils its purpose only to the extent of evoking a mere feeling of impulse associated with a certain action, but fails to arouse the feeling of energy which is needed for an intention. In that case a full-blown intention does not arise. It is clear that in both cases a person in whom the command has been wholly or partly effective would feel himself to be unfree in willing. For his impulse is determined, not by values which are significant for himself, but by the imperative form of the expression. So a feeling of inward constraint naturally accompanies the process of being influenced by a command.

Finally, it should be remarked that prohibition, with its 'Thou shalt not!', is most easily conceived as a command to avoid a certain action, i.e. to repress all conative impulses towards a certain action. Thus, according to what has gone before, this 'Thou shalt not!' expresses a feeling of conative impulse associated simultaneously with the idea of repressing in the recipient of the prohibition the impulses to a certain action. The practical 'No!' expresses either a repression, already taking place, of conative impulses to a certain action; or the idea of such a repression. The latter is just what corresponds to 'Thou shalt *not*!' In a similar way the theoretical 'No!' expresses either a rejection, already taking place, of a certain suggestion ('No! That is *not* so!'); or the idea of such a rejection ('That is not admissible!').

It may be mentioned here incidentally that the corresponding expressions for advising and admonishing are related to the 'Thou shalt!' of commanding. In advising it is sought to arouse a consciousness of intention by 'Thou shalt!' But here it is not a question of arousing it directly in the person advised. In giving advice the counsellor seeks, by use of the reasoned 'Thou shalt!' to strengthen the consciousness of a certain intention by referring to

D*

certain values which are already significant for the person whom he is advising. From the standpoint of these values he presents this action as being the best possible among the alternatives. Here, however, the 'Thou shalt!', with its peculiar appeal to volition, is on the verge of insignificance, because the essential thing here is the application of already accepted valuations. In admonishing here certainly is involved a process of arousing a consciousness of intention by suggestion and for that reason special relations to the person admonished are necessary here too. But here in contrast with the case of a command, one seeks, in conjunction with the special suggestion to the will, to inculcate also certain valuations from which the appropriateness of the action would follow. One can admonish a person to take account in his actions of his life as a whole rather than of the values of the moment. One can admonish a person to do his duty. But one does not command such things.

## 2. THE IDEA OF DUTY

*(a) On the relationship of the idea of duty to the state of consciousness of the recipient of a command, through the nature of the fundamental feeling of obligation as a feeling of conative impulse divorced from valuation.*

We pass now to the consideration of the content of the idea of duty. Its kinship with the state of consciousness which exists in a person who receives a command is already obvious from the fact that it is a prevalent opinion in the history of ethics that duty is connected with an imperative. Such a common assumption must certainly be founded in some way upon observed psychological facts. The two states of consciousness seem also to be related in so far as a person who experiences a feeling of duty feels himself driven to a certain course of action. Thus, according to the explanation given above, a feeling of compulsion occurs in immediate association with the idea of a certain action. The way in which one expresses that feeling in negating a certain action—'I must not do that'—bears witness to this. Even if 'must not' does not here express a completed intention to reject, it must at any rate be regarded as expressing a rejective impulse of the will. The expressions 'obliged to', 'bound to', which indeed indicate that we are here concerned with an unconditional impulse to a certain action, not one determined by the subject's judgments of value, point in the same direction. But the feeling of duty expresses itself also in a simple 'I *ought* to do this'. Now the ought is sometimes indubitably an expression for a mere valuation attached to a certain action. E.g. I 'ought' to go this way, as being the shortest one to the desired end. It is therefore necessary to inquire whether the feeling of duty is of the same nature as the feelings which lie at the basis of our valuations or whether it belongs to our conative feelings.

A feeling of inner compulsion towards a certain action is inseparably bound up with or inherent in the feeling of duty. To speak in Kantian terms, a feeling of necessitation. We experience a feeling of inner compulsion when, e.g., an action, which itself involves unpleasantness or at any rate does not involve pleasure, presents itself as one which ought to be done simply and solely in order to avoid a certain unpleasantness. The criminal law exerts an inner compulsion on a man who wants to steal for one reason or another, in so far as he feels that he ought to repress this inclination in order to avoid the consequences attached to theft. In so far as mere unpleasantness, or rather the thought of avoiding unpleasantness, is what determines our decision as to what action we ought to undertake, we seem to ourselves to be dependent on something external to us. Pleasure alone, as the Cyrenaics and the Epicureans say, seems to us to be an οἰκεῖον, something that belongs to us. But in such a case the compelling ought clearly indicates that the action in question is the only right one of all the possible alternatives, under the actual circumstances, from the standpoint of value. It is approved, all the others are rejected. Does, then, the inner compulsion which is experienced in the feeling of duty also refer to a selective valuation of a certain action merely with a view to avoiding unpleasantness? Various facts argue against this.

1. The unpleasantness which, on this view, it would be sought to avoid by acting in accord with duty could only be the pangs of guilty conscience. Now it should be noted that what goes by this name is often a very complex network of feelings. It may include such things as fear of public opinion, of external reactions on the part of society, and of religious punishment. But, in so far as the avoidance of such consequences of my action is *clearly* present to my consciousness as the reason why I ought to act in this way, the action demanded of me ceases to be a duty and becomes a measure of prudence, and the unpleasantness which is feared is no longer

the pangs of conscience. If I should regard such factors as reacting unjustly, the very action by which I expose myself to the unpleasantness in question may present itself as my duty, and compliance may appear as merely a cowardly measure of prudence. Consider, in this connection, the state of mind of an idealistic anarchist or a morally revolutionary innovator. These feelings are genuine factors in the pangs of conscience only in so far as they are associated with, and not definitely distinguished from, a feeling of unpleasantness of a peculiar kind. What is characteristic for this is that it is bound up with the idea of an action which is *in conflict with* one's duty. It is because I did not act as it was my duty to act that I feel pain. Therefore I cannot think of the pangs of conscience as a threatening consequence of a certain action unless I already have the feeling of duty in regard to the opposite course of action.[1] It is therefore impossible that this feeling, and the feeling of inner compulsion which is attached to it, should consist in approval of a certain action as necessary for avoiding unpleasantness (viz. pangs of conscience).

2. Suppose that a hunted murderer, in order to avoid capital punishment, is forced to submit himself to the greatest privations, to wander about in the woods without food, to hide himself from the sight of men, etc. Then he is certainly subject to the greatest possible mental compulsion. Yet the ought which concerns him here has nothing to do with duty. On the contrary, his feeling of duty may act in quite the opposite direction. And the curious thing is that, if the thought of obligation really arises in such cases, where it is a question of the right course of action in order to avoid unpleasantness, the ego, in relation to which the obligation holds, objectifies itself in a peculiar way. I, the agent, have obligations towards myself, as a person who has rights against the self which now feels itself to be under an obligation. That is to say, I feel that I ought to act in such and such a way, not from the standpoint of my own values, but with reference to a person who stands over against me and puts forward his rightful claims. This brings us to the question of the state of consciousness which exists when a person feels himself under an obligation to act in a certain way in respect of the rights of another person. Here the latter person and *his* values seem to be the only relevant factor. The value of the

[1] Kant, *Kritik der praktischen Vernunft* . . . Hrsg. von K. Kehrbach (1877), p. 47.

action for the person who is under an obligation is utterly irrelevant. For a man who feels himself under an obligation in respect of another man's right the avoidance of unpleasantness for himself is in no way the reason why he ought to act in a certain way. In so far as he regards the other man as possessed of a right, the latter stands decisively in the foreground as the person in relation to whom the duty to act in such and such a way holds. It is an essential feature in this point of view that the interests of the person who is under an obligation must here be set aside.

It should be noted here that the ascription of an inner value to a person who fulfils his duties, i.e. respect for him, is something secondary in relation to the feeling of duty itself. Action in accordance with duty seems to us *as such* to possess an inner worth. Thus the alleged *objective* value of the action is not what determines the ought of duty. From the alleged objective nature of the value of the action we cannot, therefore, derive any explanation of the feeling of compulsion which is an essential part of the feeling of duty.

If, then, the feeling of compulsion, which we experience as a factor in the feeling of duty, is not determined either (*a*) by any valuation of the action from the point of view of its being necessary in order to avoid unpleasantness, or (*b*) by reference to objective values which stand over and above the individual, it must be explained in some other way. It would seem that there remains only one possible form of explanation, viz. that we are here concerned with an impulse towards a certain action, which is felt as compulsive just because what is here determinative is not the subject's free valuation, but something which is, in that respect, external to him. The impulse imposes itself on us, no matter what evaluatory attitude we may take towards the action. That is to say, the feeling of duty is a conative feeling, and to put it more definitely, a feeling of being driven to act in a certain way. Undoubtedly a free valuation of the action is not the determining factor in this feeling.

The kinship with the state of consciousness of a person who receives a command is thus evident, not merely in so far as both cases are concerned with a conative feeling, but also in that both involve a conative feeling which presents itself as independent of the subject's own valuations.

Since Adam Smith's time the attempt has often been made to

explain the feeling of duty as a social revengeful feeling directed against anti-social behaviour. But this retaliatory feeling does not arise only in the other members of a society against an individual in so far as he has tendencies to anti-social behaviour. When he himself takes part in social intercourse, and thus becomes himself inspired with the same feeling, it works *in* him to repress such tendencies. This inner reaction against anti-social behaviour is alleged to be conscience. It should be noted here, however, that it is necessary to distinguish sharply between the subject as reacting and as reacted upon. The feeling which the subject has as reacting cannot possibly be the feeling of duty. For a feeling of obligation is in no way a part of the social retaliatory feeling. Such a feeling can arise in an individual only in so far as he is the *object*, and not in so far as he is the *subject*, of a reaction. Therefore, in order to explain the feeling of duty, we must refer to the feelings which arise in the individual when he experiences the reaction of his social ego, i.e. of 'conscience'. If, now, that state of feeling is so defined that he rejects anti-social behaviour because it exposes him to suffering through the reaction of his social ego against such conduct, it fails to explain the feeling of duty. For the feeling of duty is already presupposed in order for it to be possible to fear the unpleasantness attached to breach of duty, viz. 'the pangs of conscience', as we have just pointed out. A possible explanation of the feeling of duty (having regard to what has now been shown as to its nature) would be provided only on one assumption, viz. that the experience of the reaction of the social ego *immediately* arouses an impulse to a certain action, i.e. without the impulse being called forth by the subject's evaluation of the action from any point of view. If that be a correct account of the state of affairs on experiencing the reaction, it would imply that the social ego presented itself as commanding the individual. The individual would then be driven to regard the social ego as a commanding power within him, in order to explain to himself the state of his feelings, which would resemble that which occurs when a person receives a command. In that case the complete explanation of the feeling of duty would include the assumption that the individual objectifies the social ego into an inner commanding power.

(*b*) *Difference between the state of consciousness of the recipient of a command and the feeling of obligation. The connection of the latter with the consciousness that the action, from the objective standpoint, is a duty. Explanation of this from the form of the direct expression of the feeling.*

However, granted that the kinship between the 'I must' of the recipient of a command and the 'I am under an obligation to' of duty is obvious, we can raise the question whether the latter *really* is of the nature of an imperative. In investigating this we will consider a peculiar state of consciousness, which seems to be bound up with the feeling of impulse in the feeling of duty, and without which the latter would seem to lack the character of feeling of *duty*. The purely imperative 'Thou shalt', like the 'I shall' of a complete or incomplete intention, cannot be expressed in the form of a judgment. This was explained above as follows. What is here expressed is not a single state of consciousness, but a simultaneous association of a feeling of impulse and the idea of an action, in which the former receives its special expression. The reception of an imperative, which is only the reproduction of the simultaneous association which is expressed by the command, cannot therefore be expressed in the form of a judgment either. But the situation is otherwise with the feeling of duty. Here the expression does take the form of a judgment: 'This action is my duty' or 'I *am* under an obligation to act in this way'. It seems to follow from this that the feeling of duty involves a consciousness of duty as something real, and that this consciousness determines the expression.

Nevertheless, there seems to be an insuperable difficulty in understanding such a state of consciousness. Westermark holds that it must be understood as an awareness of the fact that omission of the action is liable to arouse moral disapproval, and this disapproval is for him the feeling of duty itself.[1] But in that case the feeling of duty itself would be possible in the absence of awareness that an action is a duty. But this seems to be impossible even on Westermark's own view. For, according to him, the moral feeling as such is marked out *inter alia* by the idea of its impartiality which is essential to it.[2] Against this there seems to be nothing to object, at any rate so far as concerns the feeling of duty. But he must define impartiality as having regard to rights which are objective.[3] But rights obviously cannot be regarded as objective unless duty,

---

[1] *Ursprung und Entwicklung der Moralbegriffe,* I, 1907, pp. 1 *et seq.* cfd. with pp. 114 *et seq.*

[2] Loc. cit., pp. 85 *et seq.*                    [3] Loc. cit., p. 101.

which is their correlate, is also objectified.[1] But it is plain from
other reasons too that his consciousness of duty in the objective
sense cannot be awareness that an action is liable to arouse moral
disapproval. For I can have that awareness as a purely disinterested spectator of my own or another's mental life without my will
being thereby necessarily directed in any way towards omitting
such an action. But it seems impossible that consciousness of a duty
to act in a certain way should be present without the will being
directed in any way towards the action in question. This 'under an
obligation to' surely expresses a conscious conative impulse, and
therefore it seems impossible that it should have any meaning unless
such an impulse is actually present. Besides, we are here concerned
with consciousness of duty, and not with consciousness of a certain
feeling of duty. It is obvious that we sharply distinguish between
duty and feeling of duty. In passing judgment upon the feelings of
duty which are present in oneself one may even decide that it is
one's duty not to allow oneself to be led by a feeling of duty which
immediately arises, either because the consequences of the action
have not been fully thought out or because the feeling seems to be
determined by 'impure' motives. In regard to other men we distinguish still more sharply between their more or less morally
imperfect feelings of duty and their real duties. We say: You
ought to develop a purer feeling of duty in yourself. All this would
be meaningless if feeling of duty were identified with duty.

But, on the other hand, it seems equally impossible to regard the
state of consciousness in question as the discovery by us of a certain quality of the action which is for us the characteristic of its
being a duty. By investigating the action we may, no doubt, discover that it has, e.g., such properties that it promotes general
welfare, and we may decide that it is a duty on that account. But
the characteristic of being a duty is certainly not for that reason
identical with the property thus ascertained to be present. If it is
the case, as has been represented above, that this 'having a duty to'
is an expression for a certain conative impulse, it seems impossible
to regard duty as a property of a certain action. As has already
been shown, it is a peculiarity of feeling that its content cannot as
such be inserted into a context of independent reality, and therefore also cannot be regarded as a real property of an object. It is

[1] Cf. my essay in *Psyche*, 1907, *On moral-psychological Questions*,
pp. 285 *et seq.* (In Swedish.)

only in the actual experience itself that such an insertion into the context of independent reality can take place.

But against this the following objection might be raised. It might be said that the very fact that we are conscious of duty as an objective characteristic in the action shows that this 'being under an obligation to' cannot, as is here suggested, be a mere expression of feeling, but that it must express a predicate in a judgment which characterizes a certain action of mine. As to this, the first point to notice is that the fact that the word 'duty' occurs as a grammatical predicate in a sentence in the indicative form, does not prove that a real judgment lies behind the sentence. This is true, however much the sentence may be the naturally forthcoming expression for a real state of consciousness which lies behind it. It is certainly not impossible that other things beside judgments, e.g. associations of different experiences, should express themselves in a sentence in the indicative form. It remains therefore to enquire in this special case whether such a sentence really does express a judgment. Let us then consider more closely how things really stand in the case of a sentence containing the word 'duty'. 'This action is a duty for me.' Such an expression is exactly equivalent to the following: 'This action ought to be undertaken by me' or 'it ought to be actualized by me'. So 'duty' is equivalent to 'ought-to-be'. But in that case I should, in the judgment which lies behind the sentence, be representing to myself a certain modification of existence itself as a real characteristic of the action. I should thus be ascribing to the modification of reality an absolute reality. But this is as impossible as that I should be able to regard a certain limitation in what is black as absolutely black. Or, to put it in another way: I should, in one and the same act of consciousness, ascribe reality in the absolute sense to the action, in so far as I take it as possessing a real characteristic, viz. oughtness-to-exist, and at the same time say that it merely ought to exist. So there cannot be a genuine judgment at the back of the utterance of the sentence. But, if what is peculiar in the 'ought' of duty cannot be a term in a judgment, because it would then be a modification of existence, it must be of such a nature that it cannot function as a cognized term in the context of reality. But this is exactly what is peculiar to a feeling-content as such. Thus it is shown that there lies at the back of the 'ought' of duty a feeling. That this feeling is a conative one follows from the fact, stated above, that in our consciousness of duty we feel ourselves driven towards a certain course of action without being determined thereto by any valuation.

It would seem, then, that here too there is only a simultaneous association of a feeling of conative impulse with the idea of an action, and that only the *verbal expression* of this association is a sentence in the indicative form. This might be explained by supposing that the idea of the determinate character of the action is predominant at the time when the speech-reflex operates, and that it forcibly inserts the expression of the feeling into the expression of the determinate character of the action. In that case the expression of the feeling would not remain independent, as it does in the imperative 'thou shalt' or the optative 'would that'. The latter expressions, in spite of being in the sentential form, do not in the least suggest that the content which they express is a property of the action commanded, or of the event desired, as the case may be. On this view, there would not really be an awareness of duty in the objective sense; there would merely be a sentence couched in such a form that it produces the misleading impression that there is a judgment at the back of it. But against this solution of the difficulty must be set the fact that the duty-sentence in its indicative form does not remain a mere *flatus vocis*; it influences my way of thinking. It really is the case that 'being under an obligation' functions as a logical term. From its supposed presence in one instance I conclude to its presence in another, exactly as if I were really dealing with a genuine property of the object itself. Here is an illustration. 'I am under an obligation to avoid *this* action because it would be a theft.' Here plainly the starting-point is that a theft is something which one is under an obligation to avoid. This action ought then to be avoided, because it would be a theft. It is impossible that this conclusion should seem to us to be cogent unless we actually thought of obligatoriness as a property which belongs to the object itself and remains the same in all the combinations into which the object may enter.

It is of interest here to consider an analogous case from the region of value. Suppose I say 'Would that he might soon arrive!' Every attempt to translate the sentence into a genuinely indicative form, e.g. 'His early arrival is something which would-that-it-might-happen', is mere *flatus vocis*. Every attempt to find a basis for the connection between the arrival and this 'would-that-it-might-happen' is doomed to failure. I cannot intelligibly ask myself

'Why would that it might happen?' The reason for this is, of course, that the expressions which are used here are by no means adapted to the genuine indicative form. This implies that here there is not attached to the sentence any idea of something as having this or that character. What determines the utterance is merely a simultaneous association of the feeling of pleasure with the idea of the person's early arrival. The expression of the feeling here keeps its independence. This checks the transition to a sentence in the genuinely indicative form, to which a genuine judgment could be attached. But suppose that the expression takes the form: 'It is desirable that he will soon come.' Even here it is certainly the case that what originally lies at the back of the utterance is a feeling of pleasure and the idea of the actuality of a certain event, provided that a meaning really is being expressed. For even here it is a genuine wish which is being expressed. It should be carefully noted that one is here by no means expressing one's consciousness of the presence of a wish, as would be the case if the utterance had taken the form 'I wish that he may soon arrive'. In the case now under consideration the utterance has, after all, taken the indicative form. And 'desirability' has here acquired the character of a property belonging to an object. It is now a logical term, as is plain from the fact that we believe ourselves to establish the desirability of this or that on the desirability of something else. It is desirable that he should soon arrive, one might say, because it is desirable that I should soon find out how a certain business transaction has gone off. Here what is secondarily desirable gets that property from the fact that it includes the more determinately specified way in which what is primarily desirable, viz. the information, comes to be; and the latter retains its value-property in this its more concrete specification. But, on the other hand, every attempt to determine what desirability, as a property of a certain event, could be is doomed to failure. It cannot be identified with the fact that the event actually is desired; nor is it a property of the latter, considered as an item in the context of reality, which might be discovered by analysis of that context.

Compare now with the above example of an expression of a valuation the following example of an expression of a conative impulse. A person feels himself tempted to commit a theft, and his overcoming of the temptation expresses itself in a simple 'No,

I will not behave so badly'. There is no genuine indicative form
to which an actual judgment could be attached. Here a simultaneous association of the feeling of a conative impulse with the
idea of omitting the action—in this case, a resolution—expresses
itself, whilst preserving the independence of the expression of the
feeling. But it may be that a motive which has influenced this
overcoming of temptation was a feeling of duty, which expresses
itself in saying to oneself 'It is my duty not to give way to temptation'. Here we do not merely have a simultaneous association of
the kind described. 'Duty', which here corresponds to 'will' in the
former example, has become a property inmanent in the omission
of the action, which one deals with as if it were a logical term.
So we have here a parallel to the psychological situations in the
two examples of dissimilar expressions for valuations.

The difficulty which is common to both cases, viz. how to
understand the possibility of regarding value or duty, as the case
may be, as an objective property, should now be capable of a single
solution. In each case there is no other ground for the objectification except the indicative form of the expression for the simultaneous association which is present. The expressions 'value' and
'duty', and others to which we ascribe similar meanings, considered
as terms in sentences in the indicative form, refer primarily to a
background of feelings in simultaneous association with ideas of
something as an item in the context of reality with its own peculiar
property. These associations express themselves in sentences in
the indicative form, because the cognitive element predominates in
determining the expression and forces the expression for the feeling in among the expressions for the objective properties of presented objects. Such sentences are, in the first place, not just arbitrarily formed conglomerations of words, e.g. 'The stone is a
gorilla', but are reflexes which arise unconditionally from the
underlying state of consciousness and are comparable with inter-
jections. Secondly, they are not characteristic of an isolated
individual, but are determined in every case by the individual's
membership of a social linguistic community, so that similar states
of mind in different persons who use the same language are
similarly expressed. But, through their unconditional and extra-
individual character, such sentences apparently acquire just the
same properties as sentences which really express underlying
judgments. It is perfectly natural, then, that the expression

leads to an attempt to form a genuine judgment in connection with it.

Suppose that a person tells me something and that I believe him. His story causes me to form judgments, bound up with my belief in the reality of the thing narrated, in connection with his utterances. Even if I do not believe the narrator, his story nevertheless leads to the formation of judgments in connection with his utterances. But in the latter case there is a consciousness that the only reality here is the idea of the event. The reason is that every idea of a certain state of affairs as real has at least a tendency to carry with it an involuntarily and extra-individually determined expression, viz. a sentence in the indicative form. It follows from this that the idea of a state of affairs is generally accompanied by the apprehension of such a sentential expression. But this makes it equally natural that the converse should happen, i.e. that the apprehension of a sentence in the indicative form (provided that the sentence is not a mere conglomeration of words, and provided that it is not a mere expression, on the part of the subject who apprehends it, of an underlying judgment) carries with it by association the idea of a certain state of affairs as real. But the idea which thus arises is not just any idea. Every ideal content, other than that which has for its involuntary and extra-individually determined expression just that sentence which is apprehended, carries with it a different expression. From the latter there would follow an apprehension of an expression which would conflict with the original apprehension. Therefore, in so far as the original apprehension persists it carries with it just that idea which has for its involuntarily and extra-individually determined expression the apprehended sentence. It should be noted that it is just the extra-individual character of the involuntary expression which makes communication possible. In making the communication, the only intention in the communicator is his intention to arouse in the person addressed certain chosen ideas, by bringing to his notice the involuntary and extra-individually determined expression-reflexes for those ideas. The utterances themselves are not in any way formed deliberately, in so far as a real community of speech exists, as is here assumed. It is only in so far as this is not the case that the communicator deliberately translates the expressions, which he would naturally use in communicating his thoughts, into sentences which will arouse the intended ideas in the person addressed, in view of the latter's ways of giving involuntary and extra-individually determined expression to those ideas. On the assumption of social community of speech, the one and only intention which need be involved in the person addressed is to pay attention to the communicator's utterances in order that the corresponding ideas may be evoked. But the ideas which are connected with the utterances attended to arise involuntarily from the apprehension of the latter, and are thus homogeneous with the communicator's own ideas in consequence of the social community of speech. It is only in so far as this community is lacking that a deliberate search for the communicator's own ideas, i.e. an effort at interpretation, is involved. But even here it depends on a translation of the given expressions into those which are natural to the person addressed. Once that has happened the ideas of the matter to be communicated arise immediately.

Let us suppose, then, that simultaneous associations of feelings with ideas of a state of affairs as actual express themselves, in the way described, involuntarily and in an extra-individually determined manner, in sentences in the indicative form and containing as elements expressions of feeling, such as 'values', 'duty', or the like. Then a peculiar consequence follows in regard to the subject's own train of ideas. When a genuine judgment-experience expresses itself in a sentence in the indicative form this gives rise to a new judgment-experience only in another subject, with the same ways of expressing himself, who apprehends the utterance. Nothing of the kind happens in the subject himself who expresses his judgment. But, in the case now supposed, the utterance necessarily reacts on the subject. For, according to what has been said above, every apprehended sentence in the indicative form, provided that it is not a mere conglomeration of words and also that it has not already behind it an actual experience of judging, carries with it such an experience. The question now is: What kind of judgment-experience results? Obviously the subject in the new judgment is the thing which is conceived as real and qualified as valuable, or the action conceived as real and qualified as dutiful, as the case may be. But what are 'value' or 'duty' as predicates? Now anything that one might think of concretely here would give rise to a judgment-experience which would have a different involuntary and extra-individual expression from that which is actually occurring, and therefore would not accord with the latter.

If, nevertheless, some judgment-experience must arise in connection with the sentence in the indicative form, this must lack all concreteness in regard to 'value' or 'duty', as the case may be, considered as predicates. That is to say, with these words one has before one's mind only the idea of a property in the abstract, a certain something regarded as present in the thing or the action of which one is thinking, without being able to form any idea of what that property is. One cannot in any way conceive this something except as a reality which determines the expression. Still, it is quite natural that, whenever the words recur as terms in sentences of the kind described, with an associated feeling behind them, one thinks that one is again in presence of the same quality, the same something to which every concrete idea is inadequate, which belongs to the word in question, e.g. 'value', 'duty', and so on. But, when once such ideas have become developed, although their only basis is in spontaneously occurring sentence-formations with expressions of feelings as terms in them, we operate with this imagined something as if it were a logical term. We are not prevented by the fact that we lack all concrete ideas of it, and that, when all is said and done, we can conceive it only as that which determines a certain expression.

We have here before our eyes a prototype in ordinary consciousness of the Scholastic way of thinking. Here too it is a question of spontaneously formed sentences, which have their basis, not in any unitary state of consciousness, but in associations, though not in this case association of feelings. Here too these sentences lead to the idea that there really is a certain something which determines the expressions, although every concrete representation of it is lacking. 'After all, the words must make us think of something.' So one works with this something as if it were a logical term, one brings it into connection with other terms, states its properties, draws conclusions with it as a term in the premises, and so on. E.g. 'That which is *causa sui* produces its own reality or exists necessarily'. The word '*causa sui*' expresses an underlying association. Into this there enter on the one hand fluctuating ideas of sensible realities, and these ideas jostle each other aside and succeed each other so that no concrete characteristic is retained before the mind. On the other hand there enter into it ideas of causal connection which jostle and succeed each other, so that here too all concrete determinateness goes up in smoke. The expression is 'a simple reality which is cause and effect in one, i.e. *causa sui*'. The simplicity comes from the first factor in the association, and cause and effect from the second. But in the sentence 'That which is *causa sui* produces its own reality and therefore exists necessarily' a third associated factor plays its part, viz. the notion of the idea of a thing as cause of that thing. This makes possible the separation between cause and effect, which is always necessary. Thus one believes that there really is something which the phrase '*causa sui*' expresses, although one has not the least idea of *what* it is. 'That which is *causa sui* has effects distinct from itself.' Here one factor in the association predominates in the expression. 'But these effects are immanent in it.' Here another factor plays its part, viz. '*causa immanens*'. In using this expression, too, one believes in the presence of a certain something which is supposed to be a property of that something which is expressed in the phrase '*causa sui*', and so on to infinity!

The final result is that there does actually exist an idea of this or that action as really a duty, bound up with a conative impulse. But that which is here thought of is merely an unrepresentable something, which is connected with the expression 'duty', 'obligation', etc., and which cannot be distinguished except by reference to just that expression. One assumes the existence of a something which is 'duty', or rather something which the word 'duty' denotes. What produces the idea is the occurrence of this expression as a term in a sentence in the indicative form, which has arisen from an underlying simultaneous association of a feeling of conative impulse with an idea of a certain action as real. The process is as follows. A feeling of conative impulse is united with the idea of the reality of a certain action. Owing to the idea being predominant when the expression is being formed, this combination expresses itself in a sentence in the indicative form, viz. 'This action is a duty'. To the sentence is attached the idea of this action as having a certain property which answers to the name 'duty'. It should be noted that in this latter idea the action is not conceived as real in the same sense as it was in the original idea of the action, i.e. it is not conceived as belonging to the context of reality whose elements are concrete and perceptible. It is conceived as real only as having that essentially imperceptible quality which is 'duty'. It exists in the world of 'duty', not in 'our' world. If it also belongs to the context of sensible reality, i.e. if it actually happens, this has nothing to do with its reality as a duty. This implies that the same action, which exists as a term in an imperceptible reality, viz. the world of duty, exists also in a term in the perceptible world.

(c) *The idea of the correctness of the action in accord with a norm which determines the feeling of obligation and its expression.*

We must now investigate more closely that idea of the action which, on our view, would be one of the two terms in the simultaneous association which lies at the basis of the idea of duty. The question is whether there is any special characteristic which is regularly thought to be present in the action. In this case the property of being a duty must be connected immediately with just this characteristic. There is actually such a peculiar property. The action is regularly thought of as being that which is *right* or *proper* under the actual circumstances. What is one thinking of here?

In consequence of the undoubted kinship between the feeling of duty and the state of feeling of the recipient of a command, one might suppose that the conceived rightness means that it is just this action which is commanded by a certain will, let us say the will of society. But, in so far as we are dealing with the consciousness of right which goes along with the feeling of duty, the primary question which always arises when confronted with a will which issues a command is: 'Is it right to obey?'

That is to say, the action, of which rightness may possibly be predicted, is not ultimately the action which is commanded, but obedience to the command. The particular action which is commanded then becomes right merely because it falls under the species of action which obedience entails. But it is, of course, meaningless to take obedience to the command as right action, if this means the action which is commanded in that very command. Certainly a superior power can command obedience to the commands of a subordinate power. And a person can command obedience to his own past or future commands. But it is impossible in a command to order obedience to that command itself.

One could, however, look at the matter from the opposite point of view and say that the rightness of an action means that the omission of it is the object of a reaction on the part of a superior will. Still, to regard such an action as right presupposes that the reaction itself is held to be righteous. But if a reaction, however powerful it may be, can always be questioned in respect of its righteousness, its righteousness can never consist in the fact that it happens, no matter what forcefulness it may possess. We must not be misled here by the circumstance that the way in which society reacts does in fact exert an influence on our judgment about the rightness of a reaction, and therefore also on our decision whether an action is right or not. We do not mean by the righteousness of the reaction of society the mere fact that it occurs. It should be noticed that the reaction of society against certain actions gets its strength from the conviction that here not only power but also right is vindicated. The individual is of course influenced by that conviction.[1]

But reference to an expected result of the action as determining its rightness is also mistaken in this connection. For it can never appear to us as a duty actually to bring about a certain external state of affairs; at the utmost our duty would be to strive for it to the best of our ability. For, otherwise, the rightness of an action would be its property of being the right means of attaining the external result. In that case an involuntary mistake about the means would imply that I had acted wrongly. But anything of the kind is unreasonable from the standpoint of the rightness which is concerned with the consciousness of duty. Yet it might seem that, when we hold that one person's right is determinative of another person's duty, the rightness of an action would mean its property

---

[1] Gareis (*Vom Begriff Gerechtigkeit*, 1907, p. 11) contends that the righteousness of a reaction originally meant its accordance with the feelings of pleasure or displeasure of society. But he lands in a curious conflict with himself when he (i) describes rightness itself as one with 'the feeling of pleasure or unpleasure' of 'the community', but (ii) immediately afterwards agrees with Windscheid's saying: 'Right is, not what I regard as right, but what the community to which I belong has recognized as right and has, on that account, asserted to be right' (p. 21). Thus 'the community' itself recognizes something as being right. It cannot therefore at the same time regard its own recognition as identical with the right, for the recognition presupposes that what is right is already there. But in that case, of course, the individual too cannot regard this recognition as one with the right; he can accept the community's point of view and its consequent way of reacting only in so far as he considers that the former really is directed to what is right and that the latter is, for that reason, right. This obviously presupposes a rightness which is above the community, and which therefore cannot be identical with the latter's way of feeling pleasure or unpleasure. There is a similar fallacy in Stark, *Die Analyse des Rechts*, 1916, p. 175.

of subserving the interest of the possessor of the right in a certain respect. In another connection we shall consider more closely the possibility of carrying out the interest-theory as applied to subjective right. But let us suppose that the idea of a person's right is the idea of a rightful interest. Still, the rightness of the corresponding action cannot be determined by its property of forwarding that interest. If I have bought and paid for an article, I have a right to demand its delivery. It is then always right for the seller to satisfy my demand. This rightness is wholly independent of whether my real interests would be hurt by the delivery of the article, which is always a possibility, e.g. if I have bought a medicine which would in fact be injurious for me. The fact is that the interest of the person who has the right corresponds to the rightness of a certain action on the part of the party who is under an obligation only in so far as the furtherance of that interest demands an action which is already determined as right. That is to say, the interest is not something which is rightful in relation to the other party when taken in abstraction; it is rightful only in so far as it is bound up with a certain determinate action on his part which it is right for him to do. But in that case it is obviously meaningless to say that the rightness of the action consists in its property of promoting the rightful interest. The latter is itself rightful only in so far as its promotion requires just that action which would be the right one. A certain action, which is assumed to promote another person's interest, has primarily the property of being the right one; and the person's interest is rightful for that reason.

It is therefore mistaken to refer (as is sometimes done)[1] the right action, in the sense which is relevant to the consciousness of duty, to certain supposedly objective values, for the realization of which a certain action on the part of certain persons would be of vital importance. No doubt we can, in such cases, also talk of a right action, in the sense of one which is objectively correct as being the condition for realizing a certain supposedly objective value. But this correctness depends entirely on the actual results of the action, and is quite independent of what the agent may have expected to be the result of it. This way of judging the rightness of an action is altogether foreign to that conception of right which belongs to the consciousness of duty. Suppose one says that it is right for the militarily trained citizens of a state to fight for their fatherland's

---

[1] See, e.g., Schlossman, *Der Vertrag*, 1876, p. 316.

existence because the latter has an objective value. As regards the sense in which rightness is used, this has exactly the same meaning as when one says that a good provision of artillery is objectively valuable as a means, because it is a condition for the existence of the fatherland. That is to say, the fight for the fatherland and the fighters themselves are treated merely as means to a value which stands above them. But the fact that a person who acts rightly, in the sense which is relevant to the consciousness of duty, stands out as having a non-instrumental objective value, is plain from the respect which is felt for him. This valuation becomes all the more marked in proportion as the sense of duty stands forth as determinative for the action, and in proportion as the motives which it overcomes are strong, i.e. in so far as the action presents itself as really right. For it is of the essence of this that the sense of duty should be determinative and that it should be strong enough to overcome the temptations to alternative actions.—What we have said does not exclude the possibility that the action which is marked out by being of essential importance for the realization of an objective value may also be marked out as just the one that is right in relation to the sense of duty. (N.B. it would be an action to the best of one's ability directed to such realization.) Our ideas of objective values are actually dominant in the world of practical thinking, and they are determinative also of the nature of our ideas of duty. But that such an action is also right from the standpoint of the sense of duty means something quite different from its objective correctness as a means.

It might, again be suggested that rightness means a maximum of immediate pleasure or a minimum of immediate displeasure concerning this action in comparison with all others which are possible on the occasion. But it is easy to see that actions which are morally indifferent or are regarded as wrong might also be chosen on such grounds. In this connection we may specially note the fallacy of referring here to aesthetic pleasure, as Herbart and others do. For, if 'beauty' is a value-predicate in an object, we are thinking of that object, not in its real character, but as the content of an image. The picture is beautiful for a spectator. It is not the cloth, together with the pigments which are spread upon it, which the beauty is thought to belong to, but only the content of an image which one gets from it. But in the case of the rightness of an action it is a question of the action itself and its real character. That a certain action is the right one means that the actual undertaking of it is right.

It seems to follow from this that nothing whatever external to an action is the criterion for its rightness from the standpoint of sense of duty. It does not matter whether the external reference be to a commanding will, or an external consequence, or the immediately greatest pleasure or least displeasure concerning the action. From this again it seems to follow that the action stands out directly as the one which is right for me, in the sense that it belongs to *me* quite literally. If I do not act in that way, there must be something external to me which has forced itself in and prevented my true self from playing its part. Such an action is, therefore, from the point of view of preserving my autonomy, something mistaken and wrong. Of course, this way of looking at the matter presupposes a distinction between an ideal ego, I as such, and an empirical ego, I in my empirically given limitations. The latter falls short of its own essence in its wrong action.

Nevertheless, such an interpretation of the state of consciousness in question, which has been common in rationalistic systems since Kant, presents certain difficulties. We must keep firmly in mind that the question here concerns that property of the action which is bound up with the feeling of conative impulse which belongs to the sense of duty. It is just with the idea of the *rightness* of the action that the feeling of obligation is bound up. We must therefore demand such an explanation of its content as really will make intelligible its power of combining with itself such a feeling of conative impulse as the feeling of obligation in fact is. Now it is undoubtedly true that the idea of self-preservation plays a most important part in our willing wherever the 'self' is endangered. But there is no experiential support for the view that this idea determines our will in such a way that we feel ourselves bound just because our own free valuation is not determinative. On the contrary, it would seem that in normal cases the strongest immediate unpleasure would attach itself to the thought of annihilation, and that this unpleasure would produce a specially high valuation of a life-preserving action and at the same time a conative impulse towards such an action. In view of this, the essential feature in the feeling of duty, according to the present theory, would be valuation of a certain action as a means to avoiding loss of one's own autonomy. The feeling of obligation would then depend on the fact that what determines the valuation of the action is the displeasure felt at this loss of autonomy. The pang of conscience would be a feeling of unpleasure at having suffered a loss of autonomy through acting contrary to my true self. The fear of the pangs of conscience need not, in that case, be an essential factor in the feeling of duty (which, as argued above, would be an impossible view); it would merely be the direct unpleasure at the thought of a possible loss of autonomy. It might then be said that the above argument, regarding the purely conative character of the feeling of duty, is unsatisfactory because it has failed to take account of this way of looking at the matter. Nevertheless, on this view, the essence of the pangs of conscience would be unpleasure at the *result of the action*, viz. the loss of autonomy, and not at the *action itself* as undutiful. That the latter, however, is the essential feature in it is most evident in remorse over wrong-doing. Here it is decidedly the infringement of another's *right* which is determinative of the unpleasure. But what is another's *right* if one's own duty towards him is eliminated in thought?

Besides this we must take account of the following fact. If I present a certain action to myself as belonging to my true self, so that any other action would mean the repression of the latter, I must so conceive the matter that the willing of the action is essential to myself in its true meaning. For an action belongs to me only through my willing it. But how can I come to regard the willing of a certain action as essential for my innermost self? One might answer, with the rationalists, that this self is one with pure reason, considered as the power of self-determined thinking and therefore in practice as a purely rational will. This is experienced in the consciousness of duty as demanding such an action as is in accordance with practical reason. Against this it needs only to be objected that self-determined thinking is the same as pure consciousness which is conscious of nothing. But this is merely a philosophic fiction. In reality there is only one reasonable answer to the question. It is only if I feel that a conative impulse to a certain action ought unconditionally to be realized that it acquires such importance that I ascribe it to my real self and regard any hindrance to its transition into an intention as a repression of my autonomy. The following point should be noted. In the idea of the inner and essential, as opposed to the outer and unessential, in the self we are thinking of something autonomous, altogether independent of everything else, and therefore determinative in respect of all else. But I cannot regard the willing of a certain action as belonging to this autonomous entity unless at least the impulse to it already exists and is assignable to it. But in what sense can a conative impulse be held to belong to what is autonomous in us? Not in the sense that its realization or transition into an intention can never be checked by anything else, and therefore always takes place and is determinative in relation to everything else. Such a conative impulse does not exist. So the assignment of a conative impulse to that which is autonomous in us cannot be based on its domination in our actual conative life.—All that remains, then, is that this assignment is something which refers to the realm of ought; that the conative impulse is dominant in so far as it unconditionally (i.e. independently of everything else) *ought* to be realized. The ego is regarded as having an inner essential will, because certain conative impulses stand out as dominant, in the sense that they, so to speak, have an unconditional *claim* to be realized. Any checking of them is a check to our autonomy, in the sense that the self which they constitute through the fact that they *ought* to be realized is not determinative in *actual* life.[1]

[1] This point of view, taken by ordinary consciousness, is reflected in philosophical attempts to deduce the ought of duty from the fact that a certain volition belongs to the essence of the ego. In reality it turns out that what is meant by the essence of the ego in this context is the willing which is essential in the sense that it unconditionally *ought* to be carried out. Thus the position is logically circular. I will take as an example Schuppe's synoptic presentation of this way of thinking in his book *Der Begriff des subjektiven Rechts*, 1887, pp. 6–7. A certain 'thinking, feeling, and willing' is to be ascribed to 'the specific notion of man, consciousness-in-general'. *Therefore* it has objective validity, in the sense that it 'is valid for everyone'. This validity does not, however, mean that it actually exists in everyone. For there is always 'the possibility of deviating from this essence of one's own'. Instead the validity is alleged to consist in the fact that such 'thinking, feeling, and willing' is demanded of everyone. This and only this is the meaning of ought. From this it is plain that the mode of thinking, feeling and willing in question does not belong to consciousness in general (which is here identified with our own essence), in the sense that it always exists in every conscious being. But, in that case, how can it be said to belong to consciousness as our essence? This can be asserted only in respect of the validity which, according to Schuppe, is a *consequence* of its belonging to consciousness as such, i.e. merely in respect of the fact that it ought to exist in every conscious being. One might object that it can always be shown to belong to the consciousness,

It follows that one is guilty of circularity if one seeks to explain the power, possessed by the idea of an action, to evoke the feeling of conative impulse which is present in the feeling of duty, by alleging that the action is essential to true autonomy. An action cannot be regarded as essential for that purpose unless the willing of it is held to belong to the initiative of the innermost ego. And this is impossible unless the feeling of duty is already present.— The real position is as follows. It is the presence of the feeling of duty, in combination with the idea of a certain action as the right one, which leads to the idea that we are here concerned with an action or a volition, as the case may be, which is of essential importance for the preservation of one's autonomy. The mediating term here is the idea, which is bound up in the way already described with the feeling, that the action or the willing of it, as the case may be, ought unconditionally to happen, i.e. that the impulse ought unconditionally to pass over into a resolution and that it is therefore a factor in my true self. This idea of the importance of the action or the volition may afterwards react on the feeling of duty, and strengthen its motivating power through its peculiar intensity as a feeling. But this idea can never be the idea of the rightness of the action, which arouses the feeling of duty.

So the question of what we mean by the rightness of an action, in the sense involved in consciousness of duty, remains unanswered. If now the view put forward above is correct, viz. that the feeling of duty is akin to the state of feeling in the recipient of a command, in so far as there is in both cases a conative impulse independent of valuation, then the proper course for pursuing the enquiry is plain. We must enquire whether, in view of our knowledge of the way in which such impulses arise, we can suggest any characteristic which could produce such an effect if it were ascribed to the action. This characteristic could then be taken to be the content of what we mean by the rightness of an action, in the sense involved in consciousness of duty.—At the same time, however, it must be ex-

which is our own *essence*, in the form of a disposition. But how can anything be described as a disposition in our own essence, i.e. in that which is determinative in us, unless it actually manifests itself as dominant? But, if the mode of action in question cannot be said to be an *essential* disposition, in the sense that it always in fact comes into action, quelling all opposition and taking the lead of all the forces in us, how can it be described as an *essential* disposition if it does not even present itself as so dominant that at least it *ought* always to take the lead in us?

plained how such a characteristic can be ascribed to a certain action.

Suppose we ask ourselves what are the factors which, in our experience, are capable of producing a conative impulse independently of all valuation. We find that there are two, viz. command and habit, which are specially relevant in explaining the idea of the rightness of an action. We have already considered the significance of command in this connection. As regards habit, it is certainly true that it primarily shows its power in the fact that certain ways of acting, which have become 'habitual', are mechanized, so that they take place automatically, i.e. without the intervention of genuine volition. But, if, for one reason or another, the habitual action does not take place, we may naturally assume that the power of habit nevertheless exerts itself, viz. in an incomplete innervation or in an incipient movement in the direction of the mode of action in question. But the check produces a feeling of unpleasure, and in that way the checked innervation or movement emerges into consciousness. The physical correlate to it is willing, which here takes the form of a feeling of conative impulse towards the action but without any intention. In this case the feeling of unpleasure is not determinative of the willing, in the sense of being its motive. The two arise together from a common cause, viz. the checked innervation or movement.

Let us now investigate the authorities with the power of command, under whose influence the individual member of society comes. First we may mention the person who brings one up. The individual in his upbringing is subject to a whole mass of orders. 'You must not do that! You must observe that!' Then there are the laws which hold in the society. The individual finds that the doing of some actions and the omission of others are bound up with reactions, in accordance with these laws, which are painful to him. It is no wonder that they come to represent for him an awe-inspiring power which commands and forbids. Then, again, the traditional belief in divine powers, who are held to issue commands and prohibitions, plays its part. And, in the present connection, the general social milieu in which one lives is particularly powerful. One's environment reacts unfavourably against the doing of certain actions and the omission of others. This acts on the individual as if an indefinite commanding power stood over him. Finally, we must mention the commanding power exercised

E

by persons in possession. Actual possession, supported by an unorganized or an organized social force, gives authority against those outside. The owner thus acquires the power to assert himself against the latter, as a power which makes the demand: 'Hands off my property!'

It should be noted that, in a primitive society, with its idea of a common origin and with less developed individuality in its members, these forces act in a unified way and support each other. But even in a modern society they co-operate to a certain extent, at any rate within certain social strata. There is *one* form of co-operation between different commanding powers which always exists, viz. between those which are effective within the social circle to which the individual belongs and with which he feels himself bound up. What, now, is the consequence of this co-operation? Well, the thought of certain ways of acting carries with it the awareness of 'That shall be done! That must be done!' or in general of an expressed command; whilst the thought of others carries with it the awareness of 'That must not be done!' or in general of an expressed prohibition or rather an expressed command to avoid them. Here the commanding authority loses its individuality, and all that is left is the word of command, presented in a fluctuating image, auditory or visual. But owing to its involuntary entry along with the thought of the action, it retains its suggestive power, i.e. it sets up the mental state corresponding to it, viz. a feeling of conative impulse in connection with the action or the omission of it. Suppose, now, that the individual finds that such a combination between the same actions and 'must be done' or 'may not be done' commonly occurs among the members of the same social group. Then the belief naturally arises that a 'must be done' or 'may not be done' belongs objectively to certain actions. Thus there is formed the idea of a system of positive or negative ways of acting as connected with an expression of command. This system 'must' or 'ought to' be unconditionally carried out, and it produces an impulse towards observance of it. When he is about to act in a way which conflicts with the system another action presents itself as that which 'must be done' or 'ought to be done'. Thus a certain action comes to stand out as that which is right in relation to the system which is bound up with the expression of command. It thus gets ascribed to it a property, the apprehension of which carries with it an immediately evoked feeling of conative impulse, which is bound up with the action which has come, in the way described, to be regarded as right. It should be noted here that one can always withdraw oneself from the influence of a commanding authority by not paying attention to it, by 'turning a deaf ear to it'. Again, such a power, through its personal character, is not exempt from the influence of all kinds of external circumstances, which make it uncertain whether it will hold to the command which it has once given. According to Homer even the gods can be bribed. But the conviction that a certain system of ways of acting is objectively connected with a 'must be done' carries unconditionally with it a judgment on any particular action in accordance with it, in so far indeed as the possibility of an action contrary to the system is contemplated at all. The idea of the 'right' mode of action, which thus arises, carries unconditionally with it a feeling of conative impulse. For here we are concerned with modes of action which seem to have this 'must be done' bound up with them *from their very nature*. This makes the conative impulse in accordance with them unconditional, and thereupon there follows attention to the special character of the particular action.

Let us now consider the conative power of habit. Here we must note that the immediate conative impulse which arises from habit has, in accordance with the above analysis of command, the same natural expression as the latter. The expression of a command is simply an expression for a conative impulse combined with the idea of another person's action. Suppose, now, that a general habit, i.e. a custom, is formed within a social group. Then it follows from the above that, in every case where any tendency to a different action arises as an obstacle in the way, there appears an unconditional 'must be done', i.e. an expression of command. Since this expression of command is regularly combined with the same ways of acting in all members of the group, it naturally follows that it is regarded as an objective property belonging to that way of acting. Thus in connection with custom there arises the idea of a system of ways of acting, having the expression of command as an objective property, which carries with it a feeling of conative impulse and leads to a judgment on each particular action, as explained above. Still, it is obvious that a person cannot, in one and the same state of consciousness, accept different systems as having the expression of command as an objective property in complete isolation from each other. We must therefore suppose that custom and the above mentioned commanding powers either co-operate to form a single system of conduct with the objective property in question, or that they lead to the formation of different systems of conduct, each of which is accepted from a different point of view, these being in conflict with each other. If the individual comes to entertain these various points of view, the consequence will be an insoluble conflict of duties within him.

In this connection it should be remarked that, in primitive society custom seems to play the predominant part here, and commanding authorities, political, religious, or social, function in accordance with it. But, as development goes on, there seems to follow a relative repression of custom in forming the system of conduct in question, and a predominance of disapproval of certain ways of acting which is derived from directly apprehended social values.—The following fact should also be noted here. Suppose that the thought that there really is a system of the kind described has arisen, through the co-operation of custom and authoritative forces, in consequence of the regular connection within a certain society between the idea of certain actions and the expression of a command. Then the way is open for filling out this system by means of interests, even of a merely individual nature. Let it be granted that the formation of the thought of the system presupposes a regular connection within the society between particular actions and the expression of a command, and that therefore the system must originally have the character of being universally valid in relation to the group. This in no way prevents this thought from becoming individualized when once it has been formed. Since a person now has the idea that a certain system of conduct 'ought' to be carried out, he can regard particular actions as belonging to this system, in so far as the latter holds for him in a certain situation. In determining such actions all kinds of factors may play a part. Still, however important individual interests may be, for obvious reasons, in determining what is the right action for me in a particular case, I always consider, in so far as the decision involves the sense of duty, that the only thing relevant is to know which way of acting is in accordance with the system of conduct which 'ought' to be carried out. It may be that, in my opinion, the system demands a peculiar action in the circumstances in which I am placed. But I always hold that the same action would be right for another person with the same individual peculiarities placed in the same situation.

It should be said that a tendency towards such individualization accompanies the development of the moral consciousness.

Suppose that the above explanation of the content of the idea of a right action, in the sense involved in the consciousness of duty, is correct. Then the idea of a 'righteous' judgment is the idea that the judgment correctly pronounces as to the actions which are right for the parties concerned in the given case, when account is taken of the system of conduct which has the objective property that it 'ought' to be carried out.

The probability that the proposed explanation is correct is increased by the light which it throws on various facts connected with the consciousness of duty.—We imagine to ourselves, under the name of 'the voice of conscience', a commanding power within us which thus determines for us the right course of action. But, if we really stood merely in the position of the recipient of a command when we hear 'the voice of conscience' there would only arise a feeling of conative impulse bound up with the idea of a certain action. The experience could not, then, give us the idea that a certain action is *objectively* right. But that is just what it does, in so far as 'conscience' acquires for us a theoretical meaning, as pointing out the right action and thereby determining the feeling of duty. So the question arises: 'Whence comes the misleading idea of a commanding power within us which is determinative of right action?' From the above explanation the answer is obvious. Conscience in its theoretic aspect is nothing but the idea, which arises in particular cases, that a certain action is in accordance with the system of conduct which has the expression of a command as an objective property, or, as we say, that it is in accord with the moral law. This action itself has therefore this 'must' or 'ought' as an objective property. But the expression of a command leads one's thoughts inevitably to a commanding will. And so one inevitably lands in the contradiction that the action, on the one hand, has the expression of a command objectively bound up with it, and yet, on the other hand, has it bound up with it only through the intervention of a certain will.

In the common notion of justice we regard certain actions as duties in relation to another person as possessing rights. Here, then, the fundamental idea is that the personality of the latter is the objective ground of the existence of certain duties. Yet it is natural for us to express the state of affairs in question by saying that the possessor of rights can make certain demands or claims on the person who has duties towards him. Here, now, are two heterogeneous ways of looking at the matter, connected with each other. On the one hand, we regard certain actions as duties because they are indicated in a certain way by another person, viz. the possessor of a right, as desired by him. According to the law, i.e. rules which are binding alike on the possessor of rights and the subject of duties, certain actions on the part of the latter, which the former indicates in a certain way that he wishes performed, thereby acquire the objective character of duties. Here it is a matter of complete indifference in principle whether the indication of the wish has the character of a claim or not. That the possessor of the right is the basis of the obligation means merely that the dutiful action derives that property through its connection, in the way described, with him. But, when one describes having a right as the possibility of making a claim, duty is conceived as arising from a demand on the part of the possessor of a right. The notion of a claim as the essence of having a right is necessarily connected with the notion of a demand as determinative of duty. This concatenation of heterogeneous points of view can also be simply explained by the hypothesis here suggested. That an action is a duty for a certain person just because it is the object of an expressed wish on the part of another means only that this is the property to which the expression of command, as an objective character of the action, is referred. But the expression of command leads to the thought of a commanding will. This must be referred in the first instance to the person whose expressed wish is the objective ground of the dutiful character of the action. He is regarded as having the power to impose an obligation by putting forward a claim to the action.

A third fact which strengthens one's confidence in the correctness of the hypothesis is the following, which we shall examine more fully a little later. This is the general tendency to regard the property of an action of being commanded by the state-authority as identical with the property of being a duty. This fact too can be simply explained by our hypothesis, as we will show in detail.

According to the point of view here put forward, what is called the moral norm is conceived as a system of conduct objectively bound up with an expression of command. Now it is certainly plain that such a notion must be completely void of truth. In conceiving the expression of command as a real property of an action one takes it as actual, not in 'our' world, but as a term in a wholly different context of reality, viz. the world of 'ought'. But this supersensible world gets its character from a factor of such palpably sensible nature as an expression of command, taken from the sensible world. This seems unreasonable in view of the reverence which is felt for the moral norm. Could such a palpably false idea produce reverence even in a consciousness steeped in modern culture? Is it not impossible to suppose that one should want to fall down and worship the very expression 'It must be done' or 'It must not be done?' As regards the first point, we must remember that the expression has a suggestive conative significance. Since it is the involuntary expression of a conative impulse, it calls forth, when it presents itself immediately as something objectively bound up with a certain action, an impulse towards that very action. But thereupon our interest is directed to the action, and any disturbing reflection is checked. Not the least question of the truth of the assumption arises. Nor is the expression of command, in so far as it is ascribed to the action, conceived as a mere expression. Certainly it arouses the thought of a commanding will, and to that extent is conceived as an expression of command. But this belongs to another context of ideas. This latter certainly acts in the same direction as the actual 'ought'-idea, but is not equivalent to it. It does not involve any kind of reflection upon *this* idea, either as regards its truth or as regards the nature of its content.

This brings us to the second question. How can we reverence a mere expression? We do not reverence it *as* an expression, we reverence it in its sensible existence as an image. There is no insuperable difficulty in understanding this. It must be noticed that the expression in question produces in us an inevitable impulse to a certain action, viz. the feeling of duty. But, as has already been mentioned, we ascribe this impulse, because it 'ought' to be fulfilled, to our own true self; so that we seem to ourselves to preserve our own autonomy only if we let it pass over into a genuine intention. But this impulse, through endowing us with a real 'self' and making possible real self-maintenance, gets attached to it the same intrinsic value which we ascribe to our ego in the proper sense. On the other hand, it arouses in us a feeling of obligation through the absence of any valuation in the conative impulse. Thus it acquires at once the character of something binding upon us and of an intrinsic value. But reverence just is a feeling which is bound up with such a context of ideas. The honouring of the flag provides an analogy to this. We honour it, not as a bit of cloth with such and such colours, but because the image of it has the power of evoking in our consciousness something else which is valuable for us. The value of the latter is transferred to its symbol.

It is far from being the case that reference to the reverenced moral norm, as that which determines for us what is right and as the ground of our obligation, constitutes a counter-instance to the theory here put forward. On the contrary, just the actual acceptance of such a norm can be made the basis of a direct proof of the essential correctness of the theory which we assert. The existence of the accepted moral norm could be expressed as the fact that there exists a rule for determining what actions ought to be done in particular cases. By this rule one does not mean an ordinance of a will. For, if that were so, one would understand by the duty which is based upon it, not a property of the action itself, but merely the fact that it is commanded. Moreover, the norm would not then be regarded as valid for the determining will itself. Even if we do insert the idea of a determining will into the thought of the moral norm, e.g. a divine will, we do not suppose that this arbitrarily legislates. We assume that it demands of us just what is in accordance with the norm, and that it derives its authority from its own moral content. Thus the moral norm itself is for us an objective rule, even though the thought of a legislator is smuggled in in an unsystematic way. This does not exclude the possibility of holding that its occurrence in its full purity in an individual depends on external circumstances which determine the degree of his moral development. But the existence of such an objective rule can be described as the fact that there exists a system of conduct which unconditionally ought to be carried out. The question now is: *What* is it that is thus described? Here the content of the grammatical predicate 'ought to be carried out' presents special difficulties. The first question is: 'Is there a genuine judgment at the back of the sentence in the indicative, in which the predicate has a meaning which accords with the suggestion made by the grammatical predicate of the sentence?' In that case, as has already been explained, we should describe a certain modification of 'being,' viz. 'oughtness-to-be', as a real characteristic. But, according to the above argument, this is meaningless.[1] The next question is: 'Is there no judgment whatever behind the sentence in the indicative, but instead a simultaneous association of states of consciousness which expresses itself in a sentence of the kind which normally expresses a judgment?' In that case one of the two terms, in reference to the expression 'ought', must be a feeling. But of what kind? Now we must notice that it is just the assumption of a moral norm which arouses in us the feeling of duty. What determines this feeling is indeed the idea that the action is right. But the feeling of duty, as has already been shown, is a feeling of conative impulse devoid of valuation. So the state of consciousness which is present in the acceptance of a norm evidently cannot be a valuation-feeling associated with the idea of a certain action. So it can only be a conative feeling which, in combination with the idea of a certain action, gets its expression inserted as a predicate-term in a sentence in the indicative form. Such a sentence would then, in its turn, produce the assumption of a certain something, which determines the expression, in the way which we have already explained. But that is just what is characteristic of the feeling of duty in contrast with other conative feelings. The expression of feeling 'must be done' or 'ought to be done' or 'bound to' is here, and here only, a predicate in a sentence in the indicative. This in turn produces, as we have already more fully explained, the consciousness of actual duty which is involved in the feeling of duty. So it might seem that it is the feeling of duty which is at the back of the 'must be done' of the norm. But this is impossible; for, as we have said, it is just the acceptance of the norm which *produces* the feeling of duty. So the state of consciousness which lies behind the expression must be an actual judgment. But, as we have already pointed out, the predicate of this judgment cannot be regarded as the content of an idea of which the grammatical predicate is an expression. Thus the only alternative left is this. The real predicate in the judgment which lies in the background can only be the grammatical predicate itself, viz. this 'must be done', as it is presented in an image. Or else it must be something else which, although it does not have the grammatical predicate as *its* expression, yet gives rise to the latter. The only way in which this can be conceived is that this other thing carries with it the image of the grammatical predicate itself, and thus causes it to be used in the

---

[1] See above, p. 113.

E*

formation of the sentence. The associative link can only be the power of the image of the predicate to function in a similar way as evoker of the same kind of feeling as that other thing itself. It should be noted that whatever we may take as the predicate in the judgment which is the acceptance of the norm becomes an object of attention only through its power to evoke a feeling of duty. This power in it must therefore be that which determines the ideas which it carries with it. Only other ideas which have similar determining power can attract attention to themselves in the consciousness of a moral norm. This suffices to show that the predicate in the normative judgment must be either (i) the grammatical predicate of the sentential expression, considered as the content of an image, or (ii) something which has the power to cause a conative impulse in the same way, but *is* not the actual meaning of the predicative expression. Now the image of the grammatical predicate of the normative sentence, i.e. 'ought to be done', can of course arouse a conative impulse merely as an expression of command or volition. So the other thing, which may possibly be the predicate of the normative judgment, must, since it acts in the same way, also be an expression of command or volition.

But a serious objection can apparently be made against the theory which we have put forward. Suppose that it is the expression of command, in its individual image-form, which is ascribed as a real property to a system of conduct conceived as something which 'ought to be realized'. Then every variation in the expression would imply that a *different* property is ascribed to the system. In that case I could not identify the moral norm which is presented to me with that which is presented to another person, if a different expression of command is natural to him because, e.g., he uses another language. Nay, if the expression in myself should glide from one form of words to another, from an auditory to a visual image, from the image of a word to that of a gesture of command, and so on, there should in each case be a different real property in the system of conduct. Here we must note the following point. We must distinguish between the actual existence of judgments with different contents in different subjects or in the same subject, whether simultaneously or successively, and a subject's power to distinguish contents from each other. The contents of judgments may be different, and yet it may happen, for one reason or another, that they are taken as identical. In reality there is a variation in the content of the judgment with every variation in the expression of command. But that does not prevent one, in viewing the varying content, from having the idea that the one thing which truly belongs to the system of conduct and which really is ascribed to it in all these judgments is something common to the varying expressions, and that the various ways in which this common content is presented are merely accompanying images. It is not surprising that one should get the idea of something common as the essential feature, since there is really something common here which alone gives to the expressions their power, viz. just their property of being expressions of command. But the following fact should be noted. The common feature which one ascribes to the system of conduct when viewing the various judgments, and which one takes to be that which really is ascribed to the system in each case, is not the property of being an expression of command. For it is impossible that one should really be able to regard the expression of command reflectively as a property of a system of conduct. Nor is that on which consciousness is focused a meaning common to the various expressions. What it is is that which is common to the expressions in the abstract. Nothing concrete whatever is before the subject's mind except these expressions themselves, in which he assumes something common to be present. In this way there is formed the idea of a moral norm which is presented to different subjects and to the same subject in all the variations of the expression of command. It must be added, however, that this idea is only the product of subsequent reflection upon certain judgments about a system of conduct which has a concrete expression of command as an objective property; viz. judgments which are the basis for determining what is the 'right' action, and which, amidst all variations in the expression of command, have in common the power of producing a feeling of duty bound up with a determinate action. What is really efficacious, however, is always the concrete sensible form of the expression.

(*d*) *The relation of the idea of a norm to the consciousness of duty.*

We must now consider in more detail the relation of the idea of a norm to the actual consciousness of duty. According to the theory here put forward, the former is merely the idea that a system of conduct has, as a real property, a certain expression of command which is presented in an image. The idea of the right action in a given case is connected with this in the following way, viz. that in this case only a certain action is in agreement with the assumed system of conduct, and it is thereby itself connected with the expression of command. The idea of a norm itself produces, through the expression of command which is present in it, a direct conative impulse towards judging of certain actions in accordance with the system of conduct. If the idea should arise that only a certain action is the one which accords with the system in the given case, then that idea produces a direct conative impulse towards just that action. This impulse is the feeling of duty. The consciousness of real duty is a phenomenon attendant on the feeling of duty. There occurs a feeling of conative impulse, free from valuation, which is directly linked with the idea of a certain action as the right one in the sense supposed. In the involuntary expression of this linkage the idea of the property of *rightness* in the action is predominant, and this makes the special expression of feeling into the grammatical predicate of a sentence in the indicative form. This sentence gives rise to the idea of a certain something, which has no place in the sensible world, but which is expressed in the characteristic expression of the feeling of duty. Thus no actual feeling of duty lies at the back of the consciousness of a norm itself, as it does in the case of consciousness of duty. If, then, I present certain actions to myself as 'duties' *in abstracto*, this has here no real obligatory significance, because the feeling of duty is lacking. In principle it is an expression of command which confronts us in imagination in the consciousness of a norm. But, once the feeling of duty has been amplified *through* the consciousness of a norm, its natural expression can function as stimulus to a direct feeling of conative impulse in the same way as an expression of command. It can then act as a substitute for an expression of command as a call to attention.

In connection with this it must now be further pointed out that there is the following difference between the idea of the right action and the idea of the action as a duty. Since the former refers to an accepted system of conduct, having the objective property 'must be done', it determines what is right in the present case only by determining what is right in *such cases as this*. But the idea of duty does not refer to a class of actions, but to one particular action determined in accordance with the idea of what is right. In so far as the feeling of duty is a feeling of conative impulse, it is necessarily bound up with a determinate present action. No doubt I can resolve in general to act in a certain way under such and such circumstances. That seems not to be a determinate present action, since I do not know when or even whether these circumstances will arise. But, even if we seem here to be concerned with a general mode of procedure, yet one does not decide on that course of procedure without reference to a particular case in which the rule is to be applied. This particular case is my own future individual life of action, in which I decide to carry out that rule. I can feel myself to be under an obligation always to pay on demand debts that have fallen due. But, even if the ground of my feeling of duty is the idea that to pay debts on demand when they fall due is always right, yet I feel myself under an obligation to apply the rule only as regards my individual future life. The feeling of duty in question is thus evidently an impulse towards setting the organism upon such a course of procedure.

But, it might be said, it can happen that the consciousness of a norm, and therefore also the idea of the right action in the present case, involve no feeling of duty. Yet it is a fact that, if the natural result of the idea of the right action, viz. the feeling of duty, does not actually occur, the idea itself vanishes. It is unable to maintain itself in consciousness. It should be noted (i) that all interest in the right action as such is determined by the feeling of duty. The thought of self-respect or avoidance of self-reproach, the idea that I can preserve my true autonomy only by doing the right action, the fear of the pangs of conscience, in fact everything which links my interest with such an action, rests upon an already present feeling of duty. But, if no interests are bound up with the action as being right, I shall also have no interest in my practical life to retain the idea of the rightness of the action. (ii) As we have already pointed out, it is just the feeling of duty and the interests which are bound up with it which are in a position to check all reflections which are disturbing to the conviction that an action is right. Without this it would be impossible to repress the suggestion that we are here really concerned only with perceptible expressions of command which cannot be genuine properties of an action, and in particular the dangerous question whether the conviction is true or not. (iii) The perceptible expression of command, taken as a real property of the action, cannot retain its perceptual character, i.e. cannot occur with the same liveliness which it has in a genuine powerful command, unless the feeling of conative impulse immediately follows. Thus the absence of the feeling of duty in connection with the idea that an action is right implies that the latter is only a weakened image of that which we actually present to ourselves when the idea is practically effective. But the occurrence of the feeling of duty always depends on peculiar psychological conditions. Therefore the maintenance of the idea of the rightness of an action does not depend *merely* on logical factors, i.e. on the correct subsumption of the action under those ways of behaving which are held to belong to the fundamental system of conduct.

Let us suppose that, before the occurrence of a feeling of duty, there are already adequate motives in a certain case for an action, e.g. an act of honesty, which appears to be right on abstract logical grounds. These motives may include as many elements as you please which are alien to the sense of duty, e.g. the thought that I shall gain certain external advantages by acting honestly in the present case. Under such circumstances what are we to say about the conditions for the occurrence of a feeling of duty in connection with the idea of the rightness of the action? The following fact should be noted here. Suppose that an action follows without any conflicting motives coming into play, bound up with the idea of another course of action, and without any special difficulties in carrying out the action which arouse the feeling of energy. Then no specially emphatic conative impulse is present in an 'I shall do this'; certainly not one which passes over into a genuine resolve. If I have already decided to go for a walk, no special conative impulse to put on my overcoat obtrudes itself. In our case where the motives, apart from the feeling of duty, can be taken for granted as tending in the direction of what is right, the action already exists in embryo in the already initiated psycho-physical adjustment. If there should be a feeling of duty, it would be concerned with the maintenance of that adjustment. But when, as in the case supposed, all motives for its cessation are powerless against the existing motives for the action, the conditions are absent for the occurrence of a special feeling of conative impulse connected with the idea of maintaining the adjustment. Since no counter-motives with real motive-force exist, there are also no difficulties in carrying out the inner intention which might lead to a special feeling of energy.

But suppose now, on the contrary, that the motives are not

decisively in favour of honesty, apart from the feeling of duty, whether it be that the motives for dishonesty exactly counter-balance those against it or that they overbalance them. Then there is a real possibility of the occurrence of a feeling of duty, bound up with the idea of honesty as right or with the idea of abolishing an incipient tendency to act dishonestly which has already arisen. And undoubtedly the more strongly the dishonest motives act, the more distinctive the feeling of duty may be. But, in view of the relation already indicated between the idea of right and the feeling of duty, it follows that the stronger the temptation to the opposite course of action is, the more impressive the idea of the right action may become. It can reach its maximum intensity when the feeling of duty is the *only* possible motive for right action. And so this idea can be more distinctive in proportion as the temptations to be overcome are stronger. Moreover, it follows also that, in judging of an already accomplished right action, the idea of its rightness presents itself with all the more liveliness the more the feeling of duty has been the dominant motive and the greater the temptations to be overcome have been. This has led to its being asserted that, in order for an action to be right, in accordance with the moral consciousness, it is *necessary* that the only motive for the action should be the idea of its rightness operating through the feeling of duty. This, however, is unreasonable. For in that case I could not have as my motive the idea of the rightness of the action, since the action could never present itself as right apart from a pre-existing idea of its rightness considered as a motive. Instead the fact is that it is always the action itself to which rightness is ascribed. But, when one contemplates the action beforehand and when one judges of it afterwards, the idea of its rightness is pushed into the background in proportion as the feeling of duty does not play, or has not played, any part in the decision. To this should be added that this circumstance has nothing to do with the fact that, in order that the result of an action may be ascribed to me, it must have been so far intended by me when I undertook the action that the idea of its resulting therefrom was present to my mind. An action is never made wrong through an effect which was not in this respect intended. This has of course nothing to do with the question whether rightness itself must be the motive for a right action.

From what has been said above the following conclusion also

follows. The wrongness of an action, i.e. its being in conflict with the line of conduct which is right in the given case, does not come into prominence, either at the moment of decision or in retro-spective judgment upon it, unless a feeling of duty is present either directly or as an after effect of one which formerly existed. (In the latter case it would be one which arouses remorse.) The following fact might seem to conflict with this. After an action has been done it may be asserted that there was a morally blameworthy lack of attention to its consequences or to its wrongness, although no feeling of duty to be more attentive was experienced at the time. It should be noticed, however, that there is a feeling of duty to be attentive in general in such matters or to practice such moral hygiene that one's attention to the consequences or to the wrongness of one's actions does not sink below a certain level. One's judgment upon a lack of attention as being wrong in a certain case should ultimately refer to the property, in this failure, of manifesting a defect in general moral self-discipline.

In this way also should be explained the fact that we, who are inclined to judge like cases alike, take account, in judging the right-ness or wrongness of other men's actions, not only of their agree-ment or disagreement with what is objectively right or wrong in the present case, but also of the agent's degree of development in respect of his consciousness of duty in general, which we estimate in accordance with our own ideas of what the moral law demands. Yet certain other factors act here in the opposite direction, and these become plain if we notice what happens in ourselves, from the psychological standpoint, when we regard others as under an obligation.

(e) *On the possibility of consciousness of another person's duty.*

It might now seem, in view of what has been said about the dependence of the consciousness of duty on the feeling of duty, as if we could not possibly have any consciousness of real duties in others. At the most this 'You ought!' would consist of a reference to the action which is right for the other person in a certain case, in the sense that it is the action which, in the given case, is in accord with the system of conduct which has a perceptible ex-pression of command as a real property. But, according to the above theory, one's idea of the rightness of an action could not occur with the same impressiveness under such circumstances when it concerns another person as when it concerns oneself, if only the feeling of duty can maintain that idea. But it is incredible that one should not be able to have as lively an idea that a certain action is right for another person as that an action is right for oneself. Now we must maintain, in the first place, that a feeling of just the same nature as that which we call a feeling of duty very well may be linked with the idea of a certain action on the part of another person. This is a feeling of conative impulse, devoid of valuation, in respect of another's action as right. In discussing command we have tried to show that a feeling of conative impulse, linked with the idea of another person's action, must be supposed to lie at the back of the expression of command in the person who gives the order. There is therefore no difficulty in principle in supposing such a feeling as we have suggested.

There are, moreover, two facts which can scarcely be explained without postulating the existence of such a feeling. One is moral indignation. It may be the case that this is at any rate intensified by all kinds of affective factors which have nothing to do with the feeling of duty, e.g. self-interest which is infringed by the wrong action, or sympathy with another person as suffering an injury. But one cannot explain in this way the specifically moral factor which characteristically enters when the feeling of right is outraged. Here the anger depends essentially on the idea that a *right* has been infringed. The indignation is not determined by the mere fact that oneself or others have suffered through the action; what is emphasized is the fact that the infliction of the suffering bears the character of an infringement of right, and is therefore a *wrong* action. But on what can one's interest in the fact that another should act *rightly* be grounded? Note that we are concerned here with an interest in this which is altogether independent of all further consequences, and one whose infringement can cause the strongest indignation. Here it cannot be a question of such interests as proceed from one's own feeling of duty. For such interests are related only to my own right action, and they are in no way infringed by wrong action on the part of another. But equally it cannot be a question of one's interests in the moral well-being of the wrong-doing party, in his preservation of his true autonomy, self-respect, or anything of the kind. In that case the reaction towards the infringement would not be anger but sorrow. It must therefore be a question of a direct interest in a certain action by another person, as that which alone agrees with the norm for the given case, i.e. as that which '*should* be done'. Now, so far as concerns oneself, the direct interest in an action as that which 'should be done' is grounded merely in the power of the expression of command to arouse a direct feeling of conative impulse. It is therefore unintelligible how an action, as that which 'should be done', could function in a different way when it concerns another person. Since in the one case the idea of the rightness of the action does not produce any direct pleasure in the latter, it cannot do so in the other case either; for in both cases that which excites interest is the same, viz. the rightness. The general rule holds also that the most immediate psychological effect of experiencing an expression of command or of *volition* is a conative impulse; just as experiencing the expression of a judgment calls forth the corresponding judgment, and as the awareness of an expression of feeling calls forth the corresponding feeling, as its most immediate psychological consequence. So in moral indignation there must occur an immediately arising conative impulse, which is bound up with the idea of a certain action on the part of another as the right one. It is this fact, that the actual action conflicts with our will, which produces displeasure and therefore anger with the guilty party. And undoubtedly this is a kind of anger which, far from being checked by moral considerations, is egged on by a feeling which, like the real feeling of duty, we ascribe to our true self and therefore regard with the same kind of respect. The same reasons which argue for the dependence of moral indignation on a certain conative feeling hold also for the dependence of esteem or disesteem for another person on the same feeling. It is plain that disesteem co-operates with moral indignation, which is closely allied with it; both these feelings are supported by the same reverence as the feeling of duty itself. *Ecrasez l'infâme!*

The other fact which is of importance here is the feeling of right in so far as it manifests itself in a demand upon another person to respect one's own or another's rights. This demand is of a different nature from that which consists in putting forward a legal claim. In the latter case we are concerned with a demand which it is right to respect because respect itself is as such the right action. But in the former case it is a question of a claim on an action, whose rightness does not consist in respect for the demand, but is valid apart from all reference to the latter. Again, this demand is not determined by interests in the background which are foreign to rightness as such, as is the case both in putting forward a legal claim and in morally indifferent or even unrighteous claims. But what is determinative is just the idea that the action demanded is right, as respecting another person's rights. Now we have already explained that in any kind of demand there occurs a feeling of conative impulse in connection with the idea of a certain other person's action. In our case what determines this feeling is the idea of the rightness of the action in question. In view of the arguments just put forward, concerning the dependence of moral indignation on a feeling of conative impulse devoid of valuation, it is impossible to suppose that a feeling of direct pleasure in what is right is inserted between this idea and the very conative impulse which it determines.

From this we can now draw the following conclusions. It is by no means *necessary* that the 'You ought!' should involve nothing more than indicating what action is in accordance with the norm in the given case for the person addressed. It can very well include consciousness of a genuine duty for him to act in a certain way. Instead of the feeling of duty, its analogue in connection with the thought of another's action can serve as the basis for the consciousness of duty. In view of the account given above, it can further be said that the idea of the rightness of a certain action on the part of another person cannot have the necessary degree of impressiveness unless this analogue to the feeling of duty is operative. Moreover, we may point out that the feeling of conative impulse, independent of valuation, directed towards another's action considered as right, must be subject to the same psychological conditions, *mutatis mutandis*, for its occurrence as the feeling of duty. That is to say, it becomes operative only if there are certain obstacles to the performance of the right action on the part of the other person. It develops to its highest intensity when, in our opinion, wrong action has already happened, and it then produces the moral indignation which we have already discussed. It is, however, also obvious that, when we judge the actions of others as right or wrong, the liveliness of the idea does not depend on the intensity of the feeling of duty in those who are the objects of our judgment. All that is needed is that a feeling of the kind described should be present in the person who makes the judgment. The feeling for rightness can react with the greatest vigour against the action of others as an infringement of right, although no definite feeling of duty is present in those who are the objects of the judgment. Yet, this tendency is counterbalanced by the fact that our judgments on our own actions as right or wrong are dependent on the intensity of the feeling of duty at the time of the actions.[1]

(*f*) *The idea of the justice of compulsion as an equivalent for neglect to act rightly.*

Bound up with the idea of the rightness of an action is the idea of the justice of compelling a person, who has acted wrongly or merely omitted to act rightly, to make a reparation equivalent to the right action which he has failed to perform. If I refuse to hand over another person's property when I have been informed of the facts, it is just, not merely that the thing should be taken from me, but also that compensation should be demanded of me for the damage done to the owner through my refusal. It should, however, be noted in the first place that, from the point of view of justice, *compulsion* to make an equivalent reparation need not be the most immediate consequence of wrong action. It may happen that justice demands in the first instance that the agent himself should make a reparation equivalent to the right action which he has failed to perform. If I have taken something, knowing it to be another's property, the immediate consequence, from the point of view of justice, of my wrong action is an obligation upon me to give it up and to compensate for the damage. But the final demand of justice is always that the equivalent act of reparation shall be enforced, so far as this is at all possible. In the field of criminal law the equivalent in question is of such a nature that only compulsion can be envisaged as a legal consequence.

It should further be noted that the reparation which is *regarded* as equivalent to the omitted right action may stand in a more or less direct relation of correspondence to the latter. In the above-mentioned examples of infringement of rights of property the right action which has been omitted consists either in handing over the thing and avoiding injury to the owner's interest in the thing, or, as the case may be, in the repression of the impulse to appropriating another's property and thereby possibly infringing the interests which he has in the property. In such cases, if the owner is regarded as the possessor of rights, whose legal claim is to be respected, the rightness of the equivalent reparation is determined by applying, to the situation which has arisen, the same norm

[1] Cf. above, p. 144.

which determines the rightness of the omitted action. The situation is different, e.g. in a case where the wrongness consists merely in failure to attend to the possibility of damaging another's property which is involved in a certain course of action, where the owner is regarded as one whose legal claim is to be respected. If, in this case, compensation for damage, if such should occur and the injured party should demand it, is regarded as an equivalent reparation, this does not result directly from applying the norm which determines the rightness of the omitted action. According to that norm, that which ought to have existed was merely a certain degree of attention as safeguarding the owner's legal claim; it was not the repression of an impulse to injure, which was not present here.—The lack of any direct connection with the omitted right action is still more obvious when the latter consists in a certain respect for the rights of the community and when the equivalent reparation consists in suffering punishment. Suppose that the wrong consists in wilful murder, and the omitted right action consists in repressing the impulse to this out of respect for the rights of the community. Then it might seem that one could only deduce, by applying the fundamental norm to the given case, that the equivalent reparation should be—not punishment, but resurrection of the dead man. It may be that in certain respects the punishment can be regarded as making recompense for injuring certain social interests, e.g. through the force of example, through bringing the law into contempt, through disturbing the general feeling of security, etc. But in general the criminal had not directed his attention to the injury which he might do in those respects. In such cases the omitted right action, for which the punishment should be the equivalent reparation, would be attention to the injurious consequences of the action to society. If so, the punishment, regarded as an equivalent reparation, would have to consist in compulsion which brings about attention in future. The greatest effect in this direction would surely be produced by compulsory courses on the social harmfulness of certain actions. But the sense of justice would certainly not regard such compulsion as in any way an equivalent reparation. Only if awareness of the social injury which results from the action demonstrably existed when the crime was committed, would recompense for the latter by a punishment in the ordinary sense present itself as an equivalent reparation, provided that such recompense is determined by applying the fundamental norm to the situation which has arisen from the negligence.—The lack of immediate connection between the omitted right action and the punishment as an equivalent compulsion is most obvious when, as happens in the idea of retaliation, the equivalence is held to consist in the criminal suffering a penalty corresponding to that which he has caused. This suffering at the most satisfies the revengeful desire of the individual or the community to triumph over the foe; it in no way offers a compensation for the injury which the criminal ought to have avoided inflicting. The victim of a robbery does not get back his property through it, and society does not get the social damage made good.

In order to understand the origin of the idea of an equivalent reparation it is necessary in such cases to go back to the social interests which evoke the demands from which the idea of the basic norm originates. A certain degree of attention to the possibly harmful effects of an action upon another person's property is regarded as respect for his rights, and therefore as the action which 'ought to take place'. This is derived from a social interest, whether universal or confined to a class, which has led to the consequence that laws, gods, and one's environment are regarded as commanding this attention. What is determinative here is the common interest in the security of the individual against damage to his property through the actions of others. But this interest is not secured merely because a 'You must pay attention', supplemented by a 'You must, if you are aware of the fact that an action will injure another's property, repress the impulse to do it', sounds in the individual's ears. For this it is necessary further that the force of the command should be strengthened by the awareness that one must make reparation, if there should be lack of attention and it should lead to damage, and that one will in fact be *compelled* to do this if one does not do it voluntarily. So, in conjunction with the formation of the idea of powers which command attentiveness, the common interest also gives rise to (i) an imperative 'You must make reparation for the ill-effects of your lack of attention', and (ii) a general inclination to demand the effectuation of compulsion. But, through this link with interest, the idea that one ought to be attentive out of respect for another's rights becomes linked with (i) the idea that one ought to make reparation for damage, if it should happen in consequence of infringing a norm and if reparation should be claimed of one, and (ii) the idea that compulsion will be exerted, if reparation is not made voluntarily, just because reparation *ought* to be made but has not voluntarily been made. In this way the compulsion itself acquires the character of something that *should* happen, as being in the last resort the reparation equivalent to the original omitted right action. In all this the original possessor of the right remains as the person whose legal claim must be satisfied, and that is why failure on his part to demand it annuls the demand for compulsion. That only a certain degree of attentiveness is regarded as right, and as entailing the consequence in question if it should be lacking, depends of course on the counterinfluence of other social interests, e.g. the common interest for that degree of freedom of movement which is essential for the individual's feeling of well-being and for such mutual intercourse as forwards social prosperity.—Similar remarks apply to the formation of the idea of powers which command certain actions. In connection with this there develops, through the social interest (whether of the community as a whole or of a class) in checking tendencies which are regarded as more or less dangerous to the community or the class, a general tendency towards a system of compulsion. This system is concerned with the omission of these commanded actions, and it is determined by the degree of dangerousness of these tendencies. It thus comes about that the thought that certain actions 'ought to be done', in view of the interests of the community or of a class, is linked with the thought of certain compulsive reactions, viz. 'punishments', as consequences of omitting such actions. In this way the compulsion too acquires the character of an equivalent reparation to the community or to the class, which 'should happen' or is 'just'. Here too the interest in question is counterbalanced by other common interests, e.g. the interest for limiting the suffering of the individual so far as possible.—When, according to the idea of retaliation, suffering 'ought' in justice to be inflicted on the criminal corresponding to that which he has inflicted, the intermediate link is a social feeling of revenge, which arises from the infringement of the interest which has led to the idea that certain actions are commanded.

But what should be particularly noted is that the justice of the compulsion does not primarily entail that any given person or group of persons should exert it. What should happen is primarily the compulsion itself, and it must of course happen as an equivalent for the right action which was originally omitted. The justice of the compulsion means simply that it rightly happens to the *object* in accordance with the norm for what 'should be done'. It is only secondarily that the idea that a person or group of persons 'should' exert the compulsion gets attached to this. Retaliatory justice is merely the counterpart to the rightness of the action which has been omitted. So the idea of it must be regarded as acting in a corresponding way, i.e. it must be supposed to cause a feeling of conative impulse, devoid of valuation, linked with the idea itself. The special reverence which is felt for such a conative impulse, as an expression of the true self, thus provides an explanation of the absolute value which is ascribed to the fulfilment of justice, and also of the special intensity of the demand for justice. From this conative feeling must also be derived the idea of compulsion as something owed by the wrong-doer. We have seen that the idea of one's own duty rests upon a simultaneous association between a conative impulse, devoid of valuation, and the idea of a certain action of one's own as right. We have also seen that the idea of another's duty rests upon a similar feeling in combination with the idea of a certain other person's action as right. We now see that the idea of the obligation to submit to compulsion rests, in the same way, upon a similar feeling in combination with the idea of compulsion as right.

(*g*) *The idea of the justice of compulsion without reference to a precedent wrong, and its connection with the feeling of revenge.*

It should, however, be noted that the idea of the justice of compulsion also arises directly, i.e. without reference to the idea of an ignored right. When Nestor, in Homer, relates that the Epeans had a debt (χρεῖος) to pay to the Pythians by reason of a previous attack,[1] a debt which could be paid only by a plundering-raid on the part of the latter, there is no suggestion that the people who made the original attack had done anything wrong. Yet they are due to pay for the evil which they wrought, in the sense that it is just that they should be subjected to suffering through a plundering-raid. The justice of the compulsion was attached to the circumstance that the Epeans had plundered in the territory of the Pythians, without any ground being alleged why it should be just. Achilles' cry that Hector or the Trojans should pay for Patroclus'

---

[1] *Il.* XI, 686 *et seq.* A similar expression as to the reason for an alleged plundering raid of Odysseus. *Od.* XXI, 16.

death is of exactly the same nature.[1] Hector had not, in Achilles'
view, done anything dishonourable in killing Patroclus in defence
of his native city. But Odysseus' words, that he would not stay
his hand until Penelope's suitors had paid for their transgressions
(ὑπερβασίην),[2] have a quite different character. In this case an
actual ground is given for the duty to pay, i.e. in other words, for
the justice of the compulsion, viz. that the action with which justice
was connected involved a wrong i.e. exceeding the right measure.
The compulsion then presented itself as a reparation equivalent
to an omitted right action, and as such it was just.—In Aeschylus'
*Eumenides* the demand that the guilt shall be more closely investigated, by enquiring whether the original action was wrong in the
actual situation, is set against the blind lust of the Erinyes for
revenge. Yet even the latter is presented in the guise of right, for
δίκη itself demanded that the matricide Orestes should be handed
over. This enquiry should take place by means of a preliminary
investigation before certain experts in the law, viz. the gods, at
which the contending parties, viz. the Erinyes as accusers and
Orestes as defendent, were to bring forward pleas and counter-
pleas. From the Erinyes' point of view this demand was an
infringement of their rights on the part of 'the younger gods'.
Here is obviously represented the progress in moral reflection which
accompanies the transition from the legal state of the blood-feud
to the settling of disputes between individuals or families by
judgments having the force of law. Even the blood-feud has its
own view of right. The demand for revenge is simply the actualization of justice in respect of the subject who originally inflicted
suffering. And neglect of it, on the part of the injured individual
or of the family which has been injured in one of its members, therefore implies a wrong which lowers personal worth. For justice
should be actualized. But it is plain from the endless circle of the
blood-feud that the action, to which the justice of inflicting
suffering on the agent is referred, is not regarded as a wrong. Since
it is just that revenge should be demanded in turn upon him who
has revenged the injury inflicted, although the latter only did his
duty, it follows that the justice of the compulsion is independent
of whether the original action was right or wrong. But with the

---

[1] *Il.* XVIII, 93, and XXI, 133.
[2] *Od.* XXII, 60 *et seq.* Cf. the analogous use of the expressions ἀτάσθαλον
*Od.* XXIV, 352. βίην ἀνδρῶν ὑπερηνορεόντων *Od.* XXIII, 31.

repression of the blood-feud through the need of peace, which demands a powerful legal order standing above the contending parties, and through social feeling, there arises the thought that compulsion is righteous only as an equivalent for a right action in regard to which the subject of the compulsion has fallen short. But such a reflection carries others in its train. It must be enquired whether the subject can be regarded as self-determining in general, and more especially at the moment when he did the wrong action, i.e. as a real practical ego to which a happening can be ascribed as its work. Otherwise, omission to act in a certain way cannot be regarded as depending on the subject as a real agent, for it is part of the notion of the latter that his inner self should really be determinative of his behaviour in practical matters. But, on the supposition that there is imputability, it must further be inquired, not merely whether, but in what way, an omission to act rightly occurs; whether, e.g., there is a deliberate fault or merely a lack of attention. This, of course, affects the nature of the just compulsion, in so far as it is to be equivalent to the omitted right action. Note that this distinction was made even in the archaic Athenian blood-tribunals:—Aeschylus' drama represents the founding of the areopagus. All such reflections are strange to the Erinyes' notions of justice, where the only relevant fact is that an injury exists, caused by the action of someone.

But what is most important of all is that the development from the idea of the justice of compulsion without regard to a precedent wrong-doing to the idea of its justice as lying in a reparation equivalent to the omitted right action provides for the first time a measure for the just degree of compulsion. It is plain that it is the feeling of revenge which is active in the primitive idea that it is right that one should suffer for inflicting suffering regardless of whether one did so rightly or wrongly. But revenge is, of its very nature, measureless. Its motto is certainly not an eye for an eye and a tooth for a tooth, but a head for an eye and a head for a tooth. So primitive justice is without measure. To do as much harm as *possible* to one's enemies is right, according to the Greek morality against which the Platonic Socrates contends. But now there enters the following curious circumstance. According to the idea of retaliation, which is still active to this day in the penal law, the amount of suffering which the culprit ought to endure is, notwithstanding the obvious kinship between retaliation and the demand for revenge, equal to

that which he inflicted but not greater. It is impossible to doubt
that this mitigation of the feeling of revenge is derived from the
thought of punishment as something which ought to be equivalent
to the crime, or rather as a restitution of just that right which the
crime has ignored but which nevertheless ought to be realized.
The feeling of revenge certainly continues to operate here in two
respects. In the first place, the fact that an agent is held responsible
for the result without regard to his intention shows that the thought
of the wrong action as the ground and the measure of punishment
has not sufficiently asserted itself against the primitive notion of
justice, and that therefore the feeling of revenge is operative.
Secondly, the fact that the reparation which is regarded as equivalent is merely a corresponding degree of suffering can be explained
only as a consequence of the feeling of revenge. It cannot be regarded either as following from a direct application of the basic
norm or as an expression of society's interest in safeguarding its
own values. But the counteracting forces must not be overlooked.
Regard to the original wrong, as the measure of the justice of the
reaction, brings with it forces which repress the importance of the
feeling of revenge in determining the equivalent reparation. In so
far as the original action is considered as a wrong, the thought of
the rights of the injured party comes into the foreground. It is
this which should be upheld by the reaction. But here the interests
come into play, which are determinative for the norm which
ordains what is right. In order that the reaction should be just,
it must be limited to upholding the right of the injured party.
Therefore, if no direct application is possible of the norm which
ordains what is right to the case of its infringement, the only factor
which can be concerned in determining the equivalence is consideration of the interest which lies behind the right. Thus, in the
first place, private punishment is transformed into a claim for
damages.[1] When the right which is infringed by the wrongful act
consists merely in the right to be immune from intentionally
harmful actions on the part of others, or again in the right to
require due attention on their part to the consequences of negative
or positive behaviour in this respect (all this within definite limits),
the just reaction can consist only in compulsion to compensate for

[1] Cf. Ihering, *Geist des römischen Rechts*, II, pp. 113 *et seq.;* Schlossman
*Der Vertrag*, 1876, p. 315, n. 1; and Regelsberger, *Pandekten*, I, 1893,
p. 222.

damage. In this way the interest on which the right is based is safeguarded. On the other hand, punishment is retained, as the just reaction against one who infringes the right of the community or of a class to a certain mode of behaviour on the part of the individual. And it is thus regulated, not from the standpoint of revenge, but from that of the interests which determine the norm underlying the right. What is needed for safeguarding those interests, and nothing else, becomes determinative for the just punishment.

Thyrén (*The General Principles of Penal Law*, 1907, pp. 47 *et seq.*, and cf. also his *The Principles for Reform of the Penal Law*, 1910, pp. 33 *et seq.* Both in Swedish) treats the idea of guilt, in the sense of deserving punishment, as being what is specifically characteristic of the notion of retaliation, but not of the notion of prevention. He seems to regard these two ideas as the only ones which can be taken into account in determining the ground and the measure of punishment. But this is hardly correct. The sharp distinction which is drawn between *dolus* and *culpa* in determining the degree of punishment has nothing to do with the idea of retaliation, which is concerned only with the actual result, but is connected only with the degree of dangerousness in the tendencies evinced in the action. Yet there is no doubt that the general sense of justice regards *dolus* as in itself more deserving of punishment than *culpa*, and that it reacts strongly against the injustice of their being put on a level in the sight of the penal law. The thought here is that punishment is just only when it is resorted to in accordance with what the rights of society or of a social class demand when those rights are infringed. But what these rights demand in such a case is determined by the same interests which are the basis for establishing certain negative or positive actions as duties towards society or that class. Since those interests are concerned with checking dangerous tendencies to action, that punishment is just which is needed for that purpose. It may be required either as a realization of a threat of punishment which acts in that direction, or to counteract tendencies which have already manifested themselves, or as a remedy for the damage which their manifestation involves. The motives for punishment may be social hygiene and in no way the feeling of revenge; but none the less, in the common-sense notion of justice punishment is connected with the idea of *guilt* in regard to the rights of society. In no department of law does so strong a reaction against 'injustice' occur as in that of penal law.

Thyrén seems here to be specially influenced by the view that guilt presupposes acceptance of the freedom of the will. The doctrine that punishment is essentially a means of prevention is alleged to be logically incompatible with that assumption, since free will as such cannot be regarded as capable of being influenced. (See, e.g., *The Principles* . . ., I, p. 37). But the situation is certainly greatly oversimplified here. (i) One may presuppose the freedom of the will as a condition of guilt, in the sense that the behaviour, in order to involve guilt, must be characterized by an omission to take account of what is right, although the agent could have freely chosen to act rightly. In that case belief in the possibility of influencing the will is not logically excluded in *every* sense. All that is assumed here is *moral* freedom as a condition of guilt. But this in no way conflicts with the view that the will is necessarily determined by the strongest motive, and therefore can be influenced, *in so far as* the will moves in the non-moral sphere when moral motives are set aside, and within that sphere has to decide for a certain motive. The criminal can certainly be supposed to have been free in his criminal behaviour, in the sense that his choice of the wrong course, in so far as it involved the setting aside of moral motives, was free. Yet it may be reasonable to wish so to influence him that, if in the future he should not allow himself to be determined by moral motives, the non-moral sphere will be so constituted that the motives within it, restraining him from action which is wrong from the external point of view, will prevail. At the very most it is belief in the possibility of *moral* improvement by influence which is logically excluded by the assumption that the freedom of the will is a necessary condition for guilt. (ii) It is very questionable whether, in demanding the freedom of the will as a condition for guilt, one has not merely the following in mind, viz., that practical behaviour must depend upon the immoral character of the practical ego, i.e. a morally bad will, if it is to involve guilt. When infancy, idiocy, or mental disease is regarded as excluding the freedom of the will, and with it guilt, the essential point is merely that the practical behaviour in such cases, even though it be in the highest degree contrary to what is right, does not depend on an immoral character in the personality itself. In the moral idiot, e.g. moral motives are never set aside, because such motives do not exist. In the idea of freedom the thought of causelessness or contingency in self-determination in certain directions is always counterbalanced by the thought of causality or necessity. For in the idea of freedom the direction of the will to this or that action is always thought of as *grounded* in the will itself, and as proceeding *necessarily* from its constitution. And in the thought of guilt *this* side of the notion of freedom, viz. the idea of the will as a cause, plays a predominant part. (iii) Owing to the illogical combination of the idea of causelessness and that of causality as regards the choice of an action, which is involved in the idea of freedom, this idea is a hybrid one from which we can equally arrive at the notion that the will can be influenced or that it cannot.

That the idea of the justice of punishment in the modern conception of justice is referred to the rights of society, and not to retribution, is specially emphasized by Heimberger in his work *Der Begriff der Gerechtigkeit im Strafrecht*, 1903.

Makarewicz, in his sketch of the development of penal law in his work *Einführung in die Philosophie des Strafrechts*, 1906, shows a complete lack of attention to the above-mentioned complex of ideas. This appears in principle in his definition of a criminal action (pp. 79-80). This is defined as an action, done by a member of a social group, which is regarded by the other members of the group as so harmful or as betraying such a degree of anti-social disposition that they react publicly and collectively by trying to deprive him of some part of his stock of values, i.e. his 'goods'. It is claimed that this is the correct way of defining it, because it preserves the essential connection between crime in the modern sense of the word and more primitive phenomena which are akin to it. The following question arises here: Is the reaction, in every instance which the author regards as a crime, really determined by the opinion of the group that the action is universally harmful or that the disposition which it betrays is anti-social? He himself mentions that the punishment is often determined by a *conviction of justice* (p. 87). Now, is this conviction, which, according to the author, may refer to supposed divine law and which certainly becomes more emphatic as the level of moral culture rises, really the same as regarding the action as universally harmful in a very high degree or as betraying a very high degree of anti-social disposition? The fact that it serves a person right that the demands of justice shall be supplemented by punishment has, as such, nothing to do with the ascription of these characteristics to an action, even if it be just the actions which have those characteristics that are regarded as rightly deserving punishment. Nor need the thought of them be active in a social reaction which is determined by the demand for justice. This is plain when the idea of the justice of the punishment is determined by moral indignation at the course of action as infringing old 'holy' customs. Even if absence of social reaction is regarded as dangerous to society, because it brings with it the wrath of the gods, it is still the divine law itself which is held to have been infringed and it is this infringement which has to be justly punished. Similarly, when the state regulates and supports 'private punishment' (which is treated by the author as genuine punishment on p. 251). Here undoubtedly the governing idea is that it is just that the criminal should suffer for the satisfaction of the injured individual. The thought of general harmfulness or anti-social disposition is here plainly subordinate. When the injured individual, according to the legal rules, has himself to take vengeance under certain circumstances, he is so far from being regarded as acting for the state that, on the contrary, when the state acts directly as an avenger on his behalf, it is regarded as representing the injured party. (See the examples adduced by the author himself in the middle of p. 257.) But the difference between the two points of view as to what is determinative of the social reaction becomes especially obvious when injury to the one person or the few who are in supreme authority is regarded as 'crime' *par excellence*. The author himself reflects on this circumstance (pp. 136 *et seq.*) but considers it to depend on the fact that what injures the mighty is held to injure all. But it is only necessary to remember how little a man from the common herd weighs in comparison with the chiefs, according to the Homeric view, e.g. in order to understand that it was not the harm done to all such men which made actions that are injurious to the mighty into crimes. The idea of the divine right of the mighty, as dominating under such conditions the whole juridical outlook and determining the notion of 'crime', is surely here ignored in a remarkable way. When the writer, in order to defend his dogmatic theory in this connection, uses such a hackneyed phrase as that a people always has 'such a form of government as the majority desires to have' (p. 239), he overlooks the compulsive activity of more or less openly superstitious ideas of law among peoples at the lower levels of culture.

It might now be questioned whether the notion of crime supported by the author could be sustained except at two opposite poles, viz. (i) in reference to the lowest stage of culture, where the people immediately takes vengeance for particular actions which are generally harmful or which exhibit an anti-social disposition, and (ii) the modern tendencies to regard the reactions of the state against so-called crime from the standpoint of the *conscious* exercise of social hygiene. Here the notions of justice which are concerned with the ideas of rights and duties do indeed lose all significance. But how is it with those actions on which punishment is imposed in the transitional stages, i.e. in point of fact the stage of development characteristic of all civilizations which have existed up to now? To this should be added that one might feel doubtful as to how far the expression *Verbrechen, crimen*, etc., may not have acquired its meaning at just that stage under the influence of the sense of justice which demands punishment, and whether for that reason such a definition as that given by the author does not altogether misrepresent the meaning which the expression has for common sense.

Our next task is to explain the idea of the justice, independently of previous wrongdoing, of compulsion or of the liability to compulsion. That liability to compulsion here means the same as that which is founded upon the omission of a right action is at once plain from the fact that the latter gradually develops out of the former. It is also plain from the fact that in both cases the justice of the compulsion is regarded as the ground of the liability to it, even though the justice is founded in the one case on a previous wrong and in the other case is independent of it. But the liability to be subjected to punishment because of previous wrongdoing corresponds, in the sphere of suffering, to the duty to act in a certain way. So the idea of liability here treated must be regarded as parallel to the idea of duty in the strict sense. That is to say, it issues from something analogous to the feeling of duty; in this case it is a feeling of conative impulse, devoid of valuation, associated with the idea of one's own or another's suffering as just. Note now also that one regards liability to suffer as a debt to be paid, just as if it concerned a genuine action which one was under an obligation to do. (A Greek expression for being the object of another's vengeance is δίκην διδόναι, i.e. to give to the avenger his right.) The justice of compulsion must be regarded in this case too as parallel to rightness in a certain action. It thus means that suffering is in a certain case right, in regard to what 'should' or 'ought' to happen, i.e. is bound up with a concretely presented expression of command; just as the rightness of an action means that in a certain case it 'should' or 'ought to' take place. The question now is: How does an expression of command here come to be regarded as objectively bound up with a certain suffering, independently of any previous wrong for which the suffering would atone?

We have already explained the idea of the objective connection of an expression of command with a certain action by the influence of commanding authorities, real or imaginary, and of custom. Neither of these factors is here in a position to provide a ground of explanation, since both command and custom relate only to actions. We need to find a third factor, which can call forth the idea of an expression of command as bound up with a suffering. Since an expression of command as such is an expression for a feeling of conative impulse devoid of valuation, and since it functions as such, we need here a factor which has the power to call forth such a feeling in connection with the thought of a person's suffering. What suggests itself immediately here is the feeling of revenge, which undoubtedly is determinative of the primitive idea of justice with which we are here concerned.

In a pure outburst of anger the action is, in the first instance, of the same kind as other involuntarily occurring affective symptoms. Its kinship with reflex action is obvious.[1] In its primitive form an outburst of anger is not directed on to any determinate object. The child breaks out against his surroundings without discrimination. Still, it is natural that, in proportion as the experienced suffering, which is the cause of the anger, is definitely associated with a certain object as its occasion, the outburst is directed on to just that object. If the object is an animal organism, the reaction includes a depressing of its vitality, and this involves infliction of suffering accompanied by a heightening of one's own vital feeling.

[1] Cf. Westermarck, *Ursprung und Entwicklung der Moralbegriffe*, I, 1907, p. 18 and Windelband, *Über Willensfreiheit*, 1904, p. 204.

The reaction is as such an element in the reacting organism's process of self-preservation, and subserves the latter in its direction *against* the attacker for the benefit of the attacked. But along with the process of reacting there follows in the subject, if the latter experiences resistance, a feeling of vital impulse or urge, which is associated with the idea of depressing the attacking organism's vitality and at the same time inflicting suffering upon it and therewith heightening one's own vital feeling. 'He shall pay dearly for his deed!' At this stage for the first time anger has become feeling of revenge. Now this feeling, as the psychical side of the reflex-like innervation, is in itself independent of all valuation. In a fit of anger I do not clench my fists because I take any special pleasure in that action, but it happens involuntarily. So the corresponding feeling of an impulse to strike down my opponent must be equally involuntary. But a consequence of its presence is the pleasure in striking out. 'As the fulfilment of every desire is attended with pleasure, so too does the fulfilment of the desire which is bound up with enmity produce its own special experience of pleasure.'[1] It is important to distinguish clearly between the reactive action which is determined by the *purpose* of self-preservation and the reaction which springs from anger. In the former case the basic state of mind is pleasure in self-preservation. From this there follows the decision and thereupon the action. But in the latter case what is primary is the action directed towards striking down the attacker and defending oneself. From this there follows, in case of resistance, the will to do so and thereupon the pleasure in triumphing over one's foe. In the first case, therefore, the pleasure in inflicting defeat is by no means measureless. It has its measure in its utility. It is possible that what is conducive to self-preservation is that the enemy should be struck down only within certain limits, and that to exceed these would be harmful. The vanquished, if preserved, may be useful, e.g. as a slave. The humiliation of an enemy may be harmful, provided that he can be made harmless without it, because of the feelings of revenge which it may arouse in him. But in the second case every mitigation, arising from the situation itself, is lacking. Since it is the reactive action, and not the pleasure in self-preservation, which is here primary, self-preservation in its concrete wholeness does not come into the picture. It enters only as self-defence *against the*

[1] Westermarck, loc. cit., p. 33.

F

*enemy*. This abstract self-preservation is of course best attained by his complete suppression. Of these two ways of reacting in the service of self-preservation, the latter, with all its inferiority in other respects, is nevertheless superior to the former in so far as it is not 'sicklied o'er with the pale cast of thought', which may be a decisive advantage in acting.—To this we need add only one further reflection on why revenge against a personal enemy carries with it a specially outstanding pleasure in inflicting suffering on him. One delights, not in depriving him of life, which would seem to be the really effective thing from the point of view of self-preservation, but in doing this in such a way that he will experience the greatest possible suffering in the process. The primitive man casts his enemy's body to the dogs in order to deprive him of the advantage which he might get from ritual burial. It might be thought that the ground of this is cruelty, in the sense of an abnormal pleasure in another's suffering. But really the state of feeling in revenge is of quite a different kind. It should be noted that the more closely akin an animal organism is to my self the easier it is for me to put myself into its state of feeling. Now suffering as such is an expression for lowered vitality. What I take pleasure in, in the feeling of revenge, is to feel my own vitality heightened at the expense of the attacker, i.e. to be superior to him. Through the connection between suffering and the lowering of the vital force the latter becomes the more striking the greater the suffering is. Suppose, now, that I am concerned with a personal being in whose state of feeling I can easily put myself. Then the pleasure of revenge must be just the pleasure of triumphing over him through seeing him suffer. One can strike down even an adder in revenge, but one's interest here is more immediately directed to annihilating him, because his suffering cannot have the same import as a sign of lowering of vitality and therefore as heightening one's own feeling of vitality. But in revenge one wants to break one's personal enemy physically and spiritually upon the wheel merely in order to see him in the dust before one's eyes.

But it should now be noticed here that the idea, with which the involuntary conative impulse is connected in the feeling of revenge against a personal object, is not so much the idea of undertaking the reactive action as of that which constitutes the goal at which it is directed. We have seen that, in so far as suffering endured is associated with the idea of a certain personal object as its cause, the original reaction, as a phase in the process of self-preservation, must be directed towards lowering the vitality of that object, and in particular inflicting suffering on it, with a concomitant heightening of one's own threatened vitality. It is therefore necessary to keep the idea of this effect vivid. Unless the idea in question acts as a point to be aimed at, the action loses its self-preserving power. So the idea follows just as involuntarily as the action itself. The idea which arises and is immediately bound up with the innervation, is therefore associated, not so much with the idea of the action itself, as with that of its effect, which latter idea is predominant at the moment of acting. Therefore, the expression for it is: 'He shall suffer for his action and give me satisfaction for it.' That is to say, the expression is a genuine utterance of a command or the expression of a feeling of conative impulse devoid of valuation, but it is essentially linked with the idea of another's suffering and not with that of one's own or another's action.

But suppose now that the members of a family or of some larger social group have feelings of revenge in common because of an injury inflicted by another person or group of persons. Each of them then eggs on the others with expressions of revenge, whether these be words or threatening gestures or other equally involuntary manifestations. When the individual perceives such expressions in himself or in the others he associates them with the idea of the suffering of the aggressor or aggressors. Since he finds the idea of this suffering associated with the perceptibly presented expression in the case of all the others too, nothing can be more natural than that he should assume there to be a factual connection between the suffering in question and the expression of revenge. But in that way the suffering becomes something which has, under the actual circumstances, the property that it 'should happen'. But at the same time and in consequence of this a norm is given, which runs as follows. He who is ever in the same situation as this aggressor, whether the sameness refers to the general character or even to the special character of the situation, 'shall' as such be made to suffer in order to heighten the self-feeling of the injured party. Therefore it is right, in view of this norm, that this person or these persons should suffer. And now the sluice-doors are open. The idea of the suffering as having the expression of command as an objective property, or as being right, produces in this respect a feeling of conative impulse. That feeling, through its association with the idea, produces, in the way already explained, the consciousness of this or that person's obligation to make recompense by suffering. At this stage the passion for the accomplishment of justice arises. Through its kinship with the feeling of duty it is the object of the same reverence as the latter. It seems to us to belong to our *true* self, and it must be fostered on pain of losing that self.

### 3. THE RELATIONSHIP AND DIFFERENCE BETWEEN THE STATE OF MIND OF THE RECIPIENT OF A COMMAND AND THAT WHICH IS ASSOCIATED WITH THE IDEA OF OBLIGATION

We have now set forth, in (1) and (2), our investigation of (i) the psychological content of command, and (ii) the nature of the idea of duty and other notions which are essentially connected with it. In this way it should have been made clear what is the kinship, and what is the definite difference, between the state of mind of the recipient of a command and that which occurs in connection with the idea of duty. In each case there is present a feeling of conative impulse, devoid of valuation, associated with the idea of a person's own action. In each case this feeling is produced through the influence of the expression of command. Finally there arises in both cases a feeling of compulsion which is referred to the expression of command as what is binding. But there the likeness ends. In command the expression acts through the recipient's peculiar relation to the giver of the order. But in the case of the idea of duty the expression acts independently in its concrete perceptible form. It appears as an objective property of the action, with the idea of which the feeling of conative impulse is associated. This action is referred to a norm, viz. the idea of a system of conduct as something which essentially goes along with the expression of command, and it stands out as the one which is right from that standpoint. Thus it comes about that a consciousness of an obligation to do the action, which is wholly absent in the case of the recipient of a command, is bound up with the feeling of duty. That which determines the feeling of conative impulse, viz. the expression of command, is here regarded as an objective property of the action. Therefore the expression of the feeling cannot retain its autonomy in the expression for the association between itself and the idea of the action as right. Instead it enters as a predicate-term in a sentence in the indicative, viz. 'The action, as being right, is my duty'. On this basis is raised the consciousness of an indeterminate something which expresses itself in duty and the like.

But, in so far as the expression of command is taken as a real property of a system of conduct, the idea becomes possible of a certain action being the right one for another person in a given case. Here the expression of command produces a conative impulse in reference to another person's action, when the idea of its rightness occurs. And in such cases the conative impulse manifests itself as moral indignation and the demands of the sense of justice, and it gives rise to a consciousness of an obligation on the part of the other person to act in this way. For the recipient of a command as such the fact that the same command may also be issued to other persons is something which is in itself of no conative significance. His desire that others shall or that they shall not obey the command, or his indifference in regard to this, depends on his own special interests.

Moreover, the idea of duty carries with it the thought that submission to a compulsion, which appears as an equivalent reparation for an omitted right action, is something obligatory, whether it concerns oneself or another. Once the expression of command has become a real property of a system of conduct, as happens in the case of the idea of duty, it is transferred to the compulsion which is regarded as equivalent to the omission to act in accordance with that system. So in any actual case the idea of the rightness of the compulsion produces a conative impulse towards it, viz. a feeling of obligation in regard to it and, along with this, also an idea of real obligation. For the recipient of a command as such the compulsion which is attached to the order, in case of disobedience to it, is merely a fact, whose consequences as regards himself he seeks to avoid so far as may be. In reference to others compulsion is signified for him only through his special interests, positive or negative.

Finally it should be remarked that the feeling of conative impulse which belongs to the idea of duty, regarded as that which 'ought' to prevail in the soul, and also other conative feelings which are allied to it, acquire a special sanctity. They do so because they are ascribed to my real self, so that I seem to myself to lose my autonomy, which has the highest affective value for me, if I fail to carry them into action. The norm itself acts through such conditions and through its power to attach reverence or respect. Esteem is attached to right action and disesteem to wrong action. This most important world of feelings is foreign to the recipient of a command as such.

Let us now imagine a social group, within which fictitious or real commanding authorities act in unanimity. The power of command necessarily suffers from certain defects so long as the expression of command is not transmuted, in the consciousness of the members, into a real property of a system of conduct identical for them all. It seems uncertain to the members that the commanding authorities will keep to their commands in every situation. So their suggestive power is not present under all circumstances. How far the individual will be positively or negatively interested or indifferent in regard to the general carrying-out of the commands will depend on circumstances external to the power of command itself. If it is an oppressive minority which bears sway, each individual may be influenced by commands addressed to himself, but on the whole his interests are opposed to the carrying-out of the system. The compulsion, which is threatened in case of disobedience, if it should affect an individual, will be merely an evil which interests him only negatively. And, if he hates the whole system because he belongs to the oppressed class, he will be negatively interested in regard to such exercise of compulsion in general. But suppose that the expression of command acquires power to act autonomously, as a supposed real property of a system of conduct identical for all. Then these defects will disappear. The idea of a possible lack of steadfastness in the will of the commanding authorities will now be irrelevant and so too will be the different degrees of suggestive force in different circumstances. When an action presents itself as that which is right in a certain case in accordance with the norm, the expression of command inevitably engenders a feeling of conative impulse, to which a mighty world of feelings, of the kind described, attaches itself, thus increasing its force. The interest in favour of the action with which the expression of command is united in a particular case is now unconditionally present, alike when it concerns oneself or others; an interest which is reinforced in its operation by the world of feeling mentioned above. The compulsion which is threatened in case of disobedience now becomes a righteous compulsion, in respect to which one feels one-self and others to be liable in that case. It is plain that the social group in which such forces are active gains in consistency and therefore in the power of self-preservation. Nevertheless there is another side to the matter. Suppose that the system of conduct which has the expression of command connected with it as an objective property acquires an opposite character for various groups or for various classes within the same group in consequence of opposed interests, so that what is right for the one group or class is wrong for the other. In that case, if enmity should arise, it takes a specially embittered form. Each one, in exerting pressure on the other, believes himself to be realizing the demands of objective rightness.

However, it is now clear, in view of the account given above, that the state of consciousness of the recipient of a command readily passes over into that which accompanies the idea of duty, and that conversely the latter carries the former with it, under certain circumstances, notwithstanding the fundamental difference between the two. It is only necessary that fictitious or real commanding authorities should assert themselves effectively and unanimously in a society, in order that the expression of command shall be transformed into a supposed real property of a system of conduct and that the idea of duty shall enter. And, if once the abstract idea arises that there is an unconditionally binding norm, there arises a tendency to connect it with commanding authorities which assert themselves affectively and consistently. This happens through regarding the expressions of command which issue from such authorities as normative. This is, of course, particularly true when he or they who command are wise enough to adapt themselves more or less to the content of already existing norms. If a tyrant's ordinances are astutely adapted to the current ideas of rightness, the people very readily come to regard them as authoritative, confirmations of real duties. That, on the other hand, there is a tendency to think of a commanding will in connection with the idea of duty, has already been shown.[1] In this way also can be explained the tendency to confuse, on reflection, the state of consciousness of the recipient of a command with the consciousness of duty.

[1] See above, pp. 133 *et seq.*

A flagrant example of this is provided by von Kirchmann's treatment of the unconditional ought in his work *Die Grundbegriffe des Rechts und der Moral* 2. Aufl., 1873. According to his view the ought is given in a feeling of respect for a commanding 'immense' physical power, which is regarded as infinite. In relation to this the individual appears as powerless. The same feeling of respect is alleged to be present in the feeling for the majestic and sublime in certain natural phenomena (pp. 51, 53, and 57). In this the fact is overlooked that the ought, in the consciousness of duty, is connected with the action itself as a real property. When it is a question of the relationship to a commanding authority as such, the ought is attached to obedience; but, as we have pointed out, this cannot be commanded in the command itself. But the ought need not in any way be connected with a commanding authority. The action which is characterized as right in respect to the 'moral law' can be regarded as having that character without any reference to such a power. The author himself mentions this (p. 56. Cf. p. 125), but regards it as involving forgetfulness of the original commanding authority. But in that case the respect, in which the ought is alleged to be given, would have acquired a quite different character from that which belongs to the feeling according to the author. The ought can also be connected at one and the same time with formal obedience and with the action commanded. This happens if the commanding power appears, not merely as commanding *in abstracto* and as entitled to do so, but as commanding the very action which is *right*. Such a double-sidedness undoubtedly exists in the child's feeling of respect for his parents' commands, and also, in the higher religions, in 'reverence' for the commands of the divine will.

But von Kirchmann also overlooks altogether the element of valuation in respect, and, with it, in the consciousness of duty which belongs to it. Respect is felt only for that which is regarded as *worthy* of respect. That is to say, the idea of an inherent inner value in the object is an essential feature in respect. A commanding power, even if it be infinite, is not respected merely as such. It is respected only if it appears as entitled to command, i.e., able, by indicating its wishes, to determine duties for others and thereby to present the respect-inspiring norm itself. In the region of personality, we undoubtedly reserve the highest reverence for a person, whether he commands or not, who stands forth through his way of life as the embodied moral norm itself. It is unreasonable to suppose that we could reverence purely natural phenomena merely because of their might.

It is plain that what von Kirchmann describes in his treatment of respect as the ought-feeling is really the state of consciousness of the recipient of a command in regard to the imposing authority which issues it and thereby with its 'thou shalt,' acts suggestively on him. But a confusion has occurred in consequence of the fact that this state of consciousness and that which is present in the consciousness of duty so easily pass over into each other.

In this way it now becomes intelligible that there should be an ever-present tendency in jurisprudence to regard legal rules as statements as to what ought to happen, *notwithstanding* that they are also regarded as imperatives. Here we are concerned with conceived imperatives, which seem to issue from an authority or a system of authorities, and which assert themselves effectively and unanimously in a society. As a result the expression of command easily transforms itself in the popular consciousness into an objective property of a system of conduct. The fact that this system is regarded as holding only for the members of the society in question, and only so long as the authorities who officially determine the system adhere to it, does not alter the fact that it is regarded as a part of the absolute system of norms. The latter appears to be adjusted for a particular society, with regard to the existing situation, by the officially determinative authorities. That the content alters means only that a change in the situation causes the authorities to decree a different content as that which 'ought to be actualized'. Conversely, the idea of such a system, with 'ought to be actualized' as an objective property of it, easily passes over into the idea of imperatives. So nothing is more natural than that one who contemplates the facts should have a tendency to regard a legal rule as at once an effectual imperative and a statement, regarded as authoritative by the members of a society, about what actions 'ought to be undertaken'.

Bierling (*Juristische Prinzipienlehre, I*, 1894, p. 17) defines a legal rule as a certain imperative, and (p. 43) the 'recognition' of it as habitually respecting it. But, two pages later, he says that, in every such recognition, there is recognized a claim on the one hand and a duty on the other. This is asserted without the slightest argument; just as if an imperative as such would involve an assertion of duty for the person commanded, based on the very fact of the command, and therefore also an assertion concerning the issuer of the command as entitled to do so. It is alleged that this assertion is recognized to be correct in and through the influence of the imperative.

According to Dernburg (*Pandekten*, 4. Aufl., 1914, p. 44) substantive law is 'that ordering of the relationships of life which is maintained by the general will'. Thus, it would seem that a legel norm can be only an assertion about the ordering of the relationships of life which the general will is prepared to uphold in a certain case. But, according to p. 88, subjective right is 'that share in the good things of life which accrues to a person in a human society'. The legal order only safeguards and models subjective right, but does not create it. Thus a legal norm which

F*

vindicates a right is an assertion about the share in 'the good things of life' which actually accrues to the individual in a certain case; or else from the standpoint of duty, it is an assertion about the action for another's advantage which actually ought to happen in a certain case.

Radbruch (*Grundzüge der Rechtsphilosophie*, 1914, p. 161) says that the content of an imperative can only be given by the words 'this ought to be'. Therefore jurisprudence, which has only to give the contents of imperatives, does quite rightly in 'making the concept of duty its own'. As if the 'thou shalt' of the imperative were the same as the 'this is what you ought to do in this case' of duty.

Salomon (*Das Problem der Rechtsbegriffe*, 1907, p. 47) takes as his starting-point a wholly unproved proposition of Lipps that the 'experience' of a foreign will acquires 'a peculiar affective character of "objectivity", i.e. a property of oughtness,' and he concludes from this that the reception of the content of a foreign will in law carries with it the idea of an objective ought.

Binder defines legal propositions as hypothetical imperatives addressed to the state-organs. (See, e.g., *Rechtsbegriff und Rechtsidee*, 1915, p. 259). As an example of such an imperative he adduces at the same place the following: 'If a person has lent money to another, and the latter has promised to repay it, the judge shall order him to make the repayment.' (B.G.B. ¶ 607.) Here the order is thought of as asserting a certain relationship as existing objectively, and the oughtness of a certain action is thought of as a term in that relationship.

In Merkel's *Juristische Enzyklopädie* ¶ 3 it is said that the judge's pronouncement, which is here held to make evident the nature of the legal rule, contains a 'You *should* respect the limits which I have laid down. You are *under an obligation* to do so'. It is further asserted that in this respect the pronouncement manifests itself as 'a command'. Of the two sentences in question only the first could possibly be regarded as a command. But the second, too, is regarded as having the same content as the first, is treated as a command. The same confusion occurs in Hellwig, *Wesen und subj. Begrenzung der Rechtskraft*, 1901. According to p. 1, declaratory judgments are authoritative declarations about the parties' legal relationships, i.e. their respective rights and duties. According to p. 5, a condemnatory judgment is an 'order to the debtor to make payment' which is put on the same footing as the 'establishment of the duty to pay'.

Opposite to the tendency to the confusion which we have just treated is the very common tendency to regard the social feeling of revenge as the essential feature in the feeling of duty.[1] We have seen that the state of mind of the recipient of a command, who is subjected to the social authority, very easily passes over into the

---

[1] Examples are Adam Smith, and John Stewart Mill, and Westermarck.

idea of duty; and that the idea of commands passes easily into the thought of an authoritative pronouncement as to what ought to be done. In the same way, the social revenge-feeling easily passes over into a definite attitude towards the infliction of suffering, which is determined by the idea of the righteousness of the suffering. As we have already shown, all that is needed is that the words 'He shall suffer for his actions!', expressive of vengeance, shall sound in the ears of all the members of a society, associated with the idea of the suffering, and straightaway the idea of an inner connection between suffering and the expression of revenge will arise. Along with it there arises also the idea of a norm concerning what 'should happen' to a person who inflicts suffering on others; and in the particular case it appears as just, in accordance with the norm, that the injurer shall suffer. At that stage there has arisen, from the social revengeful feeling, a feeling of conative impulse determined by the idea of the righteousness of suffering, which is directed towards ensuring that suffering is inflicted upon the object of the revengeful feeling. But this idea comes under the control of the idea that suffering, inflicted through compulsion, is righteous only as an equivalent to the omission of acting according to one's duty. It thus becomes necessary, in order that vengeance may function without perturbation, that the object of it should be regarded as a wicked individual. But in this way the social revengeful feeling passes over into (i) a demand for the punishment of the guilty through inflicting suffering on him which can be regarded as equivalent to the right action which he has omitted, and (ii) moral indignation, i.e. a feeling of revenge determined by the fact that the moral impulse towards, or the demand for, right action on the part of another (which is the counterpart in respect of others to the feeling of duty) is in operation. The fact that this demand is left unsatisfied causes a feeling of displeasure, which is transferred to the guilty person and calls forth a revengeful feeling. The demand for just punishment, as also moral indignation, can also be turned inwards on oneself when one impartially judges one's own actions, and it then becomes a reaction against a violation of the sense of duty. Since, now, the line of demarcation between the direct social feelings of revenge, on the one hand, and the above-mentioned feelings of moral reaction, on the other, is vague, it is easy to regard the latter as merely varieties of the former. Now the analogon of the feeling of duty in reference to other persons, or the feeling of duty itself, as the case may be, is most strongly marked in these reactive feelings. Therefore the tendency arises to regard this feeling itself as in essence identical with the social revengeful feeling.

# THREE

# PHILOSOPHY OF RELIGION

# I

## METAPHYSICAL RELIGIOSITY

### 1. FORMS OF METAPHYSICAL RELIGIOSITY

What is meant by metaphysical religiosity? Metaphysical religiosity is the opposite of the religiosity which is defined by positive religion. But this statement serves only to characterize metaphysical religiosity in a formal way. Actually metaphysical religiosity involves the following: God is not an observable person, but neither is he an impersonal power. In general, God is not comparable to anything in the world of sense. God is either reality as such or the 'I' itself—not as *this* person, but rather as that which is absolutely incapable of being objectified, as that which cannot be conceived as existing alongside another.

### Interrelations between I-metaphysics and Reality-metaphysics

If I apprehend myself, I apprehend not something which exists independent of consciousness, but something which exists only for its own consciousness. No one standing outside myself can refer to me as 'I'. Consequently it is not as 'I' that I am a reality. For in the concept of reality there is always implied the idea of something existing independent of the idea of it. Indeed, that I *am* a reality, yes, even that which is most surely known, depends upon the fact that 'I' denotes not only the 'completely inward', which cannot be objectified as can all other realities, but also a specific reality alongside other realities, which is determined through space and time. 'I' become the completely known reality, because in the 'I' are combined two distinct modes of representation, both the objectifiable reality and the 'completely inward', which is one with its own consciousness. But when one adheres only to the one side of the 'I', viz. the 'I' as one with its own consciousness, then the 'I' becomes something which, in general, does not exist, in that sense in which the word is taken in relation to a reality. From this point of view, the 'I' exists neither here nor in the future. Whenever something is said to be here or there, past or future, it is always a question of something which is conceived as existing whether it is apprehended or not. For space cannot be identical with the consciousness of space. The 'I', as the completely inward, exists only in its own consciousness in an eternal now.

The 'I' also lacks all determinateness and distinctness within itself. Otherwise it would not be one with the simple consciousness of itself. Thus the 'I', conceived purely in itself, is not a person, distinct from other persons. Everyone who apprehends himself as 'I' apprehends exactly the same thing as everyone else. The 'I' is the complete unity, without any quality for distinguishing it from something else. It is not capable of being compared with another and has no other alongside itself. Accordingly it is also absolute—it exists through and for itself. Conceived consistently, it is, indeed, the All, since it has no other alongside itself. It is reality itself, not some *specific* reality. And every determinate reality, which is always objective, is thus merely an appearance and an illusion, a dream—the Hindu *Maya*.

Nevertheless, if, constrained by one's interest in reality, one now assumes something else alongside this 'I', namely, something which is a determinate reality, the latter as such becomes only a negation of reality, a limitation of reality as such. Herein lies the paradox that the lack of reality itself is real. However, in relation to reality the 'I' is Being, the ultimate ground of all determinate reality, the innermost element in all reality. But *that* in the world of determinate reality to which this absolute 'I' is most closely related is, of course, the 'I' which is a determinate reality without being the absolute. For I apprehend myself, I have a consciousness-of-I in general, when I apprehend myself as a determinate person. The 'I' is therefore particularly the ultimate ground of the soul, the innermost element of the soul.

Therefore, taking one's point of departure from this 'I', one comes to the conclusion that the 'I' is the absolutely simple in *reality*. It is the being or the ultimate ground of all determinate reality—if, in general, such a determinate reality is assumed. It is also the innermost being of the soul, as being the absolutely inward, which is not in any way something external to my apprehension.

But just as I-metaphysics leads over to Reality-metaphysics, to the view of reality as the ultimate ground of all determinate reality, so also the metaphysics which has its point of departure in *reality* leads to I-metaphysics. For *reality* as such is only a One, itself without any property, and thus it is incapable of being distinguished from another. Thus it is the All. It has no reality alongside itself. Therefore in and of itself it is absolute. If another reality is nevertheless assumed, namely, something determinate as such, then this reality is merely a limitation of the universal reality. Reality itself is thus the essence or the ultimate ground, in just the same way as the 'I' is. But reality in fact cannot be distinguished from the 'I'. For reality must be *conceivable*—otherwise one could not have any idea of it. But the thought in which it is grasped or comprehended cannot be something different from reality itself— otherwise reality would stand in relation to another, by which it could be grasped or comprehended. Hence it not only *is* in itself, but it is also *apprehended through* itself. (Cf. Spinoza and the Eleatics.) Thus it is the same as the 'I'. So I-metaphysics and Reality-metaphysics are, properly speaking, only two sides of the same matter.

Metaphysics, with its foundation in the concept of the 'I', on the one hand, and in the concept of reality, on the other, runs like a crimson thread through the history of Indo-European civilization. The Hindu Vedanta-philosophy is a form thereof, being especially determined by the concept of the 'I'—the concept of Brahman. In relation to the eternal Brahman, everything else is merely appearance and illusion. We find it again, in the form of the philosophy of reality, in the Eleatic doctrine of the All-One, modified through the systematic thought of Plato: the absolute is certainly a unity, in relation to which all perceptible reality is merely an appearance. But the All-One has within itself a manifold of ideas. The manifold, however, ceases to be a manifold in the proper sense, for everything is comprised within the All. Every idea has all ideas as its determinations. Thus all distinction between them, in the proper sense, is destroyed. We find metaphysics again in Aristotle's doctrine of pure reason as the thought of itself and thus as an absolute unity—as itself the ultimate substance (*ursubstans*). It is found among the Stoics, less as a philosophy than as a religion. We have it in the Neoplatonic 'Ur-One', lifted up above contradictory thought and above being. The medieval mystics from the ninth to the eleventh centuries, such as Scotus Erigena and Hugo and Richard of St Victor are offshoots of Neoplatonism. We find metaphysics in the thirteenth century as a pure philosophy of the 'I' in Meister Eckhart and his followers, and in the fifteenth century in the great mystic, Jacob Böhme. But above all we find it in the seventeenth century in Spinoza as a metaphysics of reality. Later it appears, as a pure metaphysics of the 'I', with the point of emphasis on the idea of the 'I' as a unity of subject and object, during the eighteenth and nineteenth centuries in Kant, as well as in Fichte and Hegel, who proceed from Kant, and in most recent times in Bergson in France and Norström in Sweden. This metaphysics of the 'I' has a close relation to the Vedanta-philosophy even if it is not as unrealistic as the latter. But we have only touched certain high points in the giant wave of metaphysics, which runs through the entire history of civilization.

### Metaphysical Religiosity and the Feeling of Blessedness

Among the medieval mystics the metaphysics of which we have been speaking seems to have been indissolubly connected with a religiosity of a unique nature, a religiosity which included within itself a feeling of boundless joy, with which no other feeling could be compared. 'Oh rapture, sweetness, Oh joy,' cries Meister Eckhart. The soul, which has come out from God, the eternal 'I', turns back to its ultimate source—in order to become one with it. For to know Brahman is the same as to become *one* with it, inasmuch as the knowledge of Brahman is one with Brahman itself and is its own knowledge of itself. Since God is the absolute 'I', the ultimate reality, to know God and thereby to become one with him implies that one has swept aside the shackles of finiteness, that one *is* in the absolute sense. Nirvana, as the nullification of all determinate reality, is the entrance into the very being of God. According to the sage, one now lives a life without any elements which destroy or repress life, without any elements which could be experienced as pain. The contradiction which external reality presents to our purposes, which produces constant frustration, is gone, for it does not exist any more for the soul which is surrendered to God.

We may develop the thought further in the following way. Indissolubly connected with pain is a desire to overcome pain. And since this desire is not satisfied, on account of the obstacles which arise outside it, we do not overcome pain. But if one takes away desire itself, and with it the desire to overcome pain, the pain loses its significance. If I no longer desire to escape it, I am content with it—and thus it loses its sting. In fact pain as such is no longer felt. 'Oh death, where is thy sting; oh grave, where is thy victory?' But he who is divine does not need to obtain anything which he does not have, and he does not desire to escape from pain. Hence pain is nothing to him. Paralyse active desire and you thereby paralyse pain itself also.

One might say, 'But is not the result of this only a negation of pain? Whence comes the positive feeling of blessedness?' To this it may be replied that the very negation of pain is in itself a pleasure, and indeed, it is pleasant in proportion to the depth to which the pain was originally felt. But it may be asked further whether or not pleasure itself can actually be present without there being a will to preserve it. If the will to gain something which one does not have is absent, may not the pleasure be absent also? But a distinction is to be observed here. Pain I *always* choose to avoid. Otherwise it is not experienced as pain. But my will comes to be directed towards the preservation of pleasure only if some danger threatens its existence. But how is it, in this regard, with the man who is enjoying God? Does he fear the cessation of the pleasure? No! For him there is no longer any time. For him, in the same moment when he experiences God, the world is something irrelevant, a mere nothingness. Time and space have lost their significance. Every thought of a time in which the pleasure will have been lost is gone.

However this is not all. It is by no means only a matter of having the pleasure which arises with the negation of pain. For the metaphysician God is 'I' in the proper sense. Hence he is also eternal life. Now when in one's own organism the physiological functions are carried on without interference by either physical or psychological causes, when one is in possession of physical and psychological health, then one also has an altogether unblemished feeling of pleasure. God, as the unobstructed life, is also eternal blessedness. To him the metaphysician transfers his own feeling of vitality with its strong accent on pleasure. And when he sees God and knows that God is one with himself, he experiences God's own blessedness.

The forms of that blessedness which the metaphysician says he experiences through his life in God may be entirely different. It may be ecstatic (Plotinus). Thus, according to the metaphysician's view, the soul sinks into the 'Ur-One', when it leaves behind the consciousness of anything—which as such is associated with the separation of subject from object, of apprehension from being—

and enters into a life which lies beyond the consciousness of anything and in which subject and object fall together. This life is a feeling without conception. Even the consciousness of one's own existence is absent. But yet God is present to consciousness. I experience him—and this, indeed, in a feeling of absolute blessedness. Feeling is the only form of consciousness in which the content is so constituted that it cannot be placed in opposition to the one who apprehends it as existing independent of his apprehension. What remains if the experience of the feeling is thought to be absent? Therefore the word 'feeling' can be used as a designation for that psychical state in which consciousness is indeed present, but yet not a consciousness of anything in the proper sense, i.e. not a consciousness of anything which admits of being conceived as existing whether I apprehend it or not. Ecstasy is for the metaphysician just the consciousness of God, where the object which constitutes the content of that consciousness cannot be conceived as something which exists in itself, independent of the consciousness of it. And this consciousness, which is not strictly a consciousness, is a feeling of blessedness without limits and beyond measure.

But it is by no means necessary for the feeling of blessedness of the metaphysician to take the ecstatic form. It is not necessary to abandon the consciousness of the world and of one's self; it is necessary only that the world should lose its importance for me and should stand there as something of no concern to me. Then the feeling of blessedness in God becomes a quiet peace and repose, without the cessation of reflection about God. But even then this feeling of peace and repose is not a reflection about God as a reality and so is not a true experience of him. In this feeling he is merely identical with my own experience of the feeling. He is in my spirit and only there.

## 2. SCHOLASTICISM AND MYSTICISM AS
### TENDENCIES WITHIN METAPHYSICAL RELIGIOSITY

Within I-metaphysics or Reality-metaphysics two tendencies are to be observed, which are designated in the medieval terminology as 'scholasticism' and 'mysticism', according to the significance of their respective modes of thought and religious feeling. Scholasticism places the emphasis on the determination of what reality is. Mysticism thinks that reality in itself is not determinable. The determination is only something incomplete, even if it is a means to the feeling in which alone reality is given.

### Scholasticism and Metaphysical Religiosity

Properly speaking, scholasticism is inconsistent. On the one hand, reality and the 'I' are conceived as identical with the consciousness of them. Thus they cannot be conceived as realities in the ordinary sense, which exist independent of the consciousness of them. But as soon as one determines what something is, it becomes a question of determining what it is in reality in relation to some other reality, whether we apprehend it in this way or not. On the other hand, reality still must be something. It cannot be a nothingness. But in that case it possesses determinations.

Two tendencies within religious scholasticism may be distinguished, viz. pantheism and theism. Pantheism determines reality, and thus distinguishes it from its other, by reference to such determinations as give expression to its lack of determinateness: 'reality *in abstracto*', 'unity', 'being through itself', 'the consciousness of the truth through itself'. In relation to that which is the determinate reality, in the proper sense, it is the ultimate ground. All determinate reality is only a negation of reality. All the modes in which reality is determined only give expression to its lack of determinateness. For *reality* is not a determinate reality. 'Being in itself' means complete separation from everything else. Reality is incapable of being determined through something whereby it could be compared, as a specific reality, with another reality. Unity is merely lack of determinateness. For all determination is possible only with reference to that which is distinguished from the consciousness of it and is posited as something real independent of the consciousness of it. The 'ultimate ground' is Being only in relation to determinate being and therefore not in itself. Hence neither is there any real determinateness in Being. Thus pantheism makes out of the very indeterminateness of Being its determinateness—it makes it into a specific reality by determining it by reference to such determinations as indicate its lack of determinateness.

Theism goes farther and maintains that reality, in order to be itself something real, must be a positively and completely determinate reality, so that it has everything that exists as positive determinations. Thus reality is distinguished from every particular real thing precisely by being that thing with all incompleteness removed. Reality has finite reality in all its manifoldness for its determinateness in such a way that, if we only disregard the limitation of finite reality, reality has the latter entirely and completely within itself. So in Plato (in the dialogue, *The Sophist*) reality is filled with the ideas or concepts of perceptible things. In the form of ideas these things have dropped their limitations as over against one another. For any concept can be expressed as a determination of a given concept even if this is possible only through the mediation of the concept of 'being other'. In this way the manifoldness of perceptible reality enters into reality without the latter's unity being nullified and without the relation of exclusion, which is given through space and time, coming in thereby. Plato, naturally, fails to observe that if the *content* of the concept is perceptible and therefore has within itself the relation of exclusion, which belongs to space and time, the same applies to reality itself. But in that case this content is not reality as such, which does not allow any limitations within itself.

Theism in the proper sense (Descartes, Leibniz, Boström) seeks, in the determination of reality, to find a point of contact with human personality. God is the 'pure I'. Therefore the comprehensive, positive determinations which God must possess as the true reality are taken from personality, which is precisely characterized by self-consciousness. But as Descartes and later Leibniz themselves say, this requires that human personality must be conceived in abstraction from all finiteness. That is, one must conceive the consciousness and the will of man as freed from all restrictions. God thus becomes the clear and distinct consciousness of all things. As the clear and distinct consciousness, he is consciousness-through-itself and thus is not restricted in the absolute independence which belongs to him in the capacity of reality as such. As Will he creates and upholds (according to Descartes and Leibniz) all other reality and is thus independent. The fact is ignored that if God has completely clear and distinct ideas of everything—and thus actually has, like a man, the consciousness of something which is not that consciousness itself—then his consciousness is distinguished from the reality which he apprehends, and then he is not independent in relation to it. The fact is ignored that if God is Will, he is to that extent incomplete, and that he purposes something which as such is not yet realized.

It is not possible to conceive human consciousness and human will by abstraction from incompleteness. For then it ceases to be a consciousness of anything and becomes merely consciousness, without anything further. And neither is the will any longer a will. Boström, who actually seeks to maintain God's completeness as reality itself, utters merely empty words when he says that God is human consciousness and will with the finiteness removed. For God's consciousness would be pure self-consciousness. But then it is not consciousness of anything. God's will is directed only towards himself, his own existence. But if his will is grounded in himself, then there cannot be any object for his will.

## The Transition from Scholasticism to Mysticism

However no matter how much scholasticism, whether in the pantheistic or in the theistic form, wishes to determine reality itself as a definite real thing, and thus to treat it as an object for thought, it cannot avoid mysticism, or the view that God is given to us in a feeling of blessedness and for this reason cannot be conceived as a reality, since the content of feeling as such cannot possibly be treated as a reality in itself. Mysticism has its logical ground in the very point of departure of scholasticism, namely, reality: the 'I' as such, which in and of itself cannot be an object for thought. Hence scholasticism *must* pass over into mysticism.

Mysticism appears as soon as scholasticism touches on the ethical question. For Being itself always becomes the good as such. But all goodness, as such, is given in a feeling of pleasure. The complete good thus is given in complete pleasure. Plato gives us an exceedingly clear illustration of this point. Any philosophically informed person knows—or ought to know—the word assigned by Plato in the dialogue, *The Republic*, to distinguish the highest idea, the idea of ideas—the idea of the good. The idea of the good in the kingdom of ideas is compared to the sun in the visible world. Just as the sun is the ground of seeing, but itself can be observed only partially, since it blinds the eyes, so the idea of the good is assuredly the ground of all knowing, but itself can be known only partially. And just as through its warmth the sun gives life to everything that lives, but yet does not live itself, in the ordinary sense, so the idea of the good is the ground of all reality, the reality in all reality, but yet is not itself something real. In might and power it is transcendent over all being.

Now Plato treats the good throughout as identical with happiness. Thus in the same dialogue he shows that in all circumstances it is better to be just than to be unjust, on the ground that the just man as such has the greatest happiness, while the unjust is necessarily unhappy. Therefore the idea of the good also—which must be reality as such, the being of reality, although it is not itself an object of thought or something real—is for Plato happiness as such, in the sense that all actual happiness is a participation in the good and, conversely, participation in the good is blessedness. But according to Plato we gain real happiness only through directing our thought and our will towards the world of ideas itself. That is, in the feeling of blessedness which we experience when the soul turns towards the world of ideas—the very being of the ideas —we can experience being as such, but we can conceive it only partially. It is not an object of thought, nor is it a reality in the proper sense. It can be grasped only in a feeling of pure, unqualified happiness.

So like the sun breaking through the dimness, there appears, in the midst of all the unsuccessful scholastic attempts to determine what reality is in itself, the consciousness that reality itself is not something determinable, but rather reveals itself only in the pure feeling of blessedness. Dialectic, as a method of grasping the world of ideas, is relegated to a lower truth and is only a springboard to the highest truth, which we possess in and through the pure unqualified happiness which comes with the thought of the ideas. In the *thought* of reality we reach reality only partially, but the feeling of blessedness, which is given to us therewith, reveals to us reality itself.

When we turn to Plotinus, the advocate of Platonism in Hellenism, we find, indeed, all kinds of scholastic analyses of the way in which reality itself is the true being, out of which, as from a fountain which never runs dry, all other real things emanate in their varying degrees. But in all this scholasticism, Plotinus still has an unfaltering conviction that the 'Ur-One' is not any object of thought and thus does not admit of being determined as a specific real thing, of whatever sort it may be. For all consciousness of anything presupposes an opposition between subject and object. But reality itself cannot be an object which as such stands in opposition to another reality, the subject. This impossibility of setting the 'Ur-One' over against thought as an object stands, indeed, in the most intimate connection with the Platonic proposition that it is itself the good. As itself the good, it is the true, pure happiness, and is thus given in this feeling. But while for Plato this pure feeling of blessedness arises in connection with the thought of the world of ideas, for Plotinus this feeling is not the highest happiness but only a transition to the highest. In this highest happiness, ecstasy, all consciousness of anything is absent, and in that condition alone, not in thought, does man really enter into relationship with God. Thus the whole of scholasticism is, in the strict sense, false, if it also leads to the claim that there is an actual knowledge of God in feeling.

Next we move through a millennium and a half and take up the scholasticism of Spinoza, which, of course, is famous for its logical consistency. But a thousand years are as a day. We find again the same transition from scholasticism to mysticism. Indeed, according to Spinoza, deity can be conceived if anything can be conceived, and thus it is possible to determine the deity as a reality. Spinoza's ethics, however, subverts the entire thought-structure. Certainly there is nothing blameworthy in the fundamental principle of the Spinozistic ethics, viz. *Summum bonum est cognoscere deum.* This principle seems to imply nothing more than that the knowledge of God bestows on man the highest happiness, and it does not seem at all to imply that the experience of this happiness must be the experience of God himself in the feeling of happiness. But when one investigates the matter further, one comes to quite a different conclusion. For according to Spinoza the feeling of happiness which the knowledge of God bestows is, like every feeling attached to the reason, essentially an enhancement of the soul's activity. That is, the knowledge of God includes the feeling in question *as* an activity of the soul. But the soul's activity is again nothing but God's own activity operating directly, and therefore independently of everything else, through man's own soul. The principle of activity is thus God himself. But if, now, the feeling in question is essentially nothing but the activity, then it is God's own feeling of wellbeing in man. Indeed, Spinoza expressly says as much in the fourth book of his *Ethics.* The love of God, he says, is blessedness in God through the consciousness of its cause. But, he says, this love is God's own love for himself in man. That is, God enjoys himself in man's enjoyment of him. Thus he himself is present immediately in man's feeling of blessedness in the knowledge of him. Thus he is himself a content of feeling, but consequently he cannot be conceived as something real. In the midst of all rigorous scholasticism, therefore, mysticism breaks through.

If we then move on a couple of centuries, we meet the same phenomenon in the Swedish thinker, Boström. According to him God can certainly be known through reason as the completely determined reality. But he is also man's goal, his highest good, and as such he is his saviour. And certainly he is a saviour in such a way that, as Boström expresses it, he constantly invites men to partake of his life and his blessedness. God's blessedness *is*, thus, the blessedness of the man in whom God is active. In man's feeling of blessedness God himself is present. Thus God is a content of feeling. But then it is impossible to determine him through thought as a reality consisting in itself.

The transition from scholasticism to mysticism is thus mediated by the analysis of the concept of the absolute as accessible to us only in religious feeling. This transition shows clearly that the very concept of the absolute stands in an intimate connection with religious feeling. Thus it is only on the foundation of this feeling that the concept can be built up; the feeling itself is the firm bulwark on which the concept depends. The transition shows that metaphysics is, in its innermost essence, religion. But we shall now find, on the other hand, that if the scholastic passes over into mysticism in his attempt to determine being or the pure 'I', the absolute, by means of the understanding, so, conversely, the mystic cannot avoid clothing himself in the mantle of scholasticism. Thus the distinction between scholasticism and mysticism involves a difference in degree but not in kind.

## Scholasticism in Mysticism: Meister Eckhart

Meister Eckhart, perhaps the most important and deepest mystic of the West, quotes, as the text of one of his sermons from Salerno, the words, 'In the midst of the quietness of the night a birth took place within me'. And he applies the words to God's entrance into the soul in the profound experience which conversion involves. God himself becomes one with the soul, and in that moment something new is born within the soul.

Meister Eckhart sets this entry of God into the soul in contrast to the soul's relation to external things. The soul enters into relationships with external things through particular powers, which in turn require their organs. Therefore the relationship is merely external. I see by means of the power of sight, and for this power eyes are required as an organ. Thus the soul which sees cannot draw the object to itself, but rather between the object and the soul there is the organ. Therefore the soul receives into itself only an image of the state of affairs, not the state of affairs itself, and this is how it is with all other apprehensions of things. Only through such images does the soul have any feeling for things, and only through such images can it work upon and reconstruct things. But the soul enters into relationship with God not through any particular powers (in which case the relationship would be merely external and the soul would receive only an image of God), but rather by turning away from all such powers. It is in the complete stillness that God enters into the soul—in the stillness which comes when the soul abandons its interest in the operation of all these powers in the external world, when it stands empty of all desire to turn towards the external and of all feeling which relates to the external, when the very life-nerve of the earthly is severed, viz. the interest in the worldly. In this complete emptiness there is a place for God, not however in such a way that merely an image of him arises, but in such a way that he himself becomes one with the soul. In this unification with God the soul sees itself in God and sees God in itself.

Since every connection with anything external is absent here, the soul is completely lost in itself and has within itself God's own pure being-for-itself, which is the soul's highest blessedness, in that the soul enjoys its own unobstructed life. Subject and object are here completely one. If one here distinguishes between God and himself, this distinction has only a formal significance. In the abstract one needs an object in order to be conscious. Yet here this object appears not as something which exists independent of me or outside of me, but as something which is *one* with myself; so that love for God presents itself to me as God's own love for himself, and my blessedness presents itself as God's own blessedness. It is particularly in the Johannine words, 'God is love', that Meister Eckhart seeks his own foothold. God does not exist *for* me, but he is *one* with me, in such a way that the living communion, and thus love, is complete. God meets me only in love, i.e. in a positive feeling towards me, by which I am apprehended exactly as though I were God himself, and I do not meet God except in a love for him which is just as strong as it would be if it were directed towards my own life. And from either side it is certainly a love which is in repose, undisturbed by any unrest and conflict. For the soul which is surrendered to God, which God loves, is without any aspiration or wish, and his life is thus entirely without any impediments. God's love for him is therefore only an unlimited enjoyment of his own unobstructed life. The same is true from the standpoint of the soul, which unrestrainedly enjoys God's own life.

To summarize. The soul in which God has brought forth a new life through his entering into union with it is, in its communion with God, a pure self-consciousness. God, who is apprehended by the soul, is found to be one with the soul itself. But this consciousness of God is not properly a consciousness of anything, that is, it is not an idea, together with an image, for every such thing concerns itself with something which is foreign to the soul. This consciousness has instead the form of feeling and, indeed, more precisely the form of such a love for God that in God one loves oneself; and in assuming the form of love it assumes the form of a feeling of blessedness in God's unobstructed life as one's own life. Herein the significance of the feeling appears as the foundation for the idea of a pure self-consciousness. In feeling alone do we have such an experience that, if one ever considers its content to be a specific apprehended reality, this reality becomes one with the feeling itself. If God himself is *given* to us in a feeling, then he is none other than the soul which feels. But if he were given in an idea, then he would always be something other than the soul which conceives him as such. But in that case we do not have a pure self-consciousness.

Meister Eckhart, however, has other names also for the religious experience which we have been discussing. The soul which is surrendered to God is *separated*. In being filled by God, the soul is separated from the world. Neither in feeling nor in will is it determined as something which belongs to the world. And now since God is here one with the soul's innermost being, is one with the soul as withdrawn into its innermost being, the soul is independent of everything which is external to it. It reposes in itself.

Furthermore, the soul which is surrendered to God is the completely *simple*. The soul which is turned towards the world has Martha's cares. It is occupied with the manifold of things which disturb its repose. But the soul in which God has brought to birth the new life retires into itself, and there, deep within, there is no manifold. In this enjoyment of its own simplicity, the soul enjoys God. Naturally we have before us here the Hindu pure 'I', Brahman, which, precisely as 'I', lacks all manifoldness. In its innermost being the soul is nothing but this simple 'I'. And for the soul to be determined only in this way is for it to become completely simple. Certainly one may speak of the soul which is surrendered to God as having God before itself as an object of love, but it is only in and with this love for him that God exists for the soul. Therefore the object loved is the love by which it is loved. Therefore there is no actual duality in a relation to God. The two are one. In the spiritual domain, says Eckhart, there is no separation of distinct things, but everything enters into everything else.

Finally Meister Eckhart says that the soul which is surrendered to God leads an *eternal* life. For such a soul there is no time. For it has its attention centred only on God. But God exists for the soul *only* in love for him, which is immediately present. Therefore when it sees God, the soul sees only the immediately present. And since this soul is itself one with God, when it sees him it sees only the immediately present. From the soul's point of view, there is only the now. Time loses all significance. But not only has time no significance for the eye of the soul. Time, as it concerns the soul, has also in fact disappeared. For in the soul's vision of God and itself as an eternal now, the object of the vision is identical with the very soul which has the vision. Thus the soul *is* only in an eternal now. In relation to the soul there is neither past nor future, neither yesterday nor tomorrow. The soul has not been, and it will not be; it simply *is*.

But furthermore, the following is to be observed. These supersensible properties of the soul which is surrendered to God do *not* imply for Meister Eckhart, as they do for the Hindu philosophy, that the soul itself does not have anything to give to the world. In the first place, the soul which is surrendered to God has, precisely through its absorption in God, a power to awaken the good in the world. This power exceeds all human powers, because in it all particular powers, and thus all isolated powers, are combined into one. It is like a constantly overflowing fountain, which gives of its own blessedness to those who suffer in the world, without itself losing anything. It is simply lifted up above the suffering of the world, in such a way that its blessedness is not in any way affected by that suffering.

In the second place, the soul in itself and withdrawn into God is not egoistical. For as such it has discarded all its sensibly determined personality and is thus entirely universal. It has no 'ego' in *opposition* to a 'thou'. On the contrary, it sees in all other souls communion with itself. Or it sees God in them all and therefore loves God *in* them. This is the theme to which Meister Eckhart often returns: In God the soul which is surrendered to God loves all souls. Therefore it does not see any distinction between its own well-being and that of another, although on the other hand, it is lifted up above all suffering, whether it be one's own or another's. The soul gives of its own well-being, not because it suffers in the suffering of another, but because, on account of its love for God, it must share with all with whom it recognizes an essential communion, with all in whom it sees God.

But it is to be observed further that the Hindu sage turns away from the world (in the sense that he will not even share his own blessedness with another person) simply because the world does not *exist* for him. Thus on the part of the Hindu sage, it is not a question of any kind of egoism. Properly speaking, there is for him no ego, in opposition to a 'thou'. In the case of Meister Eckhart the individual is certainly separated from the world *in his thought*; consequently he cannot be glad or sorrowful about that which is worldly. But he does not deny its reality nor the existence of other persons. However, in so far as he sees God in the other person, he *must* love him. And this love consists in his doing good, without on that account attaching any importance to the perceptible good or to the good which is acquired in time. His motive is not the end which is to be attained; it is rather the quiet, in itself involuntary, love for God in man. The soul which is surrendered to God gives, because he must give of his own blessedness, but his own blessedness does not depend upon the efficacy of the giving. Meister Eckhart expresses this by saying that the individual concerns himself with the well-being of the other person, on the ground of the total power of his soul, not on the ground of any special powers. By 'special powers' here he understands such motives as are determined by images of that which is produced, i.e. what we call the interest in the perceptible result of the action.

There is a peculiar relationship between this giving of the soul which is surrendered to God and the way in which, according to scholasticism, Being or Essence is the ground of everything in the world. The former (the soul which is surrendered to God) is spiritually independent of the effect of the giving; the latter (Being) is *realiter*, in point of fact, independent of its effect, the perceptible world. Or, as Spinoza puts it, the world-effect is not something external to the Being-Cause, to which it stands in an external relation, but the world is included within God.

It is clear that if, as Boström does, one determines Being through personality, then its *de facto* independence of its effect, the world, also becomes a spiritual independence. According to Boström God is the ground of the world, without himself standing spiritually in any relationship to the world. His will is not determined by the world, and yet the world exists through his will. By the same token it is clear that this spiritual independence from effects in the world of sense which, according to Eckhart, issue from the soul which is surrendered to God is also an actual independence from these effects. For this soul *is* altogether as it apprehends itself. In so far as the soul is not determined in its own consciousness by the effect of its giving, neither is it so determined in reality. That is, we have here a relation of ground and consequent, where the ground actually stands without any relationship to its consequent. But this mode of being the ground of effects can be found only in the absolute being. That which is separated from all others can of itself cause something without entering into relation with its effect.

What shall we say then? If we inquire into the matter, we shall discover that the soul which is surrendered to God acquires, according to Meister Eckhart (the mystic), just such determinations as are characteristic, according to the scholastic, of the divine. It is consciousness through itself, it is pure subject-objectivity. As separated from others, it is the absolute, which is, purely through itself; like the Eleatic Being, it is completely simple; like God, it is eternal, for its being consists in its immediately present consciousness of itself or of God. Finally, it is a ground, without standing in dependence upon or in any relation to its consequent. The soul is God and God is the soul. Thus reality as such is regarded by Meister Eckhart also as determinable through thought as a specific reality. This reality is the soul which is surrendered to God.

And yet observe the contradiction! Meister Eckhart himself emphasizes that it is only in religious experience, in the feeling of blessedness which comes with the union of the soul with God, that God is given for the soul. *Only* therein, he says, is the *truth* found. Every definition of God through reason, he says, yields only negations—it declares what is not—or else it yields only images of him, which do not have any truth in the proper sense. Thus the determinations of God as 'creator' of the world, as 'father', etc., are only images, which are of value for those who are on the way to union with God but have not yet reached the goal. Here God is still determinable through thought. For the soul which is surrendered to God still exists as a specific reality, which he himself describes by means of a concept.

We can well understand this dialectic of Meister Eckhart's if we consider the background for the entire theory, viz. the idea of reality as such or of the pure 'I'. Reality, as such, cannot be a specific reality nor become an object for thought. The scholastic, however, seeks to determine it as a *specific* reality, different from others, in either the pantheistic or the theistic manner.

(1) In the pantheistic manner, the absolute reality acquires just such determinations as express its lack of determinateness or the impossibility of its being determined by thought. How is this carried out? From whence does one draw the concrete foundation for this reality, which in its very nature is not any specific reality? Why, from perceptible reality. But perceptible reality, as perceptible, does not serve to determine reality as such—which does not tolerate any relation of exclusion or any boundaries within itself.

Thus, for example, Spinoza clearly introduces into the concept of substance or essence the two attributes of substance, viz. consciousness and extension, in order thereby to have *something* real (Being or Thought). But he believes that he has taken away all finiteness by abstracting from consciousness or thought every particular object for consciousness or thought. God's thought, of course, includes within itself all thoughts. But God himself has no thoughts in his essence. He is merely the thought in all thoughts. In the same way, in thinking of God as extended, one must conceive of him apart from any relation of exclusion, apart from all boundaries. God is body, but he is not a body with a boundary. Spinoza does not notice that here he is really demanding that we take away the essential determinations from both thought and extension, without which these concepts possess no significance. He thus introduces finiteness into God without knowing it. Without so doing he could not conceive of God as something real. The same holds of God as *pure 'I'*, as his own consciousness. This pure 'I' cannot be an *object* for thought in the proper sense, since it is its own thought. Nevertheless, in order to have it as an object towards which one can direct one's thought, pantheism secretly introduces something which actually makes it an object for thought, viz. the perceptible. But at the same time, in order to preserve God's character of the pure 'I', the perceptible which has been so introduced is determined in such universal terms as to lose all meaning. So Spinoza introduces the attributes of thought and extension, which make God an object for thought and yet at the same time are determined so abstractly that they themselves appear only as elements in thought and therefore as immanent within thought. Thus for Spinoza these attributes are not *objects* for thought and hence are not distinguished from thought.

(2) In theism the same smuggling of the perceptible into reality as such or into the pure 'I' recurs. But in the case of theism this happens in such a way that the *particular* perceptible reality, and above all the particular human personality, is taken up into God as a result of the demand to abstract from its limitations. In this way God becomes, on the one hand, a being without any limitations in himself; thus he is not something real alongside other real things. And yet, on the other hand, God is a completely determinate reality in itself. For he has in himself everything which, in particular realities, is *actually* a mode of determinateness, and not merely a lack of determinateness. As though something remained when everything which is labelled as a deficiency in the case of finite things is taken away in thought! In the same way God becomes an *object* for thought through the introduction of the particular perceptible realities, while yet, in this formation of a reality, he coincides, in virtue of the elimination of any limitation, with the pure 'I', which is no object of thought at all.

It is to be noticed, now, that Meister Eckhart, in common with metaphysical religiosity itself, has the foundation for his view in the idea of reality as such or the pure 'I' as a *specific* reality. For the feeling of blessedness, the religious experience itself, presupposes the idea of a reality which is lifted up above everything external and is thus immediately present, just as it presupposes the idea of the pure, unobstructed life in itself and for itself—the pure 'I'. Every deficiency in that which is immediately present, every

G

obstruction of life in itself and for itself in the deity as conceived, obstructs the feeling of blessedness which is associated with the consciousness of God. Therefore Meister Eckhart and metaphysical religiosity need scholasticism. The soul cannot attain to blessedness without *knowing* something about God.

And yet scholasticism has within itself a disease-germ, in just the very respect in which it is necessary. For every firm conceptual determination makes God perceptible and thus distinguishes him from me and introduces into him the limitation which obstructs life. To that extent God becomes something external and thus excluded from other things. But then he is not *one* with the consciousness of him; rather he becomes an object which is really extraneous to my thought. Therefore if he is to realize the religious blessedness fully, the scholastic must also be conscious of the fact that he is concerning himself with images which always, no matter how much they may bring us nearer to the deity, at the same time conceal him from us. Out of concern for his own salvation, he may not remain with these images and reduce them to a firm concept of God, which claims to be the absolute truth. Such concepts kill, for they separate God from us; they defile his life, which in and for itself is inaccessible to every extraneous thought.

What has been said makes the whole thesis of mysticism understandable. God is grasped in the scholastic concepts, of course, but only incompletely. What he is in himself is not accessible to human thought. But still, even for the mystic God must be completely specific and actually accessible. For the mystic requires certainty about God in order to gain salvation. But how can one reach him, if this is not possible through the dead concepts of scholasticism? Well, he is given to us in feeling and only in feeling, because he is a reality which is one with his own immediately present consciousness, in that he is free from all relationships to anything external, even to the observing consciousness. Now feeling, however, is not an apprehension of anything. But what we require is precisely to *apprehend* God. However, if feeling itself is not an apprehension, still it itself admits of being apprehended through introspection of it. And in introspection of one's own religious experience, one actually grasps the God who is inaccessible through objective determinations. For God is your own feeling of him. Herewith the mystic gains the certainty about God which he requires. In order to arrive at this feeling, he begins with scholasticism. But at the same time, he takes his stand above scholasticism, lest he be buried in it. That is, he creates for himself an image of God, but in every moment he goes out beyond the image. In this journey on the endless sea of divination he thus discovers, in the great stillness, the new birth. In this discovery he becomes certain. Thus the mystic becomes a new scholastic, new, however, on a different base, which is relatively harmless for his feeling and in fact fortifies it.

### 3. SOME HISTORICAL EXAMPLES OF METAPHYSICAL RELIGIOSITY

Before we give ourselves to a psychological explanation of metaphysical religiosity, perhaps it is fitting that we should show further its range in the history of civilized man. Indeed, this historical account also has a certain significance for the explanation of the phenomenon itself.

#### Metaphysical Religiosity in Early Christianity

I have said earlier that metaphysical religiosity is to be distinguished from positive religiosity, not essentially with reference to their being based on reason and revelation respectively, but with reference to the manner in which the divine is determined: *either* as 'universal being' or 'pure I' regarded as a reality for itself and as the ground for all particular reality, *or* as a particular personality or a particular power, which exists alongside other persons or powers.

However even this way of establishing the boundary between the two must not be regarded in such a way that any given form of religiosity can always be actually assigned to one or the other type. Indeed, we have already found that, particularly in theistic metaphysics, the anthropomorphization of the deity is a natural thing, since theism requires something which can be thought in order to determine pure being or the pure 'I' more precisely. Of course, a pure being or the pure 'I' as such must be universal, encompassing all within itself. But still as the *true* reality, it must be completely determinate. No matter how much it is explained that in theism this personality is conceived as without limitation, still the limitation is necessarily smuggled in. For if one takes away the limitation, nothing of human personality remains, but one has at first hand only the pure, empty 'I', which has to be more precisely determined through human personality. But in this way the God of theistic metaphysics becomes a particular personality alongside others, thereby acquiring the character of the gods of the positive religions, and metaphysical religiosity passes over into positive religiosity.

The relationship can also be reversed, however. At least this is so in the positive religion which is closest to us, viz. Christianity. Even if the philosophical articulation of Christianity in medieval scholasticism and mysticism is disregarded, still the metaphysical element in Christianity is obvious. Of course, the God of the Christian, as he appears to us in the Holy Scriptures of primitive Christianity, is conceived anthropomorphically. He is supplied with a human will, which sets up a purpose for itself and thus does not already have what it needs. He is capable of being angry, sorrowful, and happy—all of which are expressions of the fact that he is not something absolute. Yet at the same time he is the creator of the world and the ruler of the world. He must be this as well, in order to be positively able to bring those who are his own to salvation. And in virtue of this his cosmic character, it is a very simple step to the line of thought which leads on to the concepts of pure being and the pure 'I', even though he has not been defined through these concepts. For the very concept of the world, with which the idea of God stands connected, is nothing but the conception of the real in general. And when God is regarded as the ground of the world, he is regarded as the ground of *the real* as such. But how can he be this unless he himself is real in the absolute sense, in opposition to *the real* for which he is the ground? Since the real for which he is the ground has its reality through him, he must have his reality in himself. Consequently he is reality as such, not *something* real.

Now, of course, there is no thorough-going metaphysics in these Scriptures. Consequently the foregoing would appear to show that, without having prepared oneself for the situation one is concerning oneself with metaphysical ideas, even if these ideas actually do not have any significance for Christian religiosity except indirectly—by securing for the believer his hope of future salvation. But for this reason this salvation can be conceived as utterly sensible. It is also obvious that the kingdom of God, of which the gospels speak, which is near at hand and in which the disciples of Christ are to occupy a place of distinction, is conceived very realistically.

Still there are two of the original Christian documents which witness to a more profoundly devised religiosity, viz. the gospel of John and the Pauline epistles. 'He who drinks of the water that I give will never thirst again.' 'I am the resurrection and the life; he who believes in me shall live, though he die.' 'My peace I give to you; not as the world gives do I give.'[1] These sentences from the gospel of John, in which Christ is regarded as giving an immediately present blessedness and peace and eternal life, lifted up above the world, have grown up upon the green tree of metaphysical religiosity. The blessedness which is not of the world is linked to the life which is lifted up above all death and thus above all barriers. This blessedness is associated, from the negative standpoint, with man's turning away from all interests which are linked to the finite life and, from the positive standpoint, with man's being determined by God as the absolutely unobstructed life, as the 'pure I'. Christ actually becomes the representative on earth of a higher spiritual reality, in which no barriers are to be found— a reality which wills nothing, since it needs nothing, a reality which reposes in immeasurable peace in itself. Christ actually becomes the true Son of God.

We discover the same thought and the same domain of feeling in the Pauline epistles. The grace of Christ, fellowship with him. immediately gives us eternal life—it lifts us up above sin and thus above death, i.e. above the misery of earthly life. 'I live, yet not I, but Christ'—understood as the Risen One, the conquerer of death —'lives in me'.[2] I, Paul belives, am also myself risen with Christ; I am lifted up above death. Certainly this thought is interwoven in Paul with all kinds of naturalistic, eschatological ideas of this life as an imminent salvation, consisting of freedom from earthly suffering. Certainly all kinds of ideas which belong properly to Hellenistic materialism enter in here—ideas of a 'pneuma', a 'holy matter', which enters into the soul and lifts it up above death. But still there is always present the thought that the Christian, in the midst of earthly distresses, is lifted up above these in his innermost life, because in *his heart*, through living with Christ, he has conquered the world and suffering with him. The earthly has become

---

[1] John iv. 14; xi. 25; xiv. 27.
[2] Gal. ii. 20.

foreign to him. He knows the earthly, yet it passes by him. It cannot penetrate through to him. For he is now a *new* man. The *old* man with his interests in the world, his feelings for the world and the evil which belongs to it, is no longer his true self. His true self is instead occupied by Christ, who through his resurrection represents the purely inward life, reposing in itself, in its opposition to the life weighed down by death and distress.

Augustine, of course, is congenial to Paul in the highest degree. However, we see that it needed only the deeper philosophical insight which Augustine possessed for the Christian God to be wholly and completely identified with pure Being. For Augustine God, precisely the Christian God, is that which is in itself. He is the truth itself and thus the absolute good: *unum, verum, bonum*, as he says. We find already in Augustine the ontological proof of the existence of God in its simple form—Being as such, Being without restriction, also is *necessarily*, i.e. it cannot be thought without being thought *to be*.

## Metaphysical Religiosity in Stoicism

If the inner connection of Christianity with metaphysics and metaphysical religiosity is calculated to cause surprise, it is likewise surprising that we should discover the same metaphysics, the same metaphysical religiosity, in purely moral systems such as, e.g., those of the Stoics and Kant. It would appear, *prima facie*, as if the Stoic wisdom had nothing to do with the metaphysical, absolute feeling of blessedness, in which one experiences God and is one with him. The Stoic wisdom is by no means merely a contemplation of, an absorption in God; but it includes an active life, a determination of the will by the World-Reason—the natural law, as being also a moral law. All willing is characterized as being *determined* for a purpose, and this involves a limitation to the extent that one does not yet have what one wants to have.

But let us look more closely! Why does the sage wish to fulfil his duty, to realize the demand of the moral law through action? Is it because the fulfilment of duty is itself something good? By no means. The fulfilment of duty belongs to the perceptible life. But everything which falls within the latter is something indifferent. Perhaps the Stoic sage wishes to fulfil his duty merely in such a way that the demand of the law comes into play in his soul against all contrary inclinations, so that he wishes to fulfil his duty on the ground of constraint, apart from any values which he wants to gain thereby? Certainly not, for the wisdom which is the ground of the fulfilment of duty is, indeed, absolute happiness, the good as such. Then is it because by fulfilling his duty the sage enters into harmony with the World-Reason in his inner being and through this harmony *becomes* happy? This would imply that the harmony is attained through something external, and in that case it would itself be conditioned by the perceptible. But harmony with the World-Reason signifies for the Stoic sage that he becomes *one* with the World-Reason itself. (Emphasize the so-called Stoic pride.) It is precisely on the ground of being one with the World-Reason that he possesses absolute happiness.

The difficulty cannot be resolved without making reference, on the one hand, to the Stoic thesis that there is in principle an absolute disparity between folly and wisdom. The transition from the one to the other takes place decisively and absolutely, so that one at once reaches absolute wisdom. On the other hand, reference must be made to the thesis that duty as such is completely independent, as regards its value, of how *long* it lasts. It is clear from this that, in the moment in which he is wise, the sage also possesses the complete good, perfect blessedness, and that he consequently has nothing to strive for—not even to preserve his wisdom. In and with his being one with the World-Reason, he is lifted up into a higher domain of time, in which time and the whole of natural life have lost all significance. From this it is also clear that the fulfilment of duty never takes place for the sake of attaining this or that, nor even for the sake of being in harmony with God's will, but rather it is a necessary *consequence* of the soul's union with God, which takes place by means of an immediate, mystical act.

With the Stoics, then, it is altogether as it is in the case of Meister Eckhart. The mystical union with God, as such, is not at all determined by some relationship to the world, nor is it dependent upon this or that action. On the contrary it implies a withdrawal from all outward life, from all special powers in the soul which can operate in the world. Indeed, this point of view is manifested pointedly in the proposition that duty as such is apathy. Therefore the sage does not will to fulfil his duty simply for the sake of achieving one end or another. In his innermost being he lives in perfect blessedness in union with God. His willing to fulfil his duty is, in fact, something entirely secondary. Even if the terms are different, Stoicism is precisely a theory regarding the mystical blessedness referred to, which one possesses through having regard for pure being or the pure 'I', when the mind turns away from the world—a blessedness in which this 'I' is itself immediately present. The Stoics' doctrine of duty is only an appendix to this theory, specifying how the man who is surrendered to God —and who is also, on the other hand, living in the world—conducts himself on the ground of his eternal life. For Stoicism there are no independent moral values. The religious is the only value. So Marcus Aurelius' highest maxim is also the same as Meister Eckhart's: Simplify yourself, withdraw yourself to the soul's innermost unity—God.

## Metaphysical Religiosity in Kantianism

If in the case of Stoicism one can find one's way to its proper source, in the case of Kant this ought to be obvious. Here only the terms are moral, not the subject-matter. We raise the same questions with regard to Kant as we did concerning the Stoics. Why, according to Kant, is the duteous will bent on fulfilling its duty? Is it because acting in accordance with duty is itself a good? Impossible. For the action as such has no value according to Kant. Is it *directly* on the ground of the demand of the law, apart from any thought of value? Impossible. For the duteous will possesses, indeed, an absolute value. It must be determined by the absolute value.

Perhaps the will submits to the demand of the law in order thereby to attain the absolute value which, as a duteous will, it possesses? Impossible. This can be made clear in two ways. (1) The submission to the demand of the law is identical with an overcoming of the superior force of inclination. But this is the perceptible side of the duteous will—it belongs to the capacity to desire. It cannot possibly be a means for attaining that in which the value of the duteous will lies. For that value lies wholly anchored in the will's being determined by reason, which for Kant —let it be carefully noticed—is the soul's innermost self, its exaltation over the perceptible, over the phenomenon. But the domination of reason in man cannot be conditioned by anything belonging to the world of the senses, and hence it cannot be conditioned by this submission to the demand of the law. The relationship is instead the opposite. The domination of reason in the will, the will's being determined by its true self, conditions the perceptible will's submission to the law.

(2) Of course, we know very well that the duteous will never submits to the law in order thereby to attain anything whatever, even if this should be its own rationality. Therefore the duteous will is *first of all* purely rational, purely self-determined, and *next*, on the *ground* of its rationality, it overcomes the superior force of inclination in the perceptible will and creates in it a new power.

The question now becomes the following: What is this fundamental power itself, the pure, self-determined will? What does it will? *It* wills nothing, least of all a certain action. For it is in itself perfect value. Thus it is not in itself a *will*, although it is so designated, because it creates in the *perceptible* will a new power of will —the power to follow the moral law in life. But what, then, is the pure will? Negatively regarded, it is freed from all perceptible determinateness, from all interests in realizing something. Positively regarded, it is permeated by its own absolute value. Now since all value, whatever Kant may say, is given for desire, the will's permeation by its own absolute value signifies nothing but its enjoyment of its own independence, i.e. the soul's enjoyment of the pure 'I' as one with itself, of its exaltation to the sphere of the purely rational. And let it be carefully noticed: in this enjoyment of itself as the pure 'I', and only therein, is the soul one with this 'I'. This is the power from which active duteousness issues—Meister Eckhart's total-power, from which the moral life issues, without the power itself being interested in this in the least way. Indeed, Kant says also that the duteous will itself pertains, at root, to the intelligible world and therefore lives a purely eternal life.

So we see, then, that for Kant morality in itself has no value whatsoever. It is merely a symptom of the soul's absorption in its essence, in perfect happiness. Why not of the soul's absorption in God? It is customarily said that in Kant religion loses all independence and is only an appendix to morality. Why? Because what Kant *calls* religion, viz. faith in God as the giver of happiness in the measure of duty, is nothing but the perceptible form of religiosity, such as we have in an extreme form in the Arabian concept of paradise. But if Kant's so-called morality were not just religion, neither would it be religiosity, but morality when Jesus says, 'My peace I give to you; not as the world gives do I

G*

give.' Kant says, 'Be determined by reason'. Paul says, 'Abide in Christ'. The background of feeling and the thought are still fundamentally the same—the feeling of blessedness in connection with absorption in the pure 'I', and the thought thereof.

### The Connection Between Mystery-Faith and Philosophical Religiosity

In one of the very oldest religious festivals in Athens, that of Zeus Polieus, the people ate together of a bullock which had been slaughtered. Obviously the bullock embodied in itself the power of the tribe. Originally, of course, it was a question of eating the totem-animal itself. But very soon the eating came to be regarded, in spite of its sacramental character, as an offence, which had to be forgiven. In this historical festival the forgiveness was to take place through a ceremony, in which the person who slaughtered the bullock was declared innocent and the guilt was transferred to the axe with which the animal was killed. The axe was allowed to bear the guilt and was cast into the sea as something accursed.

Already in this early practice we have an association of two different elements in the religious ceremony, which we often discover again, both united and separated. On the one hand, one is supposed to acquire the very power of the god, to become divine oneself. On the other hand, the ceremony served to atone the incensed, divine power. The latter element is brought to its positive completion in the offering of gifts to God for his beneficent action in one's behalf. *Do ut des* (I give as it has been given) is well known as the universal principle of sacrifice.

On the other hand, it was in the mystery cult in particular that the personal acquisition of the divine power was supposed to take place. Certainly the Dionysian cults in Boiotia at the change from winter to spring, in which Dionysos, the god of vegetation, was represented as dying and being resurrected anew, were practically nothing but vegetation-magic, through which the earth's vegetative power was supposed to be stimulated to new life after the winter dormancy. But from the side of the participants there was attached to all this—as a result of Orphic influences—the experience of ecstasy, i.e. properly speaking, a condition in which the participant's own soul left his body in order that God himself might come in instead. The participants themselves became Dionysian. They became possessed by the god, and this was expressed, as is particularly evident in Euripides' Bakkhai, in complete insanity in association with an exalted condition of blessedness.

In the Athenian state-mysteries, the Eleusinian mysteries, we find the same relationship. There Persephone, daughter of Demeter, the goddess of the seed-corn, was portrayed as rising from the domain of the dead. This portrayal was supposed to serve, of course, vegetation-magic. But the initiated, who were permitted to behold the divine images, were filled with a divine vital power, through which they could be made secure in their attainment of an eternal and blessed life.

Plato generally expresses the highest respect for the mysteries. One needs only to call attention to the fact that he likens beholding the divine images to the mystic vision of beauty as such, which is the simple unity in all beautiful particulars—itself the *reality* of the beautiful particular. This vision of the reality of beauty, of its pure being, also bestows a new vital power, according to Plato, which includes being lifted up above everything perceptible and yet is the completely unmixed blessedness.

There can be no doubt that both the Dionysian and the Eleusinian mysteries were regarded as bestowing a blessedness which was purely natural in content. One was supposed to be led over to a land where everything flowed with milk and honey. Even the god himself of whom it was a question here, who occupied the body of the individual, was a nature-god, and therefore he could bestow no other than a natural good. But with Plato it was a matter of the good, the heightened vital power, which one received through participation in pure Being, Being without any perceptible determination. In general the vision of the supernatural world of ideas, which is pure Being or reality as such, signifies for Plato the presence of this reality in the soul. Only through the presence of this reality in the soul can the highest good be achieved. It follows naturally that this pure Being is also the innermost essence of the soul. If by beholding pure Being the soul is raised to its highest vital power, then the soul and pure Being must belong essentially together.

Finally pure Being is also itself the good, the absolute value, because it bestows pure blessedness on the soul. Here and there Plato regards the absolute value of pure Being as its fundamental quality in connection with its knowability (and thus its intimacy with the soul) and in connection with its reality. Clearly the reason for this is that it is only through the blessedness which pure Being bestows that knowledge of it is possible. This brings our thought back to the Hindu Veda-philosophy, whose uniqueness consists in the belief that becoming immersed in pure Being, which is identical with the ultimate ground of the soul—the self, Atman—bestows eternal life, complete blessedness, upon the sage.

We may now follow this metaphysical religiosity forward through the centuries, either with or without a connection with the primitive belief in possession by a god who is conceived in a natural way. We discover it again in Aristotle, with his proposition that the thought of God bestows upon man the blessedness of self-realization. Aristotle's God, of course, is nothing but the Hindu Atman, the pure self, which is designated by Aristotle as a thought which has only itself for its content. In thinking of God, man becomes one with him and realizes his complete self-realization.

If we go on to Stoicism we find the same religious phenomenon in the sage's independence in relation to all perceptible value or evil, or in what is called apathy, disregard of all feeling. Of course the sage follows the law of duty; not however because of some interest in the content of the duty, but only because by being determined by that law he will be unable to become one with God and achieve that true self-realization which characterizes God, and thus to gain absolute blessedness. The sage lifts himself up above his natural self to an absolute self. And this absolute self is God, with whom he thus becomes one.

We may go on to the older Christianity as it appears, on the one hand, in the gospel of John and, on the other hand, in the Pauline epistles. Here we find an association between philosophical religiosity and the primitive mystery-faith, belief in the possibility of man's being possessed by a naturalistically conceived God, who overcomes the powers of death through his resurrection. On the one hand, Christ is regarded as assuming the place of one's own 'I'. 'I live, yet not I, but Christ lives in me.'[1] This possession by a divine power procures a number of purely natural effects, consisting above all in man's being raised up above the law of sin and death. In the same way as it happens in the Eleusinian mysteries, man through being infused with divine power acquires certainty concerning a blessed life after death, a life which certainly does not have to be conceived apart from elements of a

----

[1] Gal. ii. 20.

purely natural good. But Christ also appears, especially in the gospel of John, as the giver of an *immediately* present blessedness. This blessedness is only the other side of dying from the world and consists in the enjoyment of complete peace, of a higher life, which results from the eradication of the root of all evil, concern with what is sensible. Here the point of emphasis is placed on achieving the independence of the Hindu sage, on returning to the pure self. 'He that loses his life shall find it'.[1] 'He that drinks of the water which I give shall never thirst again.'[2] 'My peace I give unto you, but not as the world gives do I give unto you.'[3] 'I am the resurrection and the life. He that believes in me shall live, even though he were dead.'[4] Here it is a question of a blessedness given in the soul, which enters in immediately with Christ, a blessedness which has its proper mark of identification in its opposite: life in the world. Here the highest good has been rarified in fact into the *pure self*— pure Being in the Hindu sense.

If we go a step farther, we meet in Plotinus or Neo-platonism the purely philosophical form of this higher blessedness. God is the pure unity, which is lifted up above the contradiction between thought and being, and yet is Being in itself and likewise the good. Perfect blessedness is unification with him, which is achieved through ecstasy, a more momentary condition in which all consciousness, and even self-consciousness, have disappeared. Neo-platonism goes to an extreme in insisting that ecstasy is a momentary condition which arises with the loss of all consciousness, but this does not represent an essential departure from either Platonism or Christianity. Even for Plotinus there is certainly a lower form, albeit a permanent form, of purely non-sensible blessedness, which arises with the vision of God in the form of the Platonic world of ideas. It is only God's complete simplicity in his presence in the soul which leads Plotinus to demand this kind of *unio* with him, in which all consciousness of anything has disappeared.

Medieval philosophy, with its theological base, is an attempt to combine metaphysical religiosity with the *infusio gratiae* ('pouring out of grace') which occurs when Christ, the natural or the human God, takes possession of the soul. By this *infusio* man receives, according to Thomas Aquinas, not only the forgiveness of sin and the assurance of future blessedness, but also unification with the supreme God. Following Pseudo-Dionysius the Aeropagite, the

[1] John xii. 25.    [2] John iv. 14.    [3] John xiv. 27.    [4] John xi. 25.

great authority of the Middle Ages, this God is regarded as pure simple being or pure power, which is likewise the good: *unum, verum, et bonum* and *actus purus*. The blessedness which is obtained through Christ is thus an immediately present, purely metaphysical felicity, in which man becomes one with God.

With the mystics, especially Meister Eckhart, this theory is developed with a more thorough-going logic, until the point is reached where God, as pure Being or as the innermost being of the soul, the pure self, cannot be positively conceived, and is not positively given except in the metaphysical feeling of blessedness which one experiences along with the idea of God. In this feeling the soul becomes one with God. God has no positive determinations and therefore cannot be positively conceived. But in my experience of this feeling in connection with the complete negation of all determinate being, I myself become the supreme God and thus have him immediately present.

From the Middle Ages we can follow metaphysical religiosity forward even into modern times. With Spinoza, for example, insight into God's essence—pure Being, in which all particular being is included—is unification with God, in which the soul reaches its highest and purest blessedness on account of its complete independence and self-realization.

In Kant we find again the Stoic religiosity. The will which is determined by the law of duty has no interest in ends. It is determined only by the idea of its own independence, and thus it is the absolute good. And since the absolute good is one with the divine, the soul becomes one with the divine as being wholly present within the soul. Obviously Kant thinks of the accompanying feeling of blessedness as non-sensible in its content. One ought also to emphasize that Kant makes the ethical will an active moment in the intelligible world, which constitutes the ground of the sensible world. Thus I as moral stand above the whole of reality in space and time. That reality is only a moment in me.

With Hegel religion is the unity of the infinite and the finite in the form of the concept, so that the finite spirit itself becomes an absolute spirit. With Spencer 'The Unknowable', which is the principle of all things, is clearly nothing but metaphysical pure Being, and he therefore brings back religious feeling, which in its highest and present form is joined with 'The Unknowable'. With Boström God is in principle a pure, *absolute self*, and his presence in the soul in the religious feeling of blessedness makes him the absolute good, etc.

## Two Main Types of Metaphysical Religiosity

Thus metaphysical religiosity runs in a continuing stream all through the history of Indo-European culture. It can be discovered in the oldest historical times as well as in the most modern time. Its nature is one and the same, even when there are different modes of expression—although even here there are scarcely any differences of major proportions. Nevertheless we can distinguish two main types of metaphysical religiosity, one theoretically grounded and the other practically grounded, although the two forms necessarily encroach on one another. The former is found in its purest form in Hindu philosophy, Platonism, Neo-platonism, and Spinozism; the latter is found in its purest form in Stoicism, in Kantian ethics, and in certain forms of Christianity.

The theoretical form of metaphysical religiosity issues from *pure Being* or the *pure self*, as immediately present in the soul through the consciousness of it, by which the soul is lifted up above all barriers and enjoys pure blessedness in itself as identical with this pure Being or pure self. The practical form issues from a will within us, which in and for itself signifies an exaltation above natural interest. This will is most properly an alien will—a will which is suggested by or bound by the prescriptions of duty. Or one feels the presence of an alien power, e.g. Christ, whose suggestive power binds the will to itself. But in giving one's assent to the domination of this will, one has in oneself a will which is determined by its own freedom from all natural interests. For what, in fact, characterizes the suggestive determination of the will through the moral requirement or through Christ, is that one is not in this case determined by any natural interests. But a will which wills its own freedom, we are told, is a *pure self*; it is, as such, divine. Thus one has true reality within oneself, and in one's will one enjoys one's own absolute self-preservation.

Now it is of the greatest importance to understand the unique state of the soul which appears here—and above all, to avoid being deceived by the propositions which have been put forward. First, a word about the psychological implications of the supposed condition of being possessed by a god. It is plain here that the very vital feeling and, in connection therewith, the dispositions of will are altered by comparison with the usual condition. In the delirium of the Dionysian cult an entirely different temper from the usual one is diffused throughout one's life. One plainly sees life, as it were, through rose-coloured glasses. The phenomenon of conversion has a related character. One experiences the completely overpowering suggestion from Christ, who is presented by the power of hallucination, and in that moment one feels as if entirely new, undreamed-of possibilities of happiness were given. And undoubtedly one experiences altogether new feelings of will and therewith new powers with respect to that on which one previously felt dependent.

Now it is to be noticed in this connection that self-consciousness itself can by no means by comprehended in an idea of myself as a psycho-physical organism, existing in time. Apart from a reference to the immediate vital feelings and the system of feelings of will related to them, one cannot understand how 'I' come to appear to myself as something purely inward, which does not admit of being objectified. In fact, when we say, 'I', we are always concerning ourselves with a movement between the objective 'I', which is the psycho-physical organism itself, and something which is not objective, something which cannot be set over against ourselves as an object which we can observe. This is so because the feelings of the 'I' have entered into an inseparable association with our consciousness of this organism, and we thus use the word 'I' to express both these feelings of the 'I' and the idea of an objective reality.

It is natural, therefore, that if the vital feelings and the feelings of will which determine our self-consciousness have been altered, we should also seem to have become, from a purely objective point of view, different persons. It seems to us as if a person who does not belong to our own psycho-physical organism has come into it. From this arises the idea of being possessed. It is a god, it is declared, who has taken the place of one's soul in religious conversion.

There is a self-deception before us here, entirely independent of the question of the existence or non-existence of any gods. On the basis of the new feeling of life and of will, one concludes that there has been a change even of the soul-life which belongs to the actual and the objective, to the psycho-physical organism. One believes that the feeling of the 'I'—the real 'I'—is given, although, of course, a feeling cannot possibly be an apprehension of something as real.

## 4. PSYCHOLOGICAL EXPLANATION OF METAPHYSICAL RELIGIOSITY

We pass on now to a psychological explanation of metaphysical religiosity. Like Plato and Spinoza, the Hindu sages believe that they are beholding *pure Being* or the *pure* self. What is this pure Being? For it is obvious that the very concept of reality cannot be a reality, any more than, e.g., the very concept of red can be red. When we talk about this or that, a dog or a cat for example, reality undoubtedly has a meaning. But reality as such is an empty word. Then does the sage see only a word before him?

### The Pure Feeling of Certainty and the Idea of Pure Being

It needs to be remembered in this connection that what is called 'pure Being' is a reflection of the denial of the reality of the particular in the proper sense. Natural things present themselves to the sage as only a veil which obscures (the real). Indeed, they are exclusive of one another, they come into existence and they perish. Therefore they seem to him to lack reality. Such a negation carries with it as a psychological consequence the nullification of the very desire for knowledge; that is, a feeling of theoretical repose arises. This again includes a feeling of certainty, which, however, becomes a certainty without there being anything at all of which one is certain, since everything real has fallen away. But the feeling of certainty, in general, finds expression in one assertion: It *is* so. The pure feeling of certainty, the feeling of theoretical repose, finds expression in this assertion: It *is* without anything further. This expression is *pure Being*, although the sage does not know that it is here only a question of a reflexive expression for his own state of feeling.

But because it is given in a pure feeling of certainty, this 'Being' which the sage has before him also becomes one with the feeling itself. My knowledge of Being and Being itself are one and the same. Pure Being does not stand over against the 'I' as a thing and does not detract from the absoluteness of the 'I.' But in that case things, in so far as they are anything, become only ideas in me. The sage apprehends himself as simply real, everything else excluded, and experiences pleasure in this exalted condition of his.

It is to be noticed that, in regard to the relationship of the self to the external world, the ordinary consciousness is in the same psychical condition as is beautifully expressed in a verse by J. P. Jacobsen. On the one hand, all the worlds are within me, and therefore space and time as well; on the other hand, I am only a speck in the coursing of the worlds. In fact, the first type of interpretation is incorrect and depends upon an inseparable association between my apprehension of myself as an objective reality, a psycho-physical organism, and the very feeling of the 'I'. On account of this association the actual 'I' is apprehended as immanent within my feeling of the 'I' and thus as something purely inward, which exists only for itself. Now since my ideas of the world are found within me, viz. as a psycho-physical organism, they come to be ascribed to me as something purely inward, and so the reality which is conceived becomes something merely subjective, something which exists in me as a purely inward thing. But on the other hand, the ordinary consciousness cannot avoid the conception of its own self as something real in time and space. From this comes the contradiction within the ordinary consciousness between the conception of the world as existing in me and of myself as a moment in the world. But the sage breaks through the contradiction through the idea of pure Being, which is nothing but an expression for the pure feeling of certainty which has been described.

If pure Being is identical with my own feeling of certainty, then everything—even space and time themselves—becomes only a moment in my own self. My own psycho-physical organism itself becomes something merely subjective. My self-consciousness comes to be separated from the idea of the organism. The sage himself floats on the stream of his ideas and feelings and does not think of them as themselves being in time, and even less as being in space. He lives in an eternally flowing now and enjoys his feelings of independence of everything external. And the basis of the entire condition is a word—the expression of complete theoretical satisfaction, of the pure feeling of certainty. This word is 'pure Being', which at the same time becomes, through an abstraction from all natural reality, pure nothing.

We see, then, that metaphysical religiosity has such a broad scope in the history of civilized man that it cannot be explained by reference to any particular temporal circumstances, but must be explained directly by reference to the nature of the human soul-life. We pass on now to such an explanation.

*Reality and Space and Time*

When we observe an individual thing, it is natural for us to conceive its *reality* (*verklighet*) as limited to the space or the place in which it is situated. It is the most natural thing in the world for us to say to ourselves that the thing exists here and not in some other place.[1] And yet it is a question here of a confusion in human thought. For if the thing actually existed only in a certain limited space, then *the truth* regarding its existence (*tillvaro*) would also be limited to that space. For the truth of the existence of the thing means nothing other than that it exists as we apprehend it. Now if it exists only in this limited space, then the truth regarding its existence is also limited to this space.

It is obvious that the reality of the thing does not depend upon and does not have anything to do with the space to which it belongs. The thing in this space exists, although its existence (*tillvaro*)[2] does not have to encounter the limitation which its space possesses. But however that may be, human thought blends together the fact which exists with its existence itself. Something of the character of space is imposed on reality itself.

Perhaps the following will help us to see even more clearly the tendency of human thought in this way to transfer to *reality* something which really does not belong to *it* but rather belongs to *that which is real*. Nobody believes that Karl the Twelfth is still alive. Thus he does not exist any longer. He is dead and buried. And yet—if the past were nothing, the black night, it would be absolutely impossible to have knowledge of it. For what does it mean to have knowledge of something, if not that in reality the fact is as we apprehend it? Concerning that which lacks reality, which has nothing to do with reality—concerning the pure nothing —we have no knowledge. Therefore it is not true that Karl XII does not exist. He exists as surely as we have knowledge concerning him. The only correct way of putting it in the ordinary sense is that the Karl XII who exists does not have the same temporal property that we have. It is the Karl XII with the property of living in the twentieth century who does not exist—not the Karl XII with the property of living in the eighteenth century.

But how is it with human thought? Well, just as we confuse

[1] Hägerström means by 'the fact' or 'the thing', the fact or the thing *in its reality*. (Editor's note.)

[2] Existence (*tillvaro*) = Reality (*verklighet*). (Editor's note.)

reality with the space in which the existing fact is situated and say that the thing exists only here in this space, instead of saying that the thing in this space exists without any limitation, so also do we confuse reality with the point in time to which the thing belongs. And we say to ourselves not that the thing, situated in this point in time, exists without anything further, but we turn it around and say that the thing exists only in that point in time. In that case the past becomes a black night, a gaping empty space, concerning which we could not properly possess any knowledge whatever.

Therefore reality itself has nothing to do with time and space, but in our confused thought we limit it to a certain space and a certain time whenever we conceive of something real. This is a confusion of thought which belongs to the human soul.

But now observe where this confusion of thought leads! We instinctively feel and understand that reality itself cannot have its determinateness through space and time. We are thus brought to the idea of an incorporeal and non-temporal reality—reality as such. But yet the old taint of space and time remains. Thus the form of the corporeal and the temporal is imposed on reality as such. It becomes *something*, which exists on *analogy* with the corporeal and the temporal. Naturally reality as such cannot itself exist, for when we say, 'The reality of reality', we actually say nothing at all. It is a purely meaningless statement; it is the same as if we said, 'The table's table', or "The table is a table'—a mere accumulation of words without any meaning. *That* which exists must always be something different from its mere existing. But because the concept of reality has been once tainted by time and space, and because this characteristic is preserved even when we think of pure reality, reality as such, it becomes entirely natural for us that reality as such, reality in its essence, should exist in the same mode as particular things. So we have God there. For the philosopher God is reality as such, become something which itself is real. Now the way is open for uncontrolled fantasy. We believe that we know that there exists something, which is reality as such and which therefore also exists in everything which is real.

Now what is this mystical something? What is God? *One* thing that we think we know about him is that he is lifted up above all the limitations which belong to space and time. He is neither here nor there, neither then nor now. He reposes in an eternal stillness. But still human thought continues to inquire, 'What is he?' The scholastic seeks, as we have discovered, to apprehend him in concepts. But even he finally comes to a standstill before the unfathomable, he also discovers that his own thought-structure is a fragile one. This is shown in the fact that he finally appeals to feeling; that is, he recognizes that God cannot be conceived by thought. Or to put it more correctly, logic works in the direction of his coming unconsciously to recognize the weakness of his own thought-structure. The cause of this is that every quality by which he seeks to determine God displays the distinguishing characteristic of finiteness. For whatever falls within our experience, everything with which we can occupy ourselves in our thoughts as that which is real, is bound by the shackles of space and time, by which God cannot be bound.

*Conditions for the Religious Temper*

But observe, now, how through this confusion of thought a place is made for religious fantasy In his eternal repose, God is immediately present in me. He is nearer to me than everything which belongs to myself. He is nearer to me than my own thoughts and feelings, for these rise up like bubbles on the surface, only to disappear in the next moment. But God is in my innermost being without limitation and without cessation. And yet—this immediately present deity completely eludes our thought. We seek and seek, but the unknowable constantly slips away from us.

The conditions for the religious temper are to be seen here. The one condition lies in the idea of something in our innermost being, which is lifted up above all our passions and aspirations and which is also powerful enough to lift us up above the unrest of life, above the anxiety of life. By conceiving of such a reality, as abiding in our own inner being, as our own self's deepest essence, we become certain about ourselves, about our deliverance from suffering and death. For we wish first and foremost to live an unobstructed life, but this unobstructed life we find in God. For God, who is lifted up above all limitations, is our innermost self. It is not strange, then, that when one discovers him, when one sets him up before the eyes of one's soul, one believes that one has found the life-preserving source of all happiness.

To this must be added that the contemplation of what gives the impression of quietness and peace itself delivers us from our unrest. So God gives us not only the feeling of well-bring, which lies in the idea of the persistence of our innermost self, independent of all the vicissitudes and difficulties of time. I live eternally, because God is living within me. God gives us also the feeling of peace, which is bestowed by the impression of his complete exaltation over all the striving of the world.

Still in order to really believe that one has found God—the pure reality—it is required that one should be able to turn one's attention away from visible things. And for this it is demanded that one should be able to deaden one's interest in these things. Otherwise they draw attention to themselves, and God disappears from the circle of vision. A reciprocal action prevails here. We ourselves must work for the salvation of our souls, says philosophical religion; we must open ourselves to God. 'He that loses his life shall find it', says the Johannine Jesus. His meaning is that only the surrender of ourselves in the worldly sense opens our minds to the life which we possess in God. But philosophical religion also says that only through God himself can we achieve salvation. He alone can of himself draw us away from the world. The psychological import of this is that it is only the influence of the deity as our own innermost being that can draw us away from the world.

The second condition for the religious temper, and by no means the least important, lies, on the other hand, in God's unknowableness, in the impossibility of his being conceived by thought. This very soaring out into space in the continual attempt to conceive God gives rise to an altogether unique temper. Despite his immediate nearness, God becomes for us the High One, the Inaccessible, the Sublime. We experience a feeling of the sublime, which exceeds and draws to itself all similar feelings, a feeling which no visible thing whatsoever can arouse in us. What is the greatness of the surging, stormy sea compared to God's? God is not only inaccessible to human power, but he also cannot possibly be determined or thought. The sphere of the stars, which overwhelms us by its greatness, defying all comprehension, in relation to which we feel ourselves to be dust, can still be conceived by thought. The courses and greatness of the stars can be measured. Now, of course, God, as reality itself, is in the sphere of the stars, because reality as such must be in everything. But he is even more exalted over us than this. For he cannot be captured by means of any numerical measurement.

Here we must note in particular the significance of the idea of

God as omnipresent and eternal (existing in all times). There is something unique in this idea. We have previously said that the concept of God has its origin in the tendency of human thought to burden reality itself with the space and time in which an individual reality exists, and in the necessity, in spite of this, of conceiving reality itself as lifted up above time and space. This wavering between the characteristics of space and time, on the one hand, and the characteristic of being lifted up above space and time, on the other, is a product of the idea of omnipresence and the corresponding idea of eternity. Or more correctly, the fictive idea (of omnipresence and eternity) is no real idea at all, but what is present in the soul is just this wavering (between the two alternatives). The word 'omnipresence' is merely a scholastic expression for the wavering of our thought. We conceive of God as being here and there, now and then, and yet we conceive of him also as being neither here nor there, neither now nor then.

We said, however, that the feeling of exaltation, which we experience in the presence of the deity, not only exceeds all feelings of exaltation which visible things can arouse in us, but also takes them up into itself. God exists in the surging of the stormy sea, for he is, of course, everywhere. The mighty power which appears in the stormy sea therefore becomes for the religious mind God's own power and greatness. God exists in the incalculable domain of time in which the stars have their existence. For he is in all times. Thus the greatness of time becomes God's own greatness. In this way the deity draws to itself, in the case of the religious person, the feelings of supreme beauty which visible greatness can arouse in us.

Thus we discover that a complex of feelings here attaches itself to the idea of pure reality—God in the philosophic sense. We have, for example, the feeling of blessedness in the discovery within ourselves of a life, lifted up above all limitations—God is my own true self. We have the feeling of peace, which comes through the influence of the complete imperturbability which characterizes God. Finally, we have the feeling of the exalted—God is higher than all the forces of nature, for all such natural forces can yet be mastered by thought. On the other hand, God himself is also in the forces of nature. He is their true reality and therefore possesses in himself all their majesty.

And yet this reality, so familiar to our souls, this Mighty One, is nevertheless at the same time nothing but a creation of our own confused thought. He has sprung up out of the very nature of the psycho-physical organism, out of the conditions of its modes of thought. But observe carefully: he is not a figment of the imagination in the ordinary sense. If we label him that, then we must also so label our ideas of the real in general. It is just as true that God exists as it is that the so-called past has been and no longer is. It is just as true that God exists as it is that this table has its reality in this room. Indeed, we have also discovered that there is a most intimate connection between the two types of conception.

The confusion described in the preceding section is just one of the grounds of belief in God. It is also obvious from this that when, without epistemological support, one denies God, this denial does not depend upon any particular wisdom, but only on the fact that, in spite of sharing a common point of departure with those who think religiously, one does not have the same need of drawing from contradictory propositions, themselves absurd, conclusions which themselves are necessarily absurd. From the logical point of view it is neither better nor worse, once one assumes the squaring of a circle, to conclude that the relation between the diagonal of the square and the sum of the sides is the same as the relation between the diameter of the circle and its circumference. But what engenders the religious metaphysician's particular need to go farther in his thought, starting from incorrect points of departure, is undoubtedly the same as that which creates the drunkard's need to save himself—the need of escaping from the anxiety and wearisomeness of life.

## Religious Feeling and Self-Consciousness

However, the matter has another side also. There is something in the religious idea of God which, from the psychological point of view, makes it immune to epistemological objections. Of course, we have already spoken earlier of the intimate connection in which the idea of God as pure reality stands to the idea of a pure 'I'. Thus God is one with his own consciousness, one with my consciousness of him. Thus he is also given only in the feeling in which we experience religious blessedness. For the only mode in which something can be given, so that it is one with its own consciousness, is precisely the form of feeling. It is clear that in this way the

question of the reality of God in the ordinary sense becomes, from
one point of view, non-essential for religious faith.

We have represented religious feeling as a feeling linked to the
life which is free from spiritual dependence upon that which is
external. In this sense, religious feeling cannot depend upon the
idea of God as the ultimate ground of the world, because that idea
itself presupposes or has its foundation in this same feeling. This
will now be shown.

The idea of an ultimate ground of the world, naturally, is born
of our concept of causality. We apprehend one thing in the world
as having the ground of its reality in another thing. But we enter
here upon a series of progressions from effect to cause. The
particular cause is itself an effect of another cause, and so on. But
now if there were not a first cause, which was not itself the effect
of some other cause, but existed through and in itself, then it would
be impossible to terminate this series of progressions from effect
to cause; and this would mean that nothing could be determined as
real. For every effect of something else has its reality in that other,
not in itself. Therefore it cannot be determined as real except
through the recognition of the reality of the other. Now if we do
not come to something which has its reality in itself, to which we
can refer all other reality as its consequences, then, of course,
nothing can be determined as real. But in order for it to be capable
of being real in itself, this ultimate ground must be without any
relationship to any other thing. For if it stood in some relationship
to another, for example, if it existed in a specific point in time or
in a specific space, its reality would depend upon the reality of the
other. In that case it would not be the cause of itself either.

How can this complete freedom from all relationships to other
things be conceived, however? The ultimate ground of the world
must be something which is enclosed completely within itself or
something completely inward, something spiritual in the positive
sense. For everything external stands, precisely as external, in a
relationship to something else. But how can we possess any idea
of that which is enclosed within itself, of the spiritual? If there
were so such thing in our experience, we could not possibly have
any idea of it. That is, it would be impossible to conceive anything
which had its reality in itself.

But there actually is *one* such experience, namely consciousness
of the 'I'. That which is given in self-consciousness is characterized

by the fact that it exists for itself and thus is completely enclosed within itself or is something spiritual. Thus it is through the consciousness of the 'I' that the idea of that which is real in and through itself, and hence of that which is for itself, acquires any significance. Apart from this experience it would be an empty word.

Still a difficulty remains, over which we must linger a bit. How is this? Am I actually something altogether enclosed within myself? In so far as it is a question of myself, as just this determinate person, it is impossible to separate myself from a specific space and a specific time in which I exist. In general, it is impossible to divorce myself from the psycho-physical organism. But in that case I also stand in a relation to another. How does this fit together? The same 'I' which *is* enclosed within itself, which exists only for itself, is *not* enclosed within itself. That which is set free from any relationship to another nonetheless stands in a relationship to another.

The solution of the puzzle lies in an analysis of self-consciousness itself. How does it arise? Doubtless one means by the word 'I' one's own body, but also, as belonging to this body, a psychic life with a certain continuity within itself; thus one means something objective, which exists in the world. But the consciousness of this objective body, with its psychic life, still does not cover all that we mean when we say 'I'. It does not explain the unique feature of this 'I', namely that it is immediately given for itself, that it exists for itself in an existence which is enclosed within itself. There must be something else in our consciousness, to which we give expression when we say 'I'. What is that?

There is one form of consciousness which is such that its content cannot be separated from the experience in which it is given. Such a form of consciousness we call feeling. It is not possible to regard that which is experienced in the feeling of joy, the quality of joy itself, as something in itself, which can be found in the world. As soon as we try to determine what is present, we always find that we have only the very experience of joy. That which is present is the *feeling* of joy, not the bare quality of joy.

Now, however, there are a number of feelings of a special nature, such that we do not in fact have them without ascribing their contents to the living body. These are all the bodily feelings, feelings of being well and of being ill, feelings of hunger and thirst, feelings of pleasure and pain, feelings of exertion and repose, feelings of movement, etc. We feel pain in our foot, we feel hunger in our abdomen, and so on. But in this case one's living body exists for the consciousness of the organism in two ways. On the one hand, it is naturally a *reality* among other realities, with a number of manifestations of consciousness. That is, the body is apprehended through a conception which grasps its object as real. The object is thus regarded also as existing independently of the consciousness of it. On the other hand, the same living body is itself given, so to speak, from within, in a number of feelings—which are not at all conceptions of the body as real, allowing us to separate that which is apprehended and the apprehension itself as distinct realities and to set them over against one another. What would the pain in the foot be in itself, independent of my apprehension of it? No, nothing else is present except the feeling of pain itself. But in that case the living body, to which the contents of the feelings in question are nevertheless ascribed has a double character for us. On the one hand, it, together with its whole factual psychic life, belongs to the reality which is given. It exists there, whether it is apprehended or not. On the other hand, the same real body is given in a number of feelings. Hence it is something which cannot be distinguished from the apprehension of its own self. It exists as a reality in itself only in its outward aspect. In its inward aspect it is the feelings by which it is apprehended.

When we say 'I', we mean, on the one hand, the living body with its continuing psychic life as a content of feeling, and on the other hand, the same body as a reality for itself. It exists in the world, and yet it is the apprehension of its own self. Here we have both a subject, viz. the experience of feeling, and an object. viz. the real body; but both are drawn together into one reality, which is its own consciousness and is thus the completely inward. And yet this same body retains its property of belonging to objective reality in time and space. I am at one time both enclosed within myself, existing only for myself, and standing in an abiding relationship to something external; free in my inward life and yet dependent on something external.

It is clear that, in so far as I believe myself to possess an inner life for my self, it is the psychic aspects of the body that enter the foreground. These aspects present themselves as especially apprehensible, since they must exist only in my own consciousness.

But this 'I', with the double character that has been referred to, harbours within itself a number of feelings, in which its dependence on that which is external is manifested in a special way. There is a multitude of feelings of desiring and aspiration, which depend on the external world to which they pertain if they are to be transmuted into a feeling of satisfaction. This kind of attachment, now, becomes that which has real significance for me. The very fact of belonging to the external world is not troublesome in itself. But *through* experiences of desiring and of aspiration, the fact of belonging to the external world becomes something evil for me. If it were possible to control the external completely, this attachment would lose its sting. Conversely, if I did not have any experiences of desiring or of aspiration, it would not appear as something evil either.

We have previously said that the ground of the consciousness of God as that which is real in itself—and thus as that which is without any relation to anything external, and thus as that which is purely for itself—is our own self-consciousness. For there we believe that we actually experience a reality which exists for itself, which is its own consciousness. But the 'I' which is given to us appears to be inadequate, in one way, for constituting the ground of the concept of God. Certainly it is something enclosed within itself, an inner life. But still it is always attached to the external, an attachment which acquires significance for us in virtue of the fact that we are fated to be constantly desiring, constantly aspiring to something beyond that which is at hand, and consequently to be constantly frustrated. How under such circumstances can one make the leap out into space? From what does one derive the idea of the *absolute*, inner life, the idea of God? The 'I' which is given to us is finite and is at every moment painfully aware of its limits. But God is the 'I' without any limit.

The explanation is afforded by an analysis of the religious feeling as a feeling of blessedness in connection with the soul's life in freedom, a freedom which we achieve by raising ourselves up above all these experiences of desiring and of aspiration, above all the valuations, in virtue of which the external world appears to be a constraint upon us, an insurmountable barrier. Out of this a new self-consciousness arises. Even if I seem to myself to be still living in time and space as a particular individual alongside others, still I seem to myself to be spiritually independent of everything external. This state of feeling reaches its highest apex in religious ecstasy, an ideal for Neo-platonism as well as for Paul. Here we have a feeling of blessedness in combination with the nullification of all consciousness of the world and thus also the nullification of self-consciousness in the ordinary sense. In reflecting afterwards about this condition the ecstatic individual must regard himself as lifted up above everything external, everything objective, as absorbed in pure feeling—and thus as completely one with his own consciousness, as a *pure 'I'*.

But whether religious feeling is connected only with this spiritual independence of the world or simply with this expiration of all consciousness of the world and of self-consciousness in the ordinary sense, it is adequate as the ground for the idea of God as the purely inward life. It is only this that brings it about that one does not have only empty words left when one makes an abstraction from the external world and conceives of God.

We should emphasize, however, that it is characteristic of *every* self-consciousness that one does not distinguish between a content of feeling and a reality which is conceived. It is from the failure to draw this distinction that there arises the idea of a reality which is its own consciousness, which therefore exists for itself. With reference to the ordinary self-consciousness, the content of feeling is given through bodily feelings, whose content is localized in the body. The reality which is conceived is the living body, equipped with continuing functions of consciousness. By an act of synthesis the psycho-physical organism in its consciousness of itself becomes a self-consciousness—a consciousness of a reality which exists only for itself. From this point of view, however, the 'I' loses all meaning, unless I actually have feelings whose content is not separated from the reality which is conceived. But from this it follows that the idea of God, as the purely inward life, loses all meaning unless I have the appropriate experience of feeling. Thus there is no content of feeling which for me can be identified with a reality which is conceived and can give rise to the idea of the 'I'. It is only for me as *experiencing feeling* religiously that God exists, in so far as it is not a question merely of empty words. Thus it is not to be thought that God will exist for me, as long as I myself only unfeelingly contemplate the religious feeling. Only if I am myself *aflame* with the idea does God's existence have any meaning.

But on the other hand, *some* sort of reality must be conceived in an objective fashion if it is to be possible, in general, for an 'I' to be conceived. What is this reality which is conceived? It cannot be one's own body. For it is precisely the thought of being independent of the world that belongs essentially to the consciousness in question. But there belongs together with the consciousness of the body the consciousness of a desiring and aspiring 'I', which is doomed, because of its dependence on the world, to a continual suffering, a continual dissatisfaction. The second self-consciousness referred to, which is a consciousness of freedom from dependence on the world, must thus be connected with a different reality. What is that? Nothing is more natural than that it should be just the conceived-of reality which appears before me in the very moment of conversion, of liberation.

Paul says, 'Now it is no longer I who live, but Christ lives in me'.[1] The risen Christ, as the mighty conqueror of death, had revealed himself to him. It was he who had awakened his consciousness of freedom, his feeling of blessedness in connection with his spiritual independence of the powers of the world. Therefore his own religious feelings were united with the Christ of whom he conceived. But thus did Christ also become the eternal life which he thought he lived, the new 'I' which he believed he had found within himself (—take care to distinguish this self from that which is attached to the body). Christ was for him the ground of his conception of God. The fact that besides this the old Jewish God came to the fore in his consciousness and in some way combined with Christ as the ground of his concept of God, does not alter the situation.

The belief in God has thus been shown to be something secondary in relation to feeling. We have before us the idea of God as the eternal and pure spirit. The attempt to combine the Jewish God and Christ to form one essential ground for the very idea of the living God provided the occasion for a hopeless dogmatic controversy in early Christianity. In the very nature of the case, the ground of reality must be something vague and undetermined. For no conceived-of reality is equivalent to God. The idea of God becomes a consequence of the state of feeling of the person imbued with a religious sentiment, in connection with all kinds of vague ideas of a specific reality. This idea breaks forth out of warm feeling; but as a natural accompaniment of this, the idea

[1] Gal. ii. 20.

METAPHYSICAL RELIGIOSITY          223

is also especially adapted, on the other hand, to arouse the feeling
in question. In virtue of its associational connection with the
religious world of feeling and conception, the idea of God in turn
excites and inflames the feeling itself. Therefore the soul which
longs for and is in distress to gain the fullness of the condition of
religious feeling is inflamed through its crying for God. But this
only makes it more evident that at root religious feeling is by no
means identified with the idea of God, even if, as a natural consequence thereof, it is enlivened by that idea.

## LECTURES ON SO-CALLED SPIRITUAL
## RELIGION

*Quid interius deo?* is the motto which Sabatier takes for his philosophy of religion. Sabatier is especially concerned to maintain that religion is a phenomenon of the inner or spiritual life. Jesus' teaching about God as a spirit is well known, of course, especially from the gospel of John. God is not to be worshipped either in Jerusalem or on holy mountains. 'God is a spirit, and they that worship him must worship him in spirit and in truth' (John iv. 23).

Such an emphasis on the spiritual life had already been prepared, by the time of the rise of Christianity, by the prophetic religion of the Jews. This religion had a two-fold tendency. The one tendency was to free the deity from nationalistic limitations. Therewith a severe blow was also dealt to anthropomorphism— God became a world-ruler and for that reason became incapable of being represented to the senses. The other tendency was to locate the correct relationship to God not in cultic practices, but in the condition of mind of the individual.

The emphasis on the spiritual was also present in the whole tenor of Hellenistic philosophy. There matter was regarded as evil and thus as Not-being, inasmuch as in metaphysics Being and good, Not-being and evil, tend to coalesce. In opposition to matter, the World-Reason was set up as true Being. The task of man was to return from matter to the World-Reason, in order thus to gain complete self-sufficiency—a life independent of all outward things. exalted above all needs, and so a life of blessedness.

### I. SOME IMPLICATIONS OF THE SPIRITUALIZATION OF
### RELIGION

However, it cannot be denied that the spiritualization of religion, by which God becomes something purely inward and accessible only within the heart of man, has a characteristic tendency to lead to the destruction of every conceivable feature in the deity as something transcendent, as something which exists independently of the human idea of him. For existence itself, independent of the idea, is not conceivable apart from a connecting medium, in which the existing things are construed as existing alongside one another without being absorbed into one another. But the only form by means of which we can conceive phenomena as existing alongside one another without being absorbed into one another, is space. As soon as we posit a certain thing as existing independently of consciousness, we *ipso facto* think of consciousness as something which itself exists in the human body and of that other thing as something which falls outside of the body. So it would seem that in order to conceive the deity as existing independently of human consciousness, one must locate him in the same space as that in which we exist. But in that case God also becomes material. This is equivalent to saying that in proportion as the deity is conceived as something purely inward, he loses his transcendence.

The whole history of religion confirms this contention. For in proportion as God is conceived, under the influence of philosophic thought, as a spirit, he loses his transcendence. He is no longer given as something external to man. He exists only *within* him. The influence of such thinking is to be met with in the demand of mysticism that religion must be essentially feeling and will, not consciousness of an objective reality. In proportion as God is divested, under the influence of philosophic thought, of such human qualities as power, mercy, righteousness, etc.—properties which all have their source in the experience of man and presuppose a relative being which has other things existing alongside itself and hence is in space, as man is—God is reduced to pure indeterminate Being, to Being as such, the ultimate ground of all things. Critical thought cannot even ascribe cognition to him. For cognition always presupposes an awareness of an object existing independently of the thinking subject. The thinking being as such employs the categories of space.

But this pure Being, which cannot even be described as cognitive, is also inconceivable as such. For in order to conceive it as an object, thought must set it over against consciousness itself and thus make it relative, in fact material as well. Pure Being cannot exist for me except in subjective, objectless feeling, wholly shut up in itself. God and the man who is feeling God in his religious experience are one and the same. We find this in Neo-platonism. whose real aim was to separate the divine, as good, from matter,

H

as evil. For Neo-platonism the deity dissolves away into pure Being, which cannot be characterized in any way but can only be given in ecstatic, objectless feeling, in which there is no distinction between subject and object. Out of this pure Being, which cannot even be described as cognitive, the perceptible realities emanate in various stages.

This same Neo-platonic outlook dominates the religious thinkers of the Middle Ages, in so far as they attempt to take away from God all properties which are human and are thus bound up with the corporeal. We find it in Pseudo-Dionysius the Areopagite, in John Scotus Erigena, in Hugo of St Victor, in Meister Eckhart. By an inexorable logic the attempt to completely spiritualize the deity leads, under the control of thought, to mysticism. The intermediate link in this transition is the thought of pure, indeterminate Being, which, just because it is indeterminate, cannot become an object of thought. Mysticism, however, has different degrees; there is pure mysticism and there is modified mysticism. It is to be observed that there is a tendency in mysticism—and this is especially characteristic of pure mysticism—to let the intellectual factor in religion merge into feeling, so that feeling itself becomes intuitive knowledge.

All concrete characteristics ascribed to the deity, like thinking and willing—and for the *pure* mystics of the Middle Ages even those ascribed to the person of Christ—are nothing but symbols, which constitute the condition for the occurrence of that objectless feeling in which alone the deity is given. But for the mysticism which was of greatest importance in the Middle Ages, these concrete characteristics acquire reality. God's Son, i.e. the concrete God, really exists, even though he is concrete, and he leads us back to the original source, God. Assuredly he cannot be God, for he is human; nevertheless, as providing the *image* of God in the world of finitude, he too is divine. He both is and is not divine.

We all know how the problem of Christ's double nature stands in the foreground of the earliest Christian dogmatics. This problem gives expression to the intellectual difficulties which confront the religion which seeks to spiritualize God and thus to separate God from the finite, material world. For critical reflection it was natural that God should be a spirit or something immaterial. Any other view was inconsistent with his universality. Not even the conception of him as a World-Soul, with the world as his body, could be satisfactory. For in that case he would be comprised of material parts, which would depend on each other and would make the whole itself relative. God himself would then not be the absolute World-Ruler, inasmuch as he would depend on the various parts of the World-Body, which themselves would be relative. Indeed, for medieval religion the determinateness of the world was evil. The Christian lives *in* the world, but he is not *of* the world, says the so-called German Theology. But the whole tendency here was to make man's relationship to God a purely inward and spiritual one, so that God could be thought of as present in the heart of man. However, this in turn brought with it the rarefaction of God into pure Being, and therewith one came into conflict with the factual conditions of religious feeling itself. For that feeling depended on the supposition that there were divine powers outside of man, which could raise him up over the suffering and torment of the life of the senses.

So the problem of Christ's double nature gives expression to the intellectual crux of spiritual religion. As a pure spirit God loses his transcendence, and the religion which concerns itself with such a God dissolves into pure, objectless feeling. And yet religious feeling demands for its own continued existence the belief in a transcendent being.

## 2. THE INTELLECTUAL CRUX OF SPIRITUAL RELIGION, AS ILLUSTRATED IN THE THOUGHT OF SCHLEIERMACHER

The religious problem in question appears in all its force in Schleiermacher's earliest writings on the philosophy of religion, *Speeches on Religion* (1799) and *Monologues* (1800). On the one hand, Schleiermacher is clear that the Absolute, which God must be, cannot be an object which stands over against the subject. Neither is it possible, therefore, for God to be material, since in that case he would be made finite. Consequently God cannot be grasped through thought, which by its very nature objectifies. From this it follows that God can be presented to us only in such a mental faculty as does not involve objectification. This faculty is religious feeling. Only as presented in religious feeling, and thus as completely indeterminate, can God be a pure spirit.

On the other hand, Schleiermacher cannot avoid ascribing transcendence to the deity. Indeed, religious feeling as such is a feeling of passive reception. Consequently religious feeling itself presupposes something which man receives, and therefore something which thought grasps as being external to man. Now Schleiermacher believes that one can avoid the difficulty by supposing that this outer something enters into consciousness *in the very act of reception,* so that in the act of reception consciousness takes the outer something into itself without any objectification. The outer something thus loses its character of being outer in the very moment of its reception. But he does not overlook the fact that if this outer something is to be conceived by the philosopher of religion as entering into man in religious feeling, it must also be thought of by him as existing in its own right. Thus in its explanation of religion philosophy of religion comes to determine God as an object.

Schleiermacher seeks to resolve this difficulty by reducing God to the universe, which in essence is nothing but *die Menschheit,* i.e. the system of human spirits. In so far as they all enter into a system of higher and lower, in which each exists only as a necessary link in the whole, the whole is not something external to the individual. Therefore, in spite of the fact that it is not identical with the individual, it can enter into the individual's consciousness apart from any objectification.

On the other hand, Schleiermacher cannot avoid recognizing that human spirits have an essential natural element in them. The spirit is itself the unity of spirit and nature, with a greater or lesser preponderance of the spiritual element. So then God necessarily comes to be thought of as material—which Schleiermacher nevertheless thought to be impossible.

Certainly the divine transcendence is necessary as a determining condition of Schleiermacher's concept of religion. But once this point is granted, he cannot remain there. However, a more important point is the following. The transcendent object which Schleiermacher is compelled to admit into the concept of God is not the concept of God of the positive religions, particularly of Christianity. And yet it was precisely the superiority of Christianity as the spiritual religion *par excellence* that Schleiermacher wanted to maintain.[1]

---

[1] There is some uncertainty about the reading of this paragraph in the original manuscript. I have simply followed Fries's edition as published in *Religionsfilosofi.* (Tr.)

As regards the conceptions of God in the positive religions, Schleiermacher, in his earliest writings in the philosophy of religion, takes the view that they are merely symbols, in which religious feeling finds expression. Nor has he departed appreciably from this standpoint later on no matter how much he seeks to prove the religious truth of the Christian dogmas. Religious truth is contained in these dogmas only in virtue of their symbolizing the intrinsically incomprehensible, purely Absolute, in such a way that in the world of faith presented there one can obtain the purest religious feeling, i.e. experience the Absolute in the highest way.

Schleiermacher fails to notice that in adopting this standpoint he cuts the vital nerve of Christianity as a positive religion. For that consists in faith in an *objective* power, to whom one can turn and from whom one can derive strength to realize that which at bottom one is striving after: strength to stand against temptations and ultimately the hope of blessedness in a future life. He does not notice that the religious feeling of blessedness in enjoying and being caught up into the divine belongs to a world-renouncing attitude, in which all the values belonging to man's natural life fall away. Yet he represents this religious feeling of blessedness as the essential thing in religion and unites it with his conception of the deity as a pure spirit, as the purely inward. The reality, which is wholly inward within consciousness and therefore is one with its own reception into consciousness, is as such perfectly simple, and consequently it is pure, indeterminate Being. Just as surely as pure Being cannot be anything external for consciousness, so surely is the consciousness which is its own object a perfectly simple unity, pure Being. But such a consciousness presupposes, on the theoretical side, an abstraction from all determinate natural being, and devotion to it in feeling therefore presupposes a rejection of all natural values, a dying away from the world and from natural life itself.

Regardless of how prominent such a state of feeling may be in Johannine Christianity—where it appears obviously in connection with a general world-renouncing tendency within Hellenism—still it was not this line of development which become dominant in the Christian religion. Even when it survived, it was combined at any rate with another element which was equally fundamental. The latter appears emphatically in Paul, Augustine, and Luther. Through faith in the Risen One, a new power of grace, a new life, would stream into the soul. This power would not only raise the soul above the law of sin, of the world, and make it righteous before God and give it assurance of eternal life, but it would also direct the soul to social ends, to ends which pertain to the present life.

The resurrection of Christ and the work of salvation which it involved were, for these Christian heroes, by no means only a symbol, which one retained in order thereby to reach a feeling of blessedness in the reception of the Absolute. The resurrection of Christ was an *objective* reality, the most certain of all such realities. Now it was undoubtedly Schleiermacher's thought that the feeling of blessedness in the reception of the universe into the soul, which he was describing, included such a power of grace as that which Paul, Augustine, and Luther believed to arise through faith in Christ and his resurrection. But this element enters, as has been pointed out already, through a fusion of the Absolute in its pure spirituality with the kingdom of man. The result is that in so far as the religious person is determined by the Absolute, he is also determined by this kingdom. But since he does not really believe in any *objective* redeeming powers, he who is religious in Schleiermacher's way also lacks the possibility of receiving that supreme moral strength which the Christian, according to Paul, Augustine, and Luther, will possess.

When Protestant theology adopted Schleiermacher as its authority, it in fact condemned itself to death. The only task of Schleiermacher's theology as such is to set forth the so-called religious experience and the articles of faith as suitable formulas for that experience. It starts from this experience as the real. But he who identifies religious experience with the religious reality shuts himself off, if he is consistent—which, of course, he is by no means required to be—from the possibility of having any other religious experiences than such as belong to the Hindu, world-renouncing Brahma-wisdom. There is no doubt, however, that it was the need to conceive God as a spirit, and therefore as given only in the inner life, which brought Schleiermacher to this pass.

And one can well understand the influence which Schleiermacher came to exercise upon theology. In our time a naturalistic disposition of thought in regard to physical reality prevails. This excludes the acceptance of supernatural powers as intervening in existence. It has therefore become necessary for theology to withdraw religion from the critique of free-thinkers, by so-to-speak banishing God to the inner, spiritual life and excluding him from objective existence. He thus becomes the human spirit itself, regarded as lifted up into its highest potency and as living only for and in itself. God thus falls, as it were, into another world from that which is objectively given—into the world of spiritual experience, in which nothing is objectified. And so one is now struggling, as it were, for the last stronghold of religion, for the defence of the very truth-value of religious experience. Since 'truth' here *means* something entirely different from the truth of science, the assertion of the truth-value of religious experience, so it is claimed, is entirely consistent with the recognition of the truth of science. So in the philosophy of religion we have come back to the doctrine of the two truths, which was preached by the Middle Ages when dying and already corroded by free-thought. One thing is true *in foro theologico*, another *in foro philosophico*. It is forgotten that it belongs to the notion of truth to be one. It is forgotten also that the man who really believes in the double truth, and thus does not accept any *objective* divine forces, is no longer religious—at least not in the Christian sense.

### 3. THE CONCEPT OF SPIRIT IN PRIMITIVE RELIGION

In purely spiritual religion, the deity loses all natural determinateness and is therefore no longer transcendent and a real object for consciousness. It appears now that purely spiritual religion issues in a reality-renouncing mysticism. It thus loses contact also with positive religion as a moral force. We have now to inquire, on the other hand, how it stands with the religion in which the divine acquires natural reality and in which faith in its objective power lies at the basis of religious feeling.

If a savage sees a person strike a boulder which is lying on the edge of a cliff, and the boulder rolls down, he finds nothing remarkable in that. He connects the movement of the stone with the blow which is struck it and regards the blow as the cause of the movement. But suppose that the boulder has lain on the edge for a long time, so that only a slight shaking of the ground is needed in order for it to fall. Suppose that one fine day the savage, without observing the cause, sees the boulder fall to the ground with a mighty crash. Thus he has no blow coming from outside, which he can seize upon as the cause of the rock's falling. How now shall he explain the boulder's fall to himself?

He has only one analogy to help him. In the case where he himself strains his muscles in order to lift a stone from the ground, he also lacks a palpable external cause for the muscular movement. But here he discovers instead an inner, unobservable cause of the movement: the power of his own will. He knew, here, that he *wanted* to lift the stone and that he *therefore* strained his muscles. Nothing is more natural than that, when he cannot discover an outer cause for an event, he should introduce the thought of a will, connected with the state of affairs, which is the cause of the event.

For example, suppose he shoots with a cross-bow. One time he hits the target at which he is aiming, another time he misses. And yet he has aimed equally well in both cases. There must have been an invisible will-power present here, which brought about success in the one case, failure in the other. He sees lightning and hears thunder. But there is no external cause present to which he can refer the course of events. In the higher regions there must be an invisible will-power, which flings out the lightning and calls forth the thunder. He harrows, ploughs, and sows the ground, and the seed grows up. He does not see the external causes of the growth. In the earth, in the harrowing, in the ploughing, in the sowing there must lie a will-power which works. He sees that the growth of the seed depends upon suitable weather, an alternation of rain and sunshine. He cannot discover any external cause why in one year the weather should be suitable, in another the seed should rot in the field for too much rain, in a third the seed should wither away for lack of moisture. Invisible will-powers must come into play here. Or the earth opens up and belches out fire and brimstone. There must be a will in the underworld which is the cause. A cattle-plague strikes his herds. There must be an invisible, angered will which lies behind this.

He has had fortunate experiences on occasions when he was wearing a certain ring. Then he succeeded in clubbing his enemy to death. But on another occasion he was without the ring and was obliged to make an ignominious flight. Naturally enough he associates the ring with the fortunate experience, so that it becomes a bringer of luck, and keeping it is enough to protect him in the struggle for existence. But on the other hand he does not see any external, palpable connection between the ring and the good fortune. So it becomes evident to him that the same kind of invisible power is at work in the ring as he discovers in himself as will.

Here there is added another factor which confirms him in his belief in the power of the amulet. Specifically, it is doubtless the case that his original faith itself becomes his strength. It is a universal experience that the unshakable confidence that one can do a thing gives one a special ability to carry out the necessary actions. We know how the hypnotist, by instigating the belief that it is impossible to perform a certain action, also actually makes it impossible for the person who is under the power of the suggestion to perform the action. We also know that it is possible by means of suggestion, i.e. by infusing faith, to bring about purely physical changes in the organism which are not under the control of the will—e.g. to raise blisters. Therefore it is entirely certain that the savage's confidence in his fetish actually helps him, and thus his faith in it is strengthened.

So the primitive man is surrounded by invisible will-powers. These have, in fact, become realities for him, inasmuch as events take place for which he cannot discover external causes. Therefore he must resort to the same type of explanation as that which he uses in connection with his own actions, where the cause seems to him to lie in the power of his own invisible will.

In order to understand the situation, it is necessary to pause to consider the consciousness of willing. The famous American psychologist, William James, says that if we observe ourselves in an act of willing, e.g. directing our attention to something, we do not observe anything which constantly recurs except certain sensations of strain and muscular sensations. We do not even require to have an idea of an end aimed at. For example, if I go along a road as a result of an original decision to advance to a certain place, it is by no means necessary for me to have the end continually before my consciousness. My thoughts can be occupied with all kinds of other things, and yet I go straight to the chosen place. The only physical factor which is connected with the action is thus the muscular sensations which I can notice at any time through observing myself. And yet it is quite evident to me that the action depends upon my will. It is therefore obvious that the primary experience of willing must be connected with these sensations.

Now the immediate experience of willing is a consciousness of activity. In this consciousness is to be found, first of all, a con-

H*

ception of myself as the *cause* of an event, or more specifically as the cause of an event in such a way that the event comes from within or *proceeds from* within me. This in turn implies that the event is originally present in me in a different mode from that in which it is present in the real world, and that in its previous existence in me it is the cause of its subsequent appearance in the real world. The effect is present in me beforehand and is thus the cause of its own subsequent appearance in the real world. We describe this state of affairs by saying that the effect is present as the end aimed at.

It is clear that such a conception is absurd from the logical point of view. How can the effect be present before it has itself come into existence? How can the effect exist within the cause itself? This would obliterate the distinction between cause and effect. But with the obliteration of this distinction the idea of the cause-effect relation loses all significance. Thus we are left with the task of explaining the psychological possibility of the logically absurd consciousness of activity. Certainly it is a psychological fact tht we seem to ourselves to be active. Since any original consciousness of activity is a consciousness of myself as cause, we must go back to self-consciousness itself, in order to discover the basis for explaining the consciousness of activity as a psychological fact.

The 'I' has a peculiar double character, which anyone can ascertain by directing his attention to what he means when he says 'I'. On the one hand, he obviously means an object which exists independently of the consciousness of it, thus an objective reality. That I was born at a certain time and that I have continued to live in temporal reality are facts of the same kind as the fact that the sun rises in the morning and sets in the evening. To that extent the 'I' is a part of material reality. And even if, when I think of myself, I think of the psychical aspects of myself, of a continuous series of ideas, feelings, and acts of choice, still all this is nevertheless intimately connected with my bodily existence. From the consciousness of myself as a reality which exists whether I think of it or not, the material aspect is inseparable. The *de facto* unity in the various simultaneous and successive states of consciousness, which each person calls 'I', must necessarily be referred to one's body. So far, then, we have nothing at all to do with a spiritual reality, in so far as one understands by a spiritual reality a reality which itself is not in space.

It is customary to say that consciousness itself is something incorporeal, that it has no magnitude. A feeling of pleasure, for example, cannot be measured by means of a linear measure. However, it is here overlooked that the same holds for any quality whatsoever which is situated in space, if it is considered in itself in abstraction from the space in which it is present. Even the brown colour which characterizes this table, in and of itself, considered only in its qualitative determinateness, is not at all susceptible of measurement, either in length or in area. It is only the space to which it belongs that gives it extension. It is the same with consciousness. In and of itself it has no extension such that, considered in abstraction from the body in which it is present or considered only as a quality, not as a quantum, it would possess extension. Extension accrues to it only through the consideration of the space in which the consciousness is present.

But notice that, on the other hand, I am for myself not only a *de facto* unity in the various states of consciousness which occur objectively in my body. I am also that which is completely inward, or that which exists for itself, which, as such, is not an object which could be conceived as existing independently of the consciousness of the object. I am essentially self-consciousness. That is to say, the consciousness of myself, as an actual I-consciousness, is identical with its own object. This is the same as to say that I, as such, am not at all any kind of object which could be assigned a place in material and temporal reality. Any such assigning presupposes, of course, that the object is conceived as existing independently of the consciousness which apprehends it. But as the completely inward, I am precisely not something which can be conceived as existing independently of the consciousness which apprehends it. The one is merged into the other. Indeed, it can also be said that the 'I', as the completely inward, merges into the consciousness of itself. This consciousness, into which it is merged, is thus itself something which is not capable of being conceived as an object, as existing apart from the consciousness of it, because it is identical with the completely inward 'I'. I, as the completely inward and thus as not capable of being situated in space, am the spiritual 'I'. Consciousness, as an objective *de facto* reality, belongs to a certain body. It is not at all something spiritual. It is spiritual, therefore, only when it is regarded as belonging to me as the completely inward.

Let us now return to what we were discussing earlier, viz. the consciousness of activity which belongs to the primary experience of willing. We remind ourselves that to this consciousness belongs the conception of myself as the cause of something else. And I am the cause of the other in such a way that, in spite of the fact that this thing also makes its appearance in objective reality still it exists previously in me, so that it proceeds from within me, indeed bursts forth from within me. The effect has a double existence. On the one hand, it is an effect, distinct from me as the cause; on the other hand, it is itself the cause and is thus an integral part of myself. It is clear that, in so far as it is included within myself, it does not exist as an objective reality, but rather it remains entirely within myself as the completely inward, as the completely objectless being-for-itself. The consciousness of willing thus must have the same explanation as self-consciousness itself.

But now how can we explain how I can apprehend myself, on the one hand, as an objective reality and thus as in space, and yet at the same time as a non-objectifiable and thus immaterial reality, which is one with the consciousness of itself? As we have seen, it is a logically impossible position to say that the effect could be present in the cause. In the same way, it is also logically impossible that the 'I' should be present in the objective, material reality and be at the same time a completely inward being, raised above everything material—be a spirit. The psychological explanation of this logically impossible conception of the 'I' must lie in the fact that, when I apprehend myself, I join together two functions of the mind, one of which objectifies and the other of which does not. In other words, I join together a consciousness of something objective with a feeling—which by its very nature lacks an object.

It can therefore be said that, on the one hand, I exist for myself in the consciousness of an objective and thus material reality. On the other hand, this real and material self is not presented to me except in connection with a whole complex of feelings: muscular sensations, vital feelings, feelings of good health or ill health, feelings of strain and relaxation. It is to be noted, however, that we could not have these feelings without associating them with our own bodies—the same body as that to which the objective reality belongs which is in question when one calls oneself 'I'. These feelings thus enter into such an intimate association with the consciousness of myself as an objective reality, that the objectless feeling penetrates into the objectifying consciousness and colours it. Hence the object which I apprehend in the consciousness of the objective 'I' also appears to be given in an objectless apprehension, and thus it also becomes one with the apprehension of itself. This impregnation of the consciousness of an object with feelings is the secret of the concept of spirit.

The consciousness of activity is to be explained in the same way. There is bound up with my consciousness of myself as the cause of effects the so-called feeling of power or activity, that is, a muscular sensation or perhaps a peculiar feeling of innervation. Through this association the whole sequence of events, the connection between myself as cause and the effect, becomes something purely inward, something which is not an object and falls not within the world of objective reality but rather within the completely inward something which is the 'I'.

So now the primary consciousness of willing is an active consciousness. As such, it is the consciousness of a certain effect, which proceeds from myself as cause. This 'I' itself acquires thereby a double character. On the one hand, it is a real object in time and space, which exists independently of the consciousness of it. On the other hand, it is something purely inward, which exists only for myself—which is one with the consciousness of itself. Consequently it is not a real object and is not in space. For everything which we associate with space is *eo ipso* something which is objectified, something which is regarded as existing independently of the consciousness of it. In the same way the effect of my own activity has a double character for my consciousness of activity; it is at the same time something objectively real, which stands in a causal relation to myself, and something *in* me, where I myself am something purely inward and immaterial.

We explained this peculiar double character of both the consciousness of willing and the consciousness of activity as follows: In both kinds of consciousness there occurs an impregnation of the idea of objective, and therefore in each case material, relationships, with objectless feelings, which are inseparable from the idea. By this means the object appears as something objective-material, and yet at the same time as something purely inward, which exists only for itself.

Now, then, in order that he might understand those movements of things which he cannot account for by observations of externally operating causes, the primitive transfers to the active object the will which he apprehends in immediate self-consciousness—spirit as *practical spirit*. He cannot explain his own physical activity by means of an impact or a force from without, but rather he uses as the ground of explanation his own will, that inner spiritual power. In the same way he explains the stone's unaccountable fall, the unaccountable variations in the weather, the power of the amulet, etc. as due to a practical spirit which resides in the object and for this or that reason, e.g. out of wrath or of good will, works for his harm or his benefit.

(1) But it is to be observed that he transfers such a practical spirit also to his fellow-men. When he sees his enemy lift up his club to strike, the same spiritual power is active here as when he himself does this. However, there is, in the first instance, a specific difference between one man and another. One man can use only ordinary natural implements—his arms, hands, and legs, an axe, a crossbow, a club, etc.—in order to bring about external effects. But another man can bring about external effects without these implements, simply through the spiritual power of his will. The one man is equipped with the power to conjure, and thus to bring about effects without touching the object. The other lacks this power. The stronger and more preponderant his magical power is, the more profitable a person can be for the community to which he belongs and the more dangerous he becomes for his enemies.

As Frazer has shown in *The Golden Bough*, kings were originally magicians. As such they were understood to employ magic to work for the advantage of the community to which they belonged. This they did, for example, through the power to call down rain or, as with the Romans, through the ability to perform auspices correctly, i.e. the ability to obtain accurate celestial signs which indicated the success or failure of a contemplated undertaking. It is obvious that such persons would be especially suited to lead the community to prosperity.

It is to be noted that among the Romans there was a phrase which occurred very commonly: one fights *sub imperio auspicioque*. Empire, as the power of command in war, was so intimately bound up with the magical power of auspices, that the power of command or empire was identified with the ability to discern the omens of war. With the rise of the republic the power of auspices was transferred, in a mysterious way, to the consuls and other high officials, and a dreadful commotion was created if someone was made consul against the divine ordinance, i.e. in such a way that the power of auspices was not actually transferred to him. This, it was thought, could lead to ruin. For it was maintained among the Romans, as among other primitive peoples, that magic is dangerous when attempted by one who lacks the power of magic. Therefore such a consul had to resign his office, even in a ceremonious fashion with magical power, in order to purge himself completely from all connection with it.

One had to consecrate (*dicare*) the consul to his office. By this means he came into an intimate relationship to the office and to the auspices. If, now, he had been improperly consecrated to his office, his auspices would be injurious to the state. In order that the auspices should not misguide the state, attached as they were to a person who was not competent to use them, this person had to cut himself free, through a special magical counteraction, from all connection with the office to which the auspices belonged.[1] Among the Greeks the magical power with which the kings were endowed was characterized as a *holy* power, i.e. a power working in a mysterious way for good as well as for evil or as a power to bring good, but also as dangerous for one who in any way set himself up against the king.

(2) Now these magicians or kings undoubtedly had a divine character, in so far as that was possible for man, and this divine character lay in the immeasurably great power in such a man's spirit.[2] But furthermore, there are also other objects, which appear to be endowed with spirits which are supernaturally powerful by comparison with the ordinary man. Father Zeus, the god who is particularly Indo-European, is nothing but the daylight viewed as the bearer of a spirit which possesses a wonderful power of procreation, generating and maintaining life, and also the power to bring ruin upon the living. He has his female counterpart in Mother Earth, who, when fertilized by Father Zeus, gives birth to all living things and nourishes them, but also finally draws them back into

[1] This is the meaning of *abdicare*, which still remains among us in the ordinary expression, 'to abdicate'. *Dicare* means, properly, to speak in such a way that the speaking has a mysterious, magical power, so as to bring about a positive effect, thus to consecrate someone to something, particularly to a god. The opposite is *abdicare*.

[2] Cf. our expression: king by the grace of God and the so-called apostolic succession through the laying on of hands ever since Peter.

herself. They both belong together as spirits with a material substratum.

However, one may not therefore suppose that they originally were conceived anthropomorphically. It is a highly significant fact that images of the gods in human form belong to a later period in the history of Greek religion. In Rome the image in human likeness first came in through Greek influences. Vesta, the bearer of the holy fire, which, as is well known, could not be allowed to go out on the hearth of the state, was never actually conceived anthropomorphically. She was and remained the round hearth. All that was thought to be endowed with superhuman power was the mystical spiritual power, the power of the will in man, which was transferred to the object.

## 4. CERTAIN PHENOMENA IN THE HISTORY OF RELIGION AND THE ASCRIPTION OF SPIRITS TO OBJECTS

Various significant phenomena in the history of religion can be explained through this ascription of spirits to the special objects endowed with mystic power.

Spirit, as such, is immaterial. Therefore even if it is also present in a certain space which is its body, it is not for that reason bound to that body. It can be present in several bodies at the same time. This possibility for the spirit to extend itself, by reason of its being in principle detached from the body, explains how the various local cults are possible, in spite of the consciousness that God is one. It is a well-known fact that there were many gods named Zeus in Greece. The original, heavenly Zeus was broken up into different spiritual forces, which constituted the basis for the particular functions assigned to the original Zeus—Zeus the giver of victory, Zeus the progenitor, Zeus the bringer of curses. But in addition the very *same* high spirit could dwell in different altars, temples, and other objects consecrated to the god. Now this had special significance in that, through consecrating an altar or a temple here or there, one could draw unto oneself the spiritual power of the heavenly Zeus and thus also, through suitable means, lead him to work in the interests of the place in which he was located.

But now it should be observed also that the transition from polytheism to monotheism is inseparably connected with this belief in the unity of spirit which is yet present in different places. (1) In the first place, it is to be noticed that monotheism is by no means the same as the acceptance of God as a pure spirit. For I have already shown that the acceptance of God as pure spirit— i.e. to use the phraseology of Boström, as pure self-consciousness (a being which is one with its own consciousness, the purely inward)—causes God to be reduced to man's consciousness of him. Indeed, he is not even given in the consciousness of anything. For all consciousness of something as real involves one's conceiving it as existing independently of the consciousness itself. But God, as spirit, cannot be apprehended in such a way; rather he exists only in feeling, which is, in its very nature, objectless, as being free from all elements of conception—he exists only in ecstatic feeling, in which even the consciousness of one's own existence as something objective in space and time is abolished. In monotheism, however, God is a transcendent, and thus an objective, reality. Therefore he is also in space. However, this space is not a specific, limited space, or many spaces separated from one another, but it is rather the space of the world itself.

(2) In the second place, for monotheistic religion God is also wholly present in every part of space. And that is possible for him because he is at the same time a spirit independent of space. Just as Zeus, as one and the same spirit, can be both in this temple and in that temple and can work in both places, so can the one almighty God, inasmuch as he is a spirit, be wholly present in every particle of the universe. God is in the movement of the stars, he is in all living things as their sustaining power, he is also in the power of my own spirit. This is by no means the same as pantheism. For according to pantheism God is resolved into the universe itself. But the God who exists in monotheistic religion is certainly in the universe, while he is yet, as spirit, a person in himself, separated from all that can be called materiality. He has the same double nature that the 'I' has for immediate self-consciousness. The 'I' is completely inward, but yet it is at the same time something objective, present in space and time.

From the preceding it follows that there is certainly no yawning gulf separating polytheism and monotheism. In both cases the deity is both a spirit in himself and a being present in space. But in the one case he is only in a specific space or several specific spaces, and this makes him limited both in power and in interest. Rome's

*Jupiter optimus et maximus* on the Capitol does not have any greater power than this, that he is able to work for the prosperity of Rome —or for its ruin, if he becomes angered. The rural *lares*, belonging to the various country estates, can be helpful or harmful only to the fields which belong to those estates, etc. In monotheistic religion the deity is not limited to a specific area or specific areas, but he is wholly present everywhere. This is possible for him because he is a spirit. But due to his independence of any specific area, he is almighty and all-inclusive in his interests. The gulf between polytheism and monotheism is so slight that the latter is invariably coloured or modified by the former. The Allah of the Mohammedans is, of course, the one God, i.e. the only power endowed with supernatural strength; but it is obvious that he is originally nothing but the various Arabian local gods, fused into one.

In Christianity the one all-embracing God has his special revelation in Christ—a man, who lived and died in a specific time and in a specific place. This involves, of course, a distinction between the different spirits which one has in mind. But when it is a question of a relationship between spirits, difference does not mean the same as it does in the natural sphere. We have seen that one and the same Zeus-spirit can be present in different images of Zeus, and thus that the same Zeus-spirit has various bodies, and we have seen further that different Zeus-spirits, distinguished through their particular functions, can exist together with one another without their unity being lost. In the same way the Almighty God also can exist together with a human god without their spiritual unity being annulled.

In fact, the way matters stand, various spirits, as in themselves immaterial, could not be thought of as co-existent unless the material substratum separated them. For in reality spirit as such dissolves into mere being-for-itself, in virtue of being one with the consciousness of itself and being completely inward. And for this reason all spirits as such are clearly identical. Consequently we find that the Swedisn philosopher Boström, who wants to pursue to the end the concept of spirit as completely separated from the material, can conceive a distinction between God and the spirits which are included within him—God's ideas—only by introducing distinctions of quantity. The various spirits do not have the same original comprehensiveness of content in their consciousnesses.

But, of course, the concept of magnitude is borrowed from the material sphere.

The Christian doctrine of the trinity is therefore not at all extraordinary. It gives expression to something which is essential for all religions, namely, on the one hand, the separation of the various spirits from one another in respect of their material substratum and, on the other hand, their unification in respect of their spiritual nature. Thus in so far as the deity has in general a transcendent character, genuine religion is always at the same time spiritual and natural. On the one hand, there is no god—even if the god is a stone or an amulet—in which a spirit does not reside, transferred to the object from our own consciousness of willing. On the other hand, there is no religion—in which God is a reality outside the observer—which is so spiritualized that God does not have a material substratum.

This unification of spirit and body in the deity makes possible the most remarkable combinations. It is, of course, a universally recognized fact that primitive man believes that by consuming the totem-animal, whose spirit is the power which upholds the society, he also gains a share of the power of that spirit. The common sacramental meals transfer the power of the spirit of the society to the various members of the society, because the spirit lives in the body of the animal. The various sacramental meals described in Homer, e.g. the hecatombs offered to Zeus, in which one eats of the slain oxen while at the same time separating out a portion for the offering to Zeus, are especially significant. In the sacrificial animal, which must be healthy and uninjured, the Zeus-spirit lives. By appropriating the flesh one incorporates into oneself, to a certain degree, the Zeus-spirit, and this is possible because there is no absolute distinction between the spirits. But on the other hand, the Zeus-spirit itself loses something of its own power through the sacramental eating. This power must be restored if one does not wish to run the risk of encountering one's own destruction. Therefore an offering is brought to Zeus of the same material as that through which one gained a share of the power for one self. The animal's spirit-power is divided between the Zeus-spirit himself and the men who eat it.

We know well, of course, the Christian doctrine of the holy communion, as it developed during the Middle Ages. According to this doctrine one eats Christ's body and drinks his blood in the host and the wine. *Hostia* means slain sacrifice or sacrificial animal. The priest who bears the host can be regarded, on the Catholic view, as bearing the God-Christ himself. God, or Christ's own spirit, thus lives in the host, and one appropriates it to himself by eating. Compare with this the Dionysian orgies on Mount Parnassus. By eating of the raw flesh the participants in the procession of Dionysius, the *bacchantes*, come to be be-souled with Dionysius' own spirit. Their own human spirit comes out of the body (in an ecstatic flight) and instead Dionysius moves in. Thereby the human participants acquire divine powers, come into a land which flows with wine and honey, but are also seized by a holy madness.

However, as Gillis Wetter has shown in his book, *Altchristliche Liturgien* (1921-22), the primitive Christian meal of holy communion did not originally have this significance, viz. that one ate Christ's body and drank his blood. Instead, it had the character of a commemorative meal, in which Christ's death and resurrection were represented, but also realized anew through representative magic. Through the very death and resurrection of Christ *in the assembled congregation* there was transferred to the congregation the spiritual power which manifested itself there. The congregation itself died and rose again with Jesus. Compare the representation of Dionysius' death and resurrection in the Triennial Mysteries which was originally vegetation-magic, but later also acquired significance as bringing salvation to man. Compare also the contemplation of Persephone's migrations from the earth to the underworld and back again, which represented the death and the resurrection of vegetation and therefore acted as vegetation-magic, but eventually acquired significance on the human level through giving man a hope for a blessed life. Christian martyrdom itself had the same significance. With the martyr Christ once again died and rose again. Therefore the martyr-death gave the martyr a share in Christ's eternal life.[1]

So then the divine spirit, as active in the sensible world, is nothing but our own will, transferred to certain external phenomena, which we regard as the cause of those effects which we can-

---

[1] Broad's translation, printed in *Theoria*, Vol. 14, 1948 here inserts a sentence not found in the Swedish edition: 'There is a story in old Christian literature, that when St Peter was on his way to Rome, where he was to suffer martyrdom, he met his Lord and Master, who asked: "Quo vadis?" "I go", he answered, "to die along with my Lord" '. (Tr.)

not comprehend in any other way. Thus the will is transferred, for example, to the stone endowed with unusual power, to the holy animal as embodying in itself the very growth and strength of the society, to the increase of herds of livestock, to the fruitfulness of the soil, to certain men as empowered to perform wonders and signs, and finally to the whole universe as itself working life and death, good or evil.

It is also obvious, now, how this transfer comes about. I experience a feeling of power when I believe that I myself am the cause of certain effects—of a movement of an arm or a leg, of a thought, of an act of remembering—without the cause appearing, however, in an external mode in connection with the effect. I also experience this feeling of power, which is the ground of the consciousness of willing, when I think of certain external phenomena as the causes of certain effects, without the causal connection appearing in the external world. But because I am accustomed to having a feeling of power when I myself am the cause of some effect without there being any observable relationship between the effect and its cause, I experience the same feeling of power when I apprehend an external phenomenon which I believe to be the cause of a certain effect without the cause being visibly linked to the effect. When I experience an external phenomenon as causing effects in the same manner as I do myself, the feeling of power, so familiar to us from its association with our own actions, recurs, and I am led to believe that the external phenomenon is a practical spirit of the same sort as my own, i..e something enclosed within itself, which is identical with its own consciousness of itself. That is to say, I unconditionally transfer my own feelings of power from myself to the external phenomenon which I take to be the cause of certain effects. Thus the external phenomenon acquires the same spiritual character as that which I have myself. Its consciousness of itself as a cause becomes for me an objectless feeling, and so it becomes the completely inward, enclosed within itself.

The belief in the divine spirit in the stone, in the animal, in the man, or in the universe, thus has its foundation in the muscular sensations and feelings of innervation which we experience through force of habit in the moment when we think these objects to be the causes of certain effects in the same way as we ourselves are unobservable causes of the movement of our arms, etc. The belief in the divine spirit as will has its ground in these muscular sensations or feelings of innervation as transferred to the phenomena themselves.

## 5. THE CONCEPT OF GOD IN SPIRITUAL RELIGION

But the divine spirit, existing purely for itself, is by no means just a spirit in the sense of a will, conceived on analogy with our own selves. It also has other equally important attributes which betoken its property of being something purely inward.

### The Holiness of God

We are thus led to a consideration of the significance of the *holiness* of the divine spirit. 'Holy, holy, holy is the Lord', our church ritual begins. It is as though by these words we consecrated the worship of God, by creating the impression that something absolutely worthy of reverence, before which we must bow ourselves in fear and trembling, is present.

But what is holiness? That which is most prominent in the Jewish, as in the Greek and the Roman, concept of holiness is the property of taboo. What belongs to the deity is dangerous to handle or to approach without observing all kinds of special precautions. The Holy of Holies in the Jewish temple was the place into which no other person but the high priest might enter. The holiest temple in Greece was the one where the most terrible perdition was brought down upon the one who entered it without fulfilling special conditions, and above all upon the one who violated it. For this reason those who sought safety and fled to a temple especially renowned for its holiness could be secure. We employ the term 'sacrilege' even to this day to denote an action which is particularly outrageous and one which—as used to be the case—involves a particularly severe punishment.

Certainly the sacrificial animal was holy also, even though it could be eaten: thence come the words *sacramentum* and *sacrificium*. But it was also linked with a special danger which hung over one who consumed it without observing the proper ceremonial forms. One can eat and drink to one's own destruction. And it is to be noticed that, as far as we can judge, it was originally held that one actually committed a crime when one slew the holy sacrificial animal. In the very ancient Athenian Diipolia there occurs a ceremony which suggests this. After the sacrificial animal has been slain, the sacrificing priest flees and the sacrificial axe is cast into the sea as something accursed. This is explained in the ancient myths as follows: The god is angered by the slaying of the animal in which his own spirit dwelled—the holy animal. To atone for this crime, in which the whole community was involved, the priest, horrified by his deed, must be seized and held accountable for the crime. However, he is acquitted by passing the guilt on to the one who handed him the sacrificial axe. This one is acquitted in turn by casting the blame upon the axe itself. This definitely shows that it is a question of transferring the curse, which should properly fall upon the priest, to the axe, which was permitted to serve as a scape-goat. By casting out the accursed axe one set himself free from the guilt, which otherwise, through the sacrificing priest, would fall upon the whole community.

We are all acquainted with the way in which, when the plebian tribunate was to be introduced, the Roman 'plebs' demanded that the tribunes should be declared sacrosanct. By this sacrosanctity, that is, by the holiness transferred to them, they became inviolable, inasmuch as it was dangerous to attack what was holy. Even today in the talk about the holiness and inviolability of the laws there lies this taboo. To the degree that God himself becomes the bearer of the moral and juridical law, this holiness comes to include his being a mighty avenger, even to he third and fourth generations, upon those who transgress his commandment.

However, we have next to inquire whether or not holiness means only the *objective* property of fearfulness, in the sense that certain actions which affect the god become the objects of his irresistible vengeance. But one needs only to observe the god's necessary connection with the particular men and the particular community whose God he is and who are especially concerned, by means of the cult, to avert his fearful wrath. For them, of course, it is natural that his fearfulness should especially concern them. For them God is *terrible*. But this also makes it clear that they cannot remain as emotionless spectators of him. They must be seized by fear and trembling in the face of this mysterious power, upon which their entire well-being depends. So holiness, regarded as God's fearfulness, not only means the *objective* circumstance that he has the power to take a terrible revenge on the man or the community to which he belongs. Holiness also necessarily gives expression to the feelings of trembling and fear on the part of the men who belong to the god. The word 'holiness' is not merely the name for a conceptualized object, but it is also, in immediate connection with the object, a reflexive expression for a feeling—jut as the words, 'Oh dear!' or 'Alas!' are reflections of feelings, or the words 'What?' and 'Who?' are expressions of a feeling of wanting to know something

It is also obvious, of course, that even in the non-religious sense, the attribute of fearfulness is not merely a name for an objective quality in the object. It is impossible to really find an ordinary man fearful without at the same time being gripped by dread before him. How much more, then, must not fearfulness, when ascribed to a god who has power to destroy me utterly—i.e. holiness —involve a trembling before him on the part of the person who ascribes that quality to him. 'Holy, holy, holy is the Lord!' These ritual-words are obviously intended not merely to assert something objectively about the Lord, but also to arouse those feelings, for which holiness is the proper expression.

It is obvious that when one seeks to explain what it is for God to be holy, one cannot do so without taking into consideration the objectless feeling. This is so inasmuch as holiness *both* signifies a conceptualized objective attribute of the deity *and* also—as a pure reflection of our feelings—is something which we actually bestow upon the deity. God's holiness is not merely something to be thought about, in the way in which one is thinking when one says of a triangle that the two sides taken together are greater than the third; rather it is something which must be felt. He who without fear and trembling seeks to grasp God's holiness does not understand him.

Thus we have here again what we have already pointed out as being so significant for the concept of the 'I', namely the impregnation of the idea with a feeling so intimately bound up with it that when I seek to explain what the conceptualized object is, I cannot avoid taking into consideration the feeling. But this implies that the object itself is present in my own feeling. This in turn implies that the object is one with myself as experiencing it. For the feeling as such, in abstraction from the idea—to which alone the apprehension of an object pertains—is altogether without any object. God's holiness as a reflection of feeling necessarily gives rise to the awareness that he is present in my own inner being. But since he must be grasped at the same time as something objective, he necessarily becomes, as the holy one, both transcendent and immanent at the same time. As immanent within me, he is a spirit; as transcendent, the spirit is yet at the same time something material.

Something should be added here in order to avoid misunderstanding. One might say that a man can also find a roaring wild beast fearful, and yet the consequence of this feeling is not that he considers the wild beast to be a spirit present within himself. But there is a yawning gulf between the significance of the fearfulness of the roaring wild beast and the holiness of God. One can escape from the former by rendering the animal harmless or by fleeing. Consequently the fear of the animal does not have an absolute character, it is not indissolubly linked with the consciousness of the animal. The holy God, however, is something entirely different. His wrath is inescapable. Even if I hid myself in the bowels of the earth, if I gathered all the military power of the world around me to protect myself against that wrath, I should still be powerless to resist the wrath of God. He would be mighty to strike me just the same. Consequently here the feeling of dread is unconditional, indissolubly connected with the idea of God as holy. He cannot be apprehended as real without one's being seized by trembling. It is certainly true that, by means of certain types of conduct towards him, God can be appeased. The propitiation of the divine wrath is, of course, an essential part of the purpose of the cult. But this does not in any way signify any limitation in his fearful power. If he wished he *could* cast me down to burn in the flames of hell or give me up to be consumed by worms. I am still, in any case, at the mercy of his grace or displeasure.

In this connection, however, the following should be noticed. Due to its character of being, from one point of view, only a reflection of feeling, holiness is impossible to comprehend, to conceptualize. This is so for the reason that every concept, as such, has an objective meaning. But holiness, from one point of view, lacks precisely an objective meaning. Holiness is without meaning apart from the experience of the religious feeling of dread for which it is the expression. But it is impossible to think by means of feelings, because the feeling has precisely the singular characteristic that in itself it is not a consciousness of something objective. A feeling of joy or of fear cannot possibly be an awareness of something which I apprehend as existing independently of consciousness. God's holiness does not mean an actual property which he possesses. For the psychological condition which lies behind the word is not only an apprehension of something, but it is also a feeling. In order actually to possess the psychological condition of which the word is the expression, one must oneself possess the religious feeling which belongs to it. For this reason the deity appears as the completely incomprehensible. He himself is given only in a religious experience, whose content cannot possibly be conceptualized because this content lacks objectivity.

We have herewith come upon the scent of the deepest meaning of God's spirituality. He exists in our religious feeling, which in itself is objectless, particularly in the feeling of trembling before him. To that extent he is something purely inward, which cannot be grasped by objectifying thought. This is also the mystical, which Otto, in his book *The Idea of the Holy*, calls the irrational element in every religion. However, it follows from what has been said that the spiritualization of God in such a manner that he should actually *exist* in himself, as a spirit given in our feeling, is only a self-deception, a confusion of feeling and the consciousness of something objective. For it is completely absurd that anything should *actually* be given in *feeling* itself, inasmuch as feeling, by its very nature, cannot be a consciousness of something real.

We have previously maintained, however, that if the deity is not objectified in some way (and thus materialized), but is regarded as given exclusively in feeling, then neither is he something active in the sensible world, which through its objective power can assist man to realize his purposes which belong to that world. In that case the whole of religion dissolves into a completely world-renouncing experience of absolute blessedness, the feeling of peace which follows upon the death of all desire, the death of all valuational feelings pertaining to the natural life.

However, it is to be emphasized, on the other hand, that even in ordinary religion, which is bound up with the sensible world, the objectification of the deity, which is always necessary, can be more or less put aside for the sake of the feeling-elements. The result is that mysticism, irrationalism, is thrown into more or less strong relief. Perhaps this state of affairs can be made clear in the best possible way by a consideration of the religious feeling of trembling, to which the word 'holiness' gives expression. It is to be observed that we have to do here with a feeling which is irrational, in the sense that it presents itself without a reasonable ground, i.e. without a clear consciousness that the object is dangerous and of the way in which it is dangerous. Certainly I fear the wild beast, which rushes at me with a roar, because I know that it is able to crush me in its jaws. But I am also seized by trembling before the great and the mighty, without having to know that some evil or other threatens me from it. The wildness of the primeval forests, the loneliness of the desert, the deep darkness of the night can cause us to tremble and shudder, without our having any reasonable cause for fearing the sheer silence. However, since we are accustomed to feeling fear in the same way in the presence of some definite object which we regard as strong enough to injure us, we create for ourselves, in such cases, an object, to which we ascribe the property of fearfulness, in the sense that it actually threatens us with destruction. The primeval forest, the desert, the silence, the night, before which we tremble, are endowed with psychical properties. There is a god there, who can in wrath utterly destroy us.

Note, however, the enormous difference between the kind of deity which grows up out of our own natural fears and such gods as we fear because we have experienced, or believe we have experienced, their dangerousness. The Zeus of the thunder and lightning, Mother Earth, who nourishes, but also draws to herself all living things, are for us something dangerous, because we have often experienced how they can harm us. For this reason such a god acquires a clear, objective meaning. From the heavenly Zeus, when provoked to wrath, comes the deadly lightning. From the earth comes, finally, the mouldering into death. But the forest, the desert, the silence, and the night do not threaten us with any actions which are clearly understandable. Therefore these gods are dangerous, without the danger acquiring a clear meaning. The way in which they work is indeterminate and indeterminable. The objective character of these gods, consequently, recedes into the background, and one has only the indeterminate idea of something which threatens him. The mystical, irrational aspect comes into the foreground. The great Pan in the deeps of the forests is, objectively regarded, essentially nothing but a feeble attempt of primitive man to construct the object, which arouses his fear, into something which actually threatens him. In this one gets no farther than to the belief that there exists something which threatens him, but what this thing is and how it works one cannot explain. Religion is essentially merely feeling, nothing more.

## The Righteousness of God

However, it is not only holiness as an attribute of the deity which gives expression to a feeling which is unconditionally combined with the idea of the deity and which thus gives rise to the view that the deity is present in the feeling itself. The same is true also of the apprehension of the deity as the right itself. The development here is readily discernible. The deity is conceived as a law-giver. Both moral and juridical rules are referred in primitive societies to a particular communal deity, who is believed to have issued them. It is necessary, in order to heighten respect for the law, that the command be referred to the being assumed to be the highest power in the community. Through this means these commands begin to be conceived as right in themselves, whereupon their inner rightness is transferred to the deity himself. This divine will is regarded as issuing commands on the ground of their rightness or justice, and by this it is signified that the divine will is necessarily, by its own nature, determined by that which is right in itself. Thereby that which is right in itself becomes one with the divine essence, which necessarily determines God's will—or, as it is also expressed, one with the divine reason, since God is determined by reason. Such is the view found in Thomas Aquinas.

But if the deity himself is the right, i.e. justice itself, then he is also apprehended as presented in a feeling, i.e. he is spiritualized. For rightness is, as such, not an objective attribute which may be placed alongside of properties like form, size, etc., which may be presented to a disinterested observing subject. For me, as a disinterested observer of the real, there is neither right nor wrong, but only *de facto* feelings of rightness, *de facto* valuational feelings. That which is represented as right loses all meaning if it does not in some way hold sway in my will and exert pressure on it in the form of a feeling of obligation. For him who lacks a feeling of obligation, therefore, right and wrong are without any meaning. Now in so far as God is conceived as one with the right, it is presupposed that there is bound up with the idea of the divine being a feeling of obligation, which inclines one in the direction of the kind of action which God necessarily, by reason of his nature, approves. Only as an expression for this feeling of obligation as present in the individual does justice or righteousness become meaningful as an attribute ascribed to the deity.

A consequence of such an attribute of feeling, however, is the spiritualization of God. In so far as righteousness must be regarded as present only in an objectless feeling, the deity himself, *as one*, is also presented only in an objectless feeling. He is thus one with his own consciousness, existing in and for himself and thus raised up over all material reality. For material reality, as such, is distinguished from the consciousness of it and must always be conceived as existing independently of whether or not it is an object of consciousness. Inasmuch as God is one with the consciousness to which he is presented, and thus is something spiritual, he is also purely inward with reference to the individual man who is conscious of him. He exists *within* me, not outside of me. It is also obvious that in proportion as the deity is spiritualized in this way, as being one with the right, the action by means of which I come into the enjoyment of God's favour is not an external, physical sacrificial offering, but an internal one. To the extent to which the feeling of obligation is strong enough in me, the deity is also present within me and gives me a share in his own goodness.

### The Goodness of God

Thus righteousness is an attribute, ascribed to God, which is based on feeling. But besides this it is to be observed further that God is characterized also as *summum bonum*—the highest good. The development of this attribute is now as easy to establish as was the development of the attribute of righteousness. The deity is to be viewed not only as fearful, but also as the giver of good—to those, that is, who enter into the right relationship to him. Among the Greeks the highest deity is at the same time the giver of good and the giver of evil, the bringer of life and of death. Zeus, the father who nourishes all things, is at the same time Zeus, the one who casts down the lightning. Naturally which side of his nature he turns towards the individual or the state depends, in the first instance, on their behaviour towards him. The cult exists, of course, in order to appease the god's wrath or to make him positively gracious. But because the deity himself lives in indestructible blessedness, whether God brings life or death, it is also possible for me to infuse that eternal life and blessedness into myself by transferring his spirit into mine. This happens through the mysteries. The Greek mysteries were cult-acts, by which the deity himself both was infused into the human soul and poured his own life-force into it. This is possible, of course, inasmuch as the deity is spiritual. As spiritual the deity himself can be present in my own spirit and at the same time can suppress it, thereby also bringing me life and blessedness.

In Christianity the great mystery is that of man's conversion and regeneration through Christ. Among the Greeks regeneration was bound up with the external observation of Dionysius' dying and rising again, or of Demeter-Persephone's descending into the underworld and returning again, so that the god himself, through the observation, penetrated into the soul and raised it up to life and blessedness. In Christianity the mystical regeneration is bound up with the faith in the resurrection of Christ from the dead. When that faith takes hold of a man, so that he lives with Christ in his inward being, Christ himself enters into the man's spirit and raises it up to his own life of victory over death and evil and to his own blessedness. 'I live, yet not I, but Christ lives in me', is the confession of the Pauline Christian. And because Christ is a spirit, he can enter into the human spirit and from within raise man up over the power of death and of evil.

But in this way the god is no longer a giver of the good, as if the good were something external to him, which was merely imparted from without, but rather he *is* in himself the good, indeed, even the highest good. Merely feeling the presence of the god in my own spirit in itself bestows eternal blessedness, apart from the observable advantages which this may secure for me. And certainly this blessedness, which comes with the feeling of his presence, is the highest blessedness.

What we have just said also indicates the import of the divine attribute, *summum bonum*. Just as the right lacks all meaning apart from a feeling of obligation directed towards that which is conceived as right, so too the good lacks all meaning apart from a feeling of desire, a feeling of delight, in connection with the idea of the reality of that which is characterized as good. Take away this desire and the good itself is without all meaning. But if feeling God's presence within me, as such, bestows the greatest joy, then it is also clear that I must experience the greatest joy in connection with the idea of his actual presence within me. That his presence within me is the highest good is thus only an expression of the overwhelming joy which one experiences in connection with the idea of the reality of his presence. By this it is also affirmed that the deity, as the highest good, must be conceived as presented in the believer's own feeling, in the feeling which is unconditionally associated with the idea of his actual presence, and that the divine, as the highest good, is something spiritual.

From this it is clear that no matter how much the deity may be conceived as something objective and thus material, he is yet spiritualized in proportion as he is conceived as the right and as the highest good. For these attributes are nothing but expressions of feeling, and for this reason the spiritual character of the deity is evident in them. Note that as the conception of the deity as the right implies that one can apparently make the god kindly disposed towards him only by virtue of the disposition of his soul, through the strength of the feeling of obligation in him, and not by means of external actions. So also the conception of him, in his presence within, as the highest good implies that we can make the god kindly disposed towards us only by actually receiving him as present within ourselves. The cult then becomes only a means to the captivation of the soul by the deity. External actions by themselves cannot make God kindly disposed towards us. For as the highest good, he is a spirit and cannot be influenced by external actions. It is the soul's captivation by him which alone can give us a share in that good which he has to bestow. The central point lies in the mystery of conversion, of birth into a new life.

We might say that Christianity is a spiritual religion in so far as it actually locates the central point in God's being the right and the highest good. But this holds only relatively speaking. For unless the deity is at the same time conceived as transcendent, there is nothing to which the attributes of justice and highest goodness can be attached. For these attributes are mere expressions of feeling. But the feelings in question themselves presuppose for their occurrence the conception of something independent of our own consciousness, to which the feelings are attached. But this presents us with both the necessary materiality of the god and at the same time his ineluctable spirituality.

But notice that for the Pauline Christian the power of conversion does not come from the man himself, but rather from the divine being as something outside him. But more specifically, it is Christ, the one who is risen from the dead, who takes possession of man's soul. Man himself lacks the power in himself to bring about conversion. In fact it is only this faith in the risen Christ, as such a power for man, that has the instigating capacity to stimulate such a heightening of the vitality of the soul that one senses that one is experiencing an altogether unique blessedness, far beyond all other joys. Take away this faith in a power outside myself and the very possibility of the so-called new birth disappears.

## The Philosophic Concept of God as Absolute

This brings us to the tendency, which repeatedly manifests itself in the history of philosophy, to conceive God, in the Christian sense, as one with the philosophical concept of the Absolute, i.e. pure, immaterial, and timeless Being, as the only true reality, in relation to which everything else lacks reality. This all-comprehending pure Being, which can have no other reality alongside itself, is now not only the highest good, but also the good as such, alongside which no other good can exist. It is to be observed that this sort of view begins already with the Alexandrian church fathers, Clement and Origen. In Augustine it is fully developed in his identification of God with *verum, unum, et bonum*. The view is common also during the Middle Ages, under the influence of Neo-platonism.

How do matters actually stand with this philosophical Absolute? It is supposed to be reality as such, and thus the all-comprehending reality—the *ens realissimum*, which as such exists in itself, It is obvious that this pure Being lacks all determinateness. For in so far as one ascribes to it any other attribute than that of being, one delimits it as over against some other being. But then it is no longer the all-comprehending Being. Therefore in order for the concept to arise, an abstraction from every determinate being is required. Now this abstraction involves a *subjective* disregarding of determinate being, in the sense that one is not thinking at the moment of any determinate being. But in addition, what is required in order for the concept of pure Being to be actually possible is the sort of abstraction from determinate being which has *objective* significance—that is, an abstraction by which determinate being, as determinate, is declared to be nothingness. The belief in the non-being of the reality presented to us is the presupposition of the acceptance of absolute Being. But what help is it to stop *thinking* of the reality presented to me if I yet assume its existence as soon as I actually begin to direct my attention to it? The Absolute as the all-comprehending pure Being would, in that case, of course, disappear in the very moment that I was attentive to the reality presented to me. The belief in the Absolute would only be possible in a certain moment of absent-mindedness and would disappear as soon as the absent-mindedness disappeared.

But let us see, now, how the view which we have been representing, which regards the given as a mere appearance, an illusion, can serve to yield the concept of the Absolute. It certainly appears as if, on such a view, nothing else would remain but the abstract predicate 'being', without anything to which being could be ascribed. And yet one would believe that he had gained possession of that which is real without qualification.

In order to understand what has just been said, one must take into consideration the nature of the feeling of theoretical certainty. Certainty customarily makes its appearance at the moment when one has received an answer to a question, i.e. it arises in contrast to the theoretical aspiration for knowledge. When that aspiration has been satisfied and a feeling of repose takes its place, I feel certainty. Now, however, the theoretical aspiration, the raising of questions, never dies out as long as it directs itself to that which is given in the natural world. It never dies out as long as one continues to think at all. The answering of one question leads to the raising of a new one, and since the one question is really intimately bound up with the other, the theoretical aspiration is, in fact, never fully satisfied on any point. This means that complete certainty on any point is not possible, as long as one continues to move generally within the sphere of the reality presented to us. But as soon as this reality, in its determinateness, appears as a mere illusion, the theoretical aspiration ceases completely. And since certainty is the state of feeling which makes its appearance when this aspiration is, relatively speaking, satisfied, it comes about that, through the complete annihilation of that same aspiration, *absolute* certainty makes its appearance as a theoretical state of feeling. The death of theoretical aspiration becomes the birth of complete certainty.

Now, however, in all other cases the feeling of certainty is connected with the consciousness of the real. The result is that in the state of absolute certainty—which yet has its necessary condition in the fact that I am no longer visualizing any deter-

I

minate reality—I actually believe myself to be in possession of a complete knowledge of reality. This means that pure Being—which is properly nothing but the word 'being' when there is nothing real before the mind—comes to stand for the total reality. I believe that I am viewing reality in all its completeness, although actually I am viewing nothing at all. This is the so-called absolute Being, which actually has no other psychological foundation than the belief that a cognition must be at hand, even though I have nothing before myself in consciousness—a belief occasioned by the fact that the same feeling of certainty is present as is connected in other cases with cognition.

On the other hand, it is possible to explain along the same lines the belief that in the Absolute I possess absolute value, value as such. We have seen how the theoretical avowal of the nothingness of the sensible world is a condition for my achieving in my mind the state of absolute certainty, in which I believe myself to possess knowledge of something, even though I have nothing before my consciousness. Parallel with the death of the theoretical aspiration runs the death of the practical aspiration. It is natural, as Plato says, that he who has had his eyes opened to the fact that this world is a mere illusion must also become indifferent in his mind to all that pertains to it. He can no longer experience any pleasure or displeasure in connection with that which is present to the senses. Thus he finds nothing to strive after. He dies to the world practically, just as he dies to it theoretically.

Usually, of course, the relative repose and cessation of practical aspiration carry with them a state of relative joy, inasmuch as they involve a relative satisfaction of aspiration. It is thus readily understandable that the complete death of the practical aspiration —the complete repose in the soul—should carry with it a state of unmixed joy. This joy is the Neo-platonic ecstasy, the Pauline ascent to the seventh heaven. Here we have, then, a state of feeling which answers to the theoretical state of absolute certainty, a feeling of blessedness, without any object to which the feeling is attached. But since the feeling of joy finds expression in the words, 'It is good that it is so', and since this feeling of joy is one of pure, untainted joy, therefore the good which I assert as a result of this feeling is the complete good, the good as such. This good I believe to have an objective substratum in something, inasmuch as I am accustomed to ascribing the good to something objective. And so

I ascribe the absolute, complete good to the Absolute, as if it itself were something, even though the ground for this valuation is precisely the negation of every object of thought and aspiration. From this negation results the feeling of blessedness to which I give expression by the phrase 'absolute value'.

It is natural that the Absolute should be conceived as pure spirit, for the ground of its being accepted lies in a condition of the soul which, as such, is one of pure feeling without any conceptualized object. The Absolute, then, obviously cannot be an object. It itself is given exclusively in an objectless feeling; it is completely one with the consciousness of itself. The Absolute is the absolute feeling of certainty; it is itself the feeling of blessedness, as Spinoza very truly says.

However, it is obvious that nothing more preposterous could be imagined than the opinion of idealist philosophers, who think that they can regard the Christian God, with his obvious relativity, as an observable representation of the Absolute, as the Absolute itself as it is given for concrete apprehension, although not purely apprehended. The fact of the matter is that the Absolute is precisely that which arises in consciousness through abstraction from all that is presented through the senses, from all relativity.

# THE TRUTH-VALUE OF
# CHRISTIAN DOGMATICS[1]

## I. THE CONSCIOUSNESS OF THE 'I'
## AND THE RELIGIOUS CONSCIOUSNESS

In order to prepare the ground for an elucidation of the nature of religious experience, we must touch on the nature of the idea of the 'I'. The idea of my own 'I' seems *prima facie* to have the clearest meaning of anything. For it seems to every man's consciousness that nothing is so intimate, so immediately present, as he himself. But upon closer reflection it is just this apparent intimacy that poses a difficult philosophical-psychological problem.

When one says 'I', one obviously means something which exists for itself, so that it is given for itself in immediate self-consciousness. Everything else seems to be something external for my consciousness, but I myself seem to be something purely inward in consciousness, which I cannot set over against the consciousness of it as an object which is distinct from that consciousness. In this way I characterize this 'I' as that which is most intimate, most familiar to the person's consciousness.

It is certainly the case that the body is also counted as the 'I' (I run, I walk) and the body is always something external. Nevertheless it is true that although the body belongs to me, is associated with me, it is not for that reason that which is properly what I call 'I'. This is seen in the fact that one always regards oneself as the master of the body, even though it is only within certain limits. When I say, 'I run and walk', this is only a shorter way of saying that I set my body in a certain motion. This 'I', who does the setting, thus cannot be the body itself. The body here is properly only an instrument. It is certainly true also that particular psychical determinations—my own ideas, thoughts, feelings, and expressions of will—are not entirely clear to myself, and are therefore in a certain way external to my apprehension of myself. Self-knowledge

[1] Excerpted from a longer essay, *The Religious Problem of Our Time in Historical and Psychological Elucidation*. The portion translated here is taken from *Religionsfilosofi*, pp. 154–68, 219–50.

is indeed, as Socrates has said, a particularly difficult matter. But particular psychical determinations are still not the same as I myself. Certainly I *have* these or those thoughts or feelings or expressions of will, but these things are not what I *am*.

Therefore I, as such, am for myself something internal, something immediately accessible to myself. And certainly this independence is something characteristic of me as an 'I', so that it will not do to regard even the immediate apprehension of the self as something which belongs to me only accidentally. The *consciousness* of myself *is* therefore I myself. This is also seen in the fact that no one says 'I' in referring to another person, but 'you', 'he', or 'she'. That which is given in this 'I' is characterized in such a way that the consciousness thereof exists only in that person who calls himself 'I'. Why? Obviously because here the consciousness of the thing and the thing itself are identical, one and the same. This identity is seen further in the customary theory that the existence of everything else may be doubtful, but not my own existence. It is sophisticated chatter, it seems, to doubt one's own existence.

But now in this absolute intimacy of mine, in my immediate existence for myself as involving the identity of the apprehension and that which is apprehended, there lies a great philosophical-psychological difficulty. For it is in fact an absurdity that the consciousness of a thing should be the same as the thing itself. This would imply that the thing would be dissolved into consciousness. But in that case only a consciousness would be present, without this consciousness being the consciousness of anything at all.

Of course, we cannot remain with this line of thought—no matter how natural it appears to us or how inclined we are to regard it as true. As to the truth of this line of thought, it is not possible to appeal to the testimony of experience. For in the first place, it is not certain that anything is true simply because it seems to us—perhaps even from our childhood—that the situation is thus or so. Indeed, if we judge according to the testimony of our senses, it seems to us that the sun goes around the earth, but this does not make it true.

In the second place, it is to be observed that as soon as we determine that something really is characterized in a certain way, it is never a question only of a sensible experience of something, but of a *thought* regarding something, which naturally can always be a mistaken determination of the sensibly given. This is what is questionable, for example, in Bergsonian mysticism, which takes its departure from the so-called immediate experience of the self, as something which it is impossible to grasp in a concept. because the concept as such is always constant while the experience of the self is always changing. Bergson believes that such a proposition actually grasps the essence of the experience of the self. He believes that he has given a representation of this experience which actually characterizes the thing itself—as distinguished from logical analysis, which is impossible here because it loses sight of the thing. But he ignores the fact that his own proposition itself expresses only a thought about the experience of the self and not that experience itself. And certainly, in this thought he makes use of concepts—first and foremost the concept of the experience of the self, and then the concept of change. Consequently he himself makes use of that which in the nature of the case should be excluded. But then it is also clear that the truth of the judgments must be verified logically and that it will not do to take refuge in the supposed experience as the ground of knowledge when it turns out that the judgments are logically absurd.

Mysticism as a *theory*—in which mysticism itself becomes a whole of thoughts, by no means of experiences—is the most absurd of all. One makes use of thought in order to show the inadequacy of thought. One ought to distinguish carefully, however, between mysticism as a theory and mysticism as an attitude, characterized by the fact that one attaches oneself to and cultivates certain feelings, while suppressing reflection. Such an attitude is itself, naturally, neither true nor false and can often be particularly helpful.

In the third place, it should always be observed that he who remains with a self-contradiction only combines words without meaning, although he expects that there will be a meaning there. If someone says that the one God is three Gods, or that Christ is both God and man, he does not for that reason conceive one as three, or God as man. He is simply confused, in that he shifts back and forth in his own thought between the thought of *one* God and the thought of *three* Gods (or between the thoughts of Christ as God and as man). On account of this shifting he is led to say that the one God is three and that Christ is both God and man, without having any idea whatever about the matter.

*Credo quia absurdum.* I believe on the ground of a combination of words, on the ground of a confusion. It is a mistake to say, however, that I believe in the thing itself, because that presupposes that I actually can conceive something by the word. I do not believe in the thing itself, but I believe only that the combination of words has a meaning. This I believe on the ground of a shifting of thought, which has the result that in the expression I determine the one as the other.

If we now return to the question of what 'I' am as 'I', then the theory which we have been considering in line with the customary interpretation must be false, in the sense that a shifting of thought enters into it. This shifting finds expression in such a proposition as was just now advanced, viz. that I as such am characterized by a coincidence of consciousness and the thing of which I am conscious. But now the task becomes that of explaining what are the things that are being confused with one another here, or, broadly speaking, what are the psychical factors which cause such propositions to be advanced.

For purposes of this investigation, attention ought first to be directed to a peculiarity which characterizes feeling as distinguished from conception. This peculiarity is that while feeling is always, certainly, an experience of something, it is impossible to distinguish this something from the experience itself, in such a way that one could say that it exists for itself, apart from the experience. For example, what would the pain in one's tooth be in itself, without regard to the very experience of the pain? What would pleasure be, without regard to a conscious being which experiences it? What would hunger be, without regard to a feeling of hunger? The object of conception, on the other hand, can always be grasped as something real in itself, whether the conception itself is merely a phantasy or a real cognition. Compare in this connection colour or circularity with hunger. The colour and the circularity exist, so it seems to us, in the real object and are to be carefully distinguished from the apprehension of the thing which is present in myself. By contrast hunger does not exist in my body in such a way that it is *one* reality and my feeling of hunger *another*.

Sometimes a feeling and a conception are so intimately associated with one another that we cannot think of the one without also thinking of the other, or are so intimately associated that we confuse them with one another. It is now easy to see how one might say in such a circumstance that the object which is conceived as real is itself given in feeling. But now since the feeling cannot be conceived as a reality alongside of its content, one is led to say also that the object which is conceived as real is its apprehension of itself, its own experience. The consciousness of the thing is the same as the thing itself. That is, the customary view in connection with the significance of this 'I myself', as that in which the thing coincides with the apprehension of it, must depend simply on a shifting of thought from feeling to conception.

What feeling and what conception are in question here? To answer this question we need only to consider that there is an external object which presents itself at the same time in feeling and in conception. If I have a toothache, I feel pain in my tooth. It is not the case that I first have the feeling of pain, without perceiving the pain in the tooth, and then afterwards locate the pain in the tooth. I cannot have the experience of pain itself without locating the pain in the tooth. That is to say, to the feeling belongs this content: the pain in the tooth. Or when I have a feeling of general physical health, I feel this in the body. So also with the feelings of hunger and thirst, of inner muscular tension, or weariness, of vitality, etc. In a word, we have a whole group of feelings which have this unique character, that we do not experience them except as being in the body. From this it follows that it is certainly false that the feeling itself cannot have a physical content.

The customary psychological theory is certainly quite different in this respect. I suppose that I first have the feeling and then I locate it in the body, which can be apprehended through sensations or touch, so that the feeling would be *one* act of consciousness and the sensible apprehension of the body another. But this is not a correct representation of the actual psychological situation. For in the toothache, for example, I have a completely unified apprehension of the pain in the tooth. I permit myself to be confused here, as so often happens elsewhere, by the fact that one and the same psychic act can have a manifold of causal conditions. Of course the feeling of a toothache presupposes sensations of sight and feeling to the extent that the total apprehension which is present there presupposes for its possibility my having had sensations of sight and of feeling through which the image of my own body (in which the tooth is included) could originally develop. But the feeling of a toothache is still not a feeling of pain plus sensations of sight and of feeling, or visual or tactile images. In that case nothing would be present in me except a feeling of pain and in addition a conception of the tooth—not an experience of pain *in* the tooth.

But notice; it is not possible to regard the pain in itself as something real in itself, without regard for the experience of it. Therefore the aching tooth itself, in its character as aching, is not an external reality which can be regarded as existing without regard for the unified experience which is the feeling of pain. This means that in the group of feelings in question—we can characterize them, if we wish, as inner sensations—my own body appears in the feeling, so that my body itself as experienced here does not have its character of reality in the same sense as, for example, in the case of a colour with a circular form.

Now it is to be observed, however, that precisely the same bodily content which appears in the feeling, on the one hand, and which is thus real only as an experience of feeling, is also the object of a conception. I conceive my body also as a reality in the proper sense, so that in its past, present, and future existence it has a reality which I definitely distinguish from my present apprehension of this reality. To that extent I do not experience it in a feeling— for example, in feeling well or feeling ill—and hence I can conceive this condition as subsisting independently of the feeling in which it is experienced.

However, the group of inner sensations which are in question here are joined with this conception of the reality of the body, not in such a way that the conception itself is a feeling, much less a complex of feelings, but in such a way that, precisely in their character as experiences of feeling, as acts of consciousness, the feelings constitute moments in the *object* of the conception. That is, I do not *feel* in the conception in question, but I am *conscious of* the reality of the feelings. But it is also the case that different conditions of consciousness are unconditionally located in the body which is conceived as real. For the apprehension it would be a dead body, with the same character in that respect as a stone, if in my apprehension of it it did not possess what is called an inner life—if I did not ascribe to this body my soul-life.

Therefore at the same time I feel my body, although the only thing that is real is the feeling itself, and I conceive my body as a reality independent of the conception, which has existed, does exist, and, one may well suppose, will exist, equipped with certain functions of consciousness. Thus in connection with the appre-

I*

hension of the body we have to do with an association of conception and feeling of the most intimate character possible, inasmuch as the content of the feeling is in essential respects the same as the content of the conception. And certainly they are so intimately associated in the psycho-physical organism that when one apprehends the living body one always *feels* it. Thus nothing is more natural than that, when one thinks of the conception which is in question here, one should shift over to the accompanying feeling, which has the same content, and should be unable to keep them explicitly and clearly apart.

What is the result? It is that the real object, which exists for the conception, itself comes to be described as an object for feeling. Now in so far as it is a question of feelings, the only thing that is real is the feeling itself; it is not possible to isolate the content of feeling and to regard it as real independent of the experience of the feeling itself. Hence the real object which is conceived is the feeling in which it is experienced. The real thing itself, the body which lives in time, endowed with functions of consciousness, becomes its apprehension of itself.

In order to elucidate what has been said we now consider that when I say 'I', it is certainly, on the one hand, a question of the person who is speaking, taken in his totality. But because of the intimate relationship which a living conscious organism assumes towards itself, or—more correctly—because of the manifold of inner sensations which the organism always has, inasmuch as their content is ascribed to one's own body, this world of feeling always lies behind the expression 'I'. Let it be noticed carefully that it is not only a question of a reflection regarding this world of feeling, but also a question of the world of feeling itself. Thus nothing is more natural than that, when one seeks to explain what this 'I' signifies, it becomes impossible to think one-sidedly of an objective reality, which I can place before myself and observe as an external observer, in the same way that I investigate a stone. 'No,' I say to myself, 'I am not an externally understandable object, but something hidden, which exists only for myself in my feeling. Outside of this feeling of mine it does not exist.' And so we have mysticism.

There is a pretty little ballad of the Dane, Erick Bøgh, in which it is told how a man went to a goldsmith to have his beloved's name engraved. The goldsmith said that he well understood what was wanted, and he repeated the words which the man wished to have engraved—but he did it in a dry, businesslike tone. 'No, my dear Mr. Goldsmith,' said the man, 'it was not thus that I meant it, but thus.' And he repeated the same words, but with that colouring added which the lover has when he talks to his beloved, fraught with feelings of love. It was this, he said, that the goldsmith was to engrave, not the dry words which he himself had spoken. This indicates that the words intended for engraving had become so intimately associated in the consciousness of the lover with these feelings of love, that he had lost the sense of their objective character. They are not the same words if they are not spoken with the colouring of love. In order that their objective character might be correctly apprehended, the man demanded that one must also, in his inner being, so to speak reproduce the feeling of love which he himself experienced.

We have the same phenomenon before us when the religious person seeks to explain to the unbelieving person, who stands outside the sphere of the religious, what he means by God. When his meaning is taken up in a dry reflection—'Then you mean this or that, e.g. an all-powerful, all-good, righteous, etc., person who has created the world'—the believer does not recognize his own reflection, because for him God is not merely an objective object which can be grasped in feelingless thought. When he says, 'God', he gives expression not to a mere thought, but to a thought fraught with feeling, so that the word does not have any meaning if the feeling is not there. The God is *his* God through the most intimate association with God himself, and thus it is not possible for him to be conceived unless a whole circle of feelings is attached to the conception.

The same holds true, and in an altogether specific sense, when a person stands before himself and seeks to describe what is properly to be understood by that which he calls 'I'. A whole world of feeling lies behind that word. To attempt to determine the thing through concepts of this or that objective reality is therefore an impossibility for him. And still he does not want to deny, naturally, that it is a question of a reality in the proper sense. On the contrary, he is more firmly convinced of the fact that he himself is real than of anything else. But still, this reality, as it is for him, exists only in and for his own feeling. This he must say to himself, of course, because the word 'I' itself gives expression to a whole

complex of feelings in him. The result is that he says that he himself is a reality, which is one with his own experience or feeling of
it. For as soon as one thinks of a feeling, it is impossible, as we have
said, to constitute the content as something real in itself. The only
thing that is real is therefore the feeling itself. However, since in
this word 'I' one is thinking of an objective reality—the psycho-
physical organism as actually living in time—this reality is identified with the feeling itself, in which that which is determined is
given.

Of course there is a mediating agency, which makes possible the
transition of thought to which such propositions give expression
—namely the transition of thought from the objective reality to
the feeling. This mediating agency is the manifestations of consciousness which belong to the objectively conceived psycho-physical
individuals. It is only as a *conscious* being that one can be one with
the consciousness of himself. Only as a conscious being can one be
a self-consciousness, something purely inward within consciousness. Therefore one is led to characterize this 'I', given in self-
consciousness, as something specifically spiritual, independent of
the body. And so we have the unique relationship in which the
body stands to 'I myself' in the customary manner of viewing or
rather representing it. Certainly the body itself belongs to me. It is
impossible for anyone to abstract away entirely from his own body,
when he thinks about himself. But on the other hand, corporeality
is not compatible with my character as being one with my own
consciousness. Therefore one distinguishes the body, on the one
hand, from oneself as a spiritual person, which is properly that
which is inward, that which is immediately known. One says,
'Certainly the body belongs to me, but only as an instrument for
my spirit'.

The particular manifestations of consciousness in the psycho-
physical organism undergo a similar fate, although not altogether
the same. Of course I must always think of them when I try to
represent myself in order to be able to identify myself and my own
consciousness of myself. But the difficulty with the manifestations
of consciousness in the psycho-physical organism is that they occur
in time. Therefore they belong to the past and the future as well as
to the immediate present.

By contrast, the spirit, which is 'I', exists only in and for my own
feeling or the complex of inner sensations, to which I give expres-

sion when I say 'I'. But this feeling or this complex of sensations, naturally, is just that which is immediately present in every case. Indeed, it is this complex of sensations which, because of its intimate association with the idea of the psycho-physical individual, is the cause of the whole drama of thought which is being unfolded here. Therefore the spirit, as always immediately present, acquires a character which conflicts with the identification of the spirit with the temporal manifestations of consciousness. Hence one says that the spirit only supports the manifestations of consciousness, but that these are not what it *is*. In order for such an idea to be possible, however, it is necessary that something elevated above change should appear in the manifestations of consciousness. This, indeed, seems to be the case, in so far as the psycho-physical organism finds a continuity or connection among its manifestations of consciousness. In the idea of the 'I' this connection is referred to the inner, personal unity, elevated above time. Thus the idea of the 'I' or personality is explained.

Now we must touch briefly on the possibility of apprehending other organisms than one's own as persons. Other men are, just like ourselves, organisms endowed with consciousness, feeling, and will, and they exhibit continuity in their conscious life. It is obvious that this objective similarity to ourselves actually causes us to transfer the idea of 'I' or personality to them. They are endowed by us with the same inner personal unity, with which we ourselves are endowed.

However, the idea of others as persons is necessarily a pure abstraction without any real significance—it is without the necessary foundation of experience, in so far as the supposed spirit of the other person stands there for us as a pure *object*. Spirit is precisely that which by its very nature conflicts with the concept of reality in the customary sense, in so far as it cannot be regarded as existing independently of the consciousness of it. In its very essence, spirit is self-consciousness. Hence to carry through the apprehension of personality with reference to other people would require that the other personality could not stand as something external to my own consciousness of it but would have to appear as present *in* it and thus as present in myself. But this in turn presupposes an actual communion of feeling, that I am united with this feeling, so that I transfer the content of my own feeling to him and localize it in him. For it is only in feeling that something is given to us in such a way that we can regard what is given as one with our own apprehension of it. Therefore only a sympathetic unity of feeling with other people gives us the concrete idea of them as being themselves personalities. That the other person becomes 'You' and not 'I' myself, depends on the fact that the original idea of the 'I' is attached to one's own organism, so that this 'I' is, so to speak, already occupied. But in this 'You!' in which an experience of the personality of the other person is really expressed, there also lies implied the thought of something present in myself and for myself.

Observe in this connection a peculiar situation with reference to the ground of certainty for assuming my own existence. There is present here not only the usual empirical certainty. Indeed I as such am given in self-consciousness, where the identity of subject and object obtains. Therefore one cannot ask whether consciousness through which I apprehend myself, is true. The thing itself, indeed, is this consciousness. Inasmuch as the consciousness of myself exists, I exist also. But that I came to be regarded as self-consciousness, as one with my own consciousness, depends on the fact that the 'I' is given in feeling, the content of which is regarded not as real in itself, but as real only in the very experience of that content.

In this way also we are given the same kind of distinctive ground of certainty as it pertains to the belief in the existence of other persons. Even if, from the objective point of view, another person's being given to me might be an illusion, still if, from the psychical point of view, I can live with him and am united in feeling with him, he presents himself to me as a spirit which is immediately present in my feeling. Thus he becomes just as certain for me as my own feeling. This is the ground of certainty for the so-called religious experience. The God given in the image may be uncertain, regarded purely objectively. But as I am united in feeling with him, spiritually live with him, he also becomes for me something immediately present. He becomes one with my own feeling of him and therefore acquires the feeling's own certainty. The question of reality in the ordinary sense—the question of existence independent of consciousness—loses its significance, and another question of reality presents itself, which cannot be answered in more than one way. Indeed, it is necessary to consider this, if we are to understand metaphysical religiosity, as based on the idea of pure, absolute spirit. This idea has its foundation not in any images or even hallucinations of a personality foreign to us, but immediately in the consciousness of my own spirit—my own 'I'.

To this it should be added that other feelings besides the purely physical ones also contribute to the apprehension of the 'I'. In this connection one should consider especially the affections—great enjoyment, deep sorrow and despair, anger. Because of the intimate association between these states of mind and the so-called affective symptoms—e.g. turning red or clenching one's fists in anger, beating one's breast in despair—people have wished to explain them as nothing but pure bodily feelings. However that may be, it is certain that they stand in the most intimate association with bodily feelings. Therefore they contribute in their own way to the forming of the idea of something purely inward within us, a spirit. One should further mention the feelings of psychical good or bad health, of psychical vigour or weakness, which we cannot help referring to our own body, because of the intimate relation between our psychical and our physical lives.

Finally one must mention the will as perhaps the most important of the feelings which are operative here. It is easy to show that the will is essentially a feeling. By no means would the will be counted as an element in psychical life if we did not experience something in the will. But the very experience of the will cannot be a conception of the will as something real. For the experience of the will is something which belongs to the will itself, something indissolubly bound up with the thing itself, so that it is not possible to regard the will as *one* reality and the experience of the will as another. But this is to say that the will is a feeling. Feeling is characterized precisely by the fact that the content cannot be regarded as something real, to be distinguished from the very feeling in which it is experienced.

What the feeling of will is does not need to be analysed here. It is certain that it stands in the most intimate union with the feelings of tension and strain, the content of which we ascribe to our own bodies. These feelings appear in connection with the idea of a certain *activity* in the organism, so that they become causes of certain effects. This makes it understandable also that the idea of something inward within ourselves, of spirit, our innermost 'I', is formed especially upon the foundation of our feeling of will. We ascribe to the active psycho-physical organism the content of the feeling of will, at least with reference to the feelings of tension and strain which are always connected with it. Therefore the activity itself acquires an inner side, inasmuch as it is given in our own feeling of will. And since, in the sphere of feeling, the feeling itself is the only thing that is real, the activity of the psychophysical organism is dissolved into the very feeling of will. Thus we reach a purely inward spiritual activity, which is one with the experience of that activity and belongs to our innermost 'I'. Our innermost 'I' is thus given above all as a will. Nothing in our psychical life seems to proceed from our spirit, our 'I', as much as does our willing.

## 2. THE QUESTION OF TRUTH IN RELIGION

The conclusion of what has been said is the following. In so far as we regard ourselves as a spirit or as an inner 'I', accessible only to itself, this depends on a shift of thought from the actual conceived-of organism over to the feelings, the content of which is located in the organism. In this way the organism presents itself as given in our feeling, but thus also as one with the experience of it—as the completely innermost. Naturally it can be said, therefore, that our apprehension of ourselves as a spirit, as an inner 'I', is properly speaking meaningless. We shift back and forth between different thoughts, the contents of which we do not distinguish, but just for that reason we have no determinate, particular object before ourselves.

Still it is not correct to say for this reason that the apprehension of the spirit as such, taken in its immediacy, is false, For it is to be noticed that because we ascribe the spirit to the feeling in which it is given, we say, indeed, that it is not a question of something which may exist whether we apprehend it or not. But if one is to raise the question, 'True or false?' this always demands that it must be asked concerning something which is presupposed as existing independently of the apprehension. This is implied in the very question of truth: Is the thing in reality the way it is apprehended to be, or is it only that there is an apprehension of the thing as so constituted? This makes it clear, then, that one cannot ask whether or not an opinion is true if there is no intention to determine reality in and for itself. But by the spirit, as the inward, as the innermost thing in me, one intends precisely that which is in the feeling, in the experience, and which is thus also one with its own apprehension. Therefore it is meaningless to ask if the spirit actually exists. It is meaningless to ask whether or not the apprehension of it is true.

In Viktor Rydberg's poem *The Thinker* (*Grubblaren*) the religious question is put thus: Is he, or is he not, he who is given in our vital feeling? It is precisely because of this question that religion has become embarrassed in our time. Dogmatics is the greatest danger for contemporary religion. As long as one's whole way of thinking was impregnated by magic and superstition, the blue flowers of religion could grow up under their powerful protection. But with the progress of human scientific study, with the triumph of human thought, there is the prospect that dogmatics will fall like a house of cards. Then must religion also be smothered in the wreckage?

One can understand those who seek to connect religion with dogmatics and then hold tenaciously to the dogmas against all reason. They are really fighting, so to speak, for their own souls, for their highest delight, because for them the religious delight has its foundation in certain dogmatic ideas. This struggle, like religious fanaticism in general, is closely related to the tigress's struggle for her young and the lover's struggle for his beloved. However, it is to be observed that the connection of religion with dogmatics also always implies its connection with faith in and hope for certain external advantages, even if it is eternal salvation as a result of a certain relationship to the divine. Therefore one is struggling also in order to preserve such a faith, such a hope.

But in their blindness these fanatics do not understand that through such a firm connection with the dogmas they are in fact leading religion to its demise and are thus defiling one of the very highest values of the human race. For in the long run superstition cannot survive against man's desire for knowledge and scientific study, which are the foundation for his survival in the struggle for existence. There is only one way to rescue religion from collapse, and that is to tear it loose entirely from the question of truth, which is, in fact, just as meaningless there as it is when someone who has a toothache asks himself, 'Does the pain which I feel actually exist in reality—i.e. does it exist independently of my feeling of it?'

It is certainly characteristic that one finds it being vigorously maintained in contemporary philosophy of religion, for example, in

Eucken and James, that an inseparable aspect of the religious outlook is a vital feeling for and will toward the religious content. But these thinkers fail to draw the only reasonable conclusion that could be drawn, viz. that it is therefore meaningless to ask if the outlook is true or false, since as a content of feeling or a content of will as such, nothing else can be present except a determinate form of our own feeling and will. Rather they suppose that in making such a statement as the above they have upheld the truth of the religious content although this truth, as is also said, is of a different sort from objective truth. It is clear, however, that if by 'truth' one does not mean that something is in reality or in itself such as one apprehends it to be, then one is only playing thoughtlessly with words. For the question here concerns only objective truth. But now we are offered—even though it may be in a golden dish—something entirely different, which is presented as truth, although it is not truth in the ordinary sense. The preparation is offered, I say, in a golden dish, for it is also maintained that this truth is the truth which concerns the innermost essence of all existence.

It would be absurd, therefore, to investigate the truth-value of religious experience. But let us investigate the truth-value of the dogmatics, which in part constitute the background for the experience, in part are based upon it. Before doing this, however, we must touch on one other matter, for the treatment of which we may employ as a motto the words, 'Those who are well have no need of a physician, but those who are sick'.

### 3. THE RELIGIOUS TYPE AND THE IRRELIGIOUS TYPE

Westermarck notes, in the beginning of his work, *The Origin and Development of the Moral Ideas* (New York, Macmillan, 1906–1908), that Jesus represents the moral life as the only essential value for everyone. The importance and significance which the moral person as such attaches to morality is thus transferred, for natural reasons, to other persons, as if immorality were necessarily the supreme suffering for them also. One can say that the statement is in principle correct. But let it be noted that if it is made in the right way, the contention, coming from the lips of the preacher of morality, that immorality is the supreme evil, itself can *bring it about* that the person to whom it is addressed actually comes to recognize it as the most extreme suffering to betray his conscience.

Actually what constitutes the ground for the conviction of the preacher of morality that immorality is the greatest of all suffering, is the idea of that spiritual death which he connects with immorality. We have already noted that the character of unavoidability in the feeling of duty and the sense of one's own mission in life, gives rise to the unique idea that it is precisely in these feelings that our true and real 'I' is given. Since a certain action appears in the consciousness of duty as that which is right *in itself*, as that which in itself ought to be done, it gives rise to an unconditional inclination in the will. We cannot think of the right action, when it is something which lies close at hand, without being inclined towards it. And we cannot think of a past action, when it went contrary to our conviction about the right, without feeling in our wills an inclination in the opposite direction, *towards* the right. For the consciousness that our actual action has been other than the right necessarily gives rise to a feeling of dissatisfaction. In this way the feeling of duty takes on the character of unavoidability.

As we have said earlier, our feelings, and particularly our feelings of will, which are localized in our own organism, are the ground of our idea of the 'I', for the organism as actually conceived appears as itself given in the feeling and thus necessarily as one with the apprehension of itself. But for this reason the feeling of duty in particular, with its unavoidability, becomes the ground of our apprehension of the 'I'. That 'I' which seems to be given to us in the feeling of duty must also, so it seems, be our true, real 'I', since the feeling here, in which the 'I' is given and with which it is given and with which it is also identical, is so permanent, so unavoidable. But it therefore seems to us also that a lack of agreement with the feeling of duty implies a departure from our true self, a death in the supreme sense. Therefore just this reflection on the feeling of duty as belonging to our moral self becomes the cause of our thinking that transgressing the feeling of duty is the deepest of all suffering.

But it is to be noted that everything also hangs on this introspective reflection. This reflection is not always present, because one's attention can generally be centered more on outward things. The interest in what is within one's own 'I', then becomes of secondary significance. To be sure, the moral consciousness may continue to have its power at all times, but this does not mean that it is stretched so taut that immorality appears particularly as suffering.

How many men there are who, unconcerned about their duty and their mission in life, are occupied with the pleasure of the moment, without immorality becoming a real evil for them. But on the other hand, how many there are who are occupied with what they have found to be their duty and their mission in life without considering that they are saving themselves from spiritual death, being interested only in fulfilling their duty, just because it is their duty, and in being able to accomplish the work which they feel is their mission. Neither the one nor the other of these types of men needs either the forgiveness of sins or power for a new life, in which the inclination towards the worldly is in principle nullified. The absolute opposition of *sin and duty* does not exist for them.

But if the preacher of morality, with his attention turned inwards towards himself, should actually succeed in directing their attention towards the inward, towards the fact that they possess within themselves an inner 'I', which is to be preserved as the only thing of ultimate value—an idea which, like all ideas of the inward, the spiritual, is neither true nor false—then it may happen that, as one says, they are 'awakened'. Then they begin to brood about the extremity in which they find themselves, and so they seek the consolation of religion.

Now it is undoubtedly the case that, from a purely physiological point of view, the individuals who, in their robust morality or immorality, do not allow themselves to be awakened are the healthy, sound natures, who do not need any physician of the soul. The second group, who are by nature inclined towards the introspective life and therefore are themselves spiritually awake or allow themselves to be awakened, lack that robust soundness which characterizes the others. Naturally it is only to confuse the concepts if one characterizes the introspective type of man, who broods about his sins and seeks his consolation in religiosity, as mentally deranged. But on the other hand it is altogether indubitable that a religious state of mind, with its brooding about sins, is related to insanity—above all on account of the hallucinatory elements which go with it and which indeed may at times acquire such strength that actual insanity results. The relation between the age of puberty—the time when the danger of one's mental equilibrium is the greatest —and conversion also points in the same direction.

Now there is one thing that healthy natures will never experience, namely, the entirely unique felicity, surpassing all other pleasure, which the religious repose in God bestows. But in return they also miss the deep anxiety of soul, the doubt, which he who has been awakened but has not yet been converted can experience in his inner being. Indeed, on account of his permanent bent towards the inward, even the convert himself necessarily has his hours of profound anguish, so that he cannot recover the feeling of religious bliss. Then one is in despair about oneself, one believes that one is separated from God. Indeed it is a question, in this respect, of a supremely natural psychical phenomenon: the unnatural high tension directed towards the positive stage, which the religious feeling of bliss includes, has a natural tendency, because of the law of the relativity of the feelings, to turn into its opposite.

If one asks now which of these types is the better, no objective answer can be given. It will not do to advance the proposition of Plato and of Stuart Mill: 'It is better to be Socrates dissatisfied than a pig satisfied', and to seek to show that he who has experienced both the pig's pleasure and spiritual pleasure (which the pig does not have) regards the latter pleasure as the only significant one. For it is not at all true that a Socrates, who, just in virtue of being Socrates, has developed a distaste for the pleasure of the pig, is a reliable judge in the matter. Nor is it possible to exhibit the one type as better than the other according to a moral standard of measurement. The extrovertive, naturally sound person can also possess the strongest feeling of duty and can also follow that feeling without therefore taking time to brood over his sins.

Finally, if one looks at the matter from the point of view of man's ultimate goal and asks which type is the better as the means for achieving that goal, then naturally the answer to that question depends upon what one actually regards as the ultimate goal. And the way in which this question is answered may just be dependent on the kind of man one is. Mark well, it is a natural and necessary tendency for the moral-religious type to find the ultimate goal for the life of the race in the spiritual and eternal, which affords the highest pleasure for this type of person. The kingdom of God, indeed, becomes for the Christian a universal human brotherhood, where mutual love, supported by love for God, is what is essential

—apart from any relation to such cultural goals as have to do with worldly things. On the other hand for the more extrovertive type, who is dependent in feeling and will upon external things, the goal of man too is infected by external elements. Either the *summum bonum* becomes happiness in general, as a sum-total of feelings of pleasure, or the highest good becomes culture, regarded as the mastery of the understanding or of the will over nature, pleasure in God, pleasure in the inward in the proper sense, the spiritual and the eternal.

John Stuart Mill, Spencer, and the utilitarians in general define happiness as a *sum-total* of feelings of pleasure. For them happiness, as the goal of the race, can be at least relatively produced through external means—the useful. It is to be noted that when one defines happiness in this way, the definition may by no means be taken in such a way that the sum-total of pleasure which is intended is of a non-spiritual sort, in the sense that intellectual, moral and aesthetic feelings are not comprised therein. Still this definition does exclude that purely inward pleasure, that repose in God, which is ultimately a repose in one's own innermost self and with which moral pleasure as pleasure in living in fathfulness to one's true self is closely related. For he who has a disposition towards this pleasure is not in a position to regard it as one possible pleasure *alongside* others. For him this pleasure stands as the only necessary one, as the only one which merits the name of happiness. Indeed, to the religious man, through an illusion which is easy to understand, it seems that the man who is manifestly least disturbed, the happy man in the ordinary sense, is in his innermost being profoundly unhappy. For the man who is religiously inclined, in the essential sense, all other pleasure (and likewise all suffering), which is not of a religious nature, stands as something secondary, something of which the fullness of his happiness is independent, and even more, something of which one must be independent in order to possess happiness and avoid unhappiness.

This does not necessarily imply that, as seen from the religious person's point of view, one must be insensitive to all pleasure or all suffering of a non-religious nature. Such is the case only in Hindu religiosity. Rather the situation is simply that one is seeking the source of pleasure, in virtue of which one is happy on the whole, *in spite of* all suffering, and without which one finds all other pleasure to be incapable of remaining the universal condition of unhappiness. The inner pleasure of the religious person neither rises nor falls with the vicissitudes of life. Rather the inner pleasure is for him the only essential one. When this pleasure declines, everything becomes desolate and dark and cold. On the other hand, when it rises up, untrammelled happiness is there, even if the cup of outward suffering is filled to the brim.

Religious happiness—salvation—and conversely the feeling of not being at peace with God is for the religiously disposed person an absolute master, which suppresses any reference to another pleasure or suffering. The non-religious pleasure or suffering does not strike at the very centre of happiness or unhappiness. Therefore happiness as a sum-total of feelings of pleasure cannot be for a man a goal which includes the religious pleasure as one element alongside others. If one has set up happiness in this sense (i.e. as a sum-total of feelings of pleasure) as the goal of the race, then it would be possible to include in it only that moral and even so-called religious pleasure which consists of one's feeling pleasure when one has fulfilled his duty or carried out his responsibility, or one's believing that he is receiving certain external help from God. But the true religious pleasure does not come in as an element here.

In the same way culture, as man's mastery over nature, both the inner and the outer, may be set up as the goal of the race. One may very well include here the thought of man's moral perfection as, on the one hand (formally) his mastery over momentary impulses and on the other hand (positively) his being determined by that which is the ultimate goal, viz. the refinement of the race. But here also it is not possible to include the race's religious perfection, the kingdom of God, as *one element* alongside others. For if anyone has a disposition for this perfection, so that it becomes an integral part of his moral task, then this also becomes the absolute goal for him, for which all others are only a means. So it is, therefore, that for the religiously inclined person the goal of the race is in principle different from the goal which can present itself to the extrovertive type. It is as though there were two worlds, which can only be in conflict with one another. This is not to say, however, that it is not possible for the individual man, who does not have to be a permanent and consistent unity, to compromise here.

But now if the goal which is set up in either case is dependent upon what type of man one represents, with reference to an inward or an outward orientation, then it is clear that any decision as to which type—the introvertive or the extrovertive—is the better, in relation to the objective of the race, is impossible. It is therefore impossible, from the one point of view or the other, to show that one or the other of these types is to be preferred to the other. But this is not to say that religion is not actually a consolation for the man who has once become spiritually sick in the sense that he turns himself inward towards himself and broods about his soul's salvation. He needs a physician, because he is sick. 'Blessed are they who hunger and thirst after righteousness, for they shall be filled.' 'Blessed are the poor in spirit, for theirs is the kingdom of heaven.' These words possess an unfathomable significance, not in the sense of its being true that those who do not hunger and thirst after righteousness in the deepest sense, and those who do not feel this spiritual emptiness, cannot achieve true happiness, but in the sense that for those who are suffering within themselves there is a remedy through which they may become well.

To this it must also be added, finally, that a certain element in every spiritual religion can possess significance for all, from the point of view of happiness and from the point of view of the possibility of achieving the goal. It is especially characteristic of the neurasthenic person that he cannot work unless he can see immediately with his own eyes a result of his work. He is unable to work, so to speak, with a long-range view. The cause of this, naturally, is that his desire to achieve the goal operates too much in the form of inciting him, of egging him on, with the result that the lack of an immediate satisfaction causes such suffering, such unrest, that he is paralysed and is unsuccessful. Now neurasthenia, as such a tension directed towards the particular desire, is naturally not absolutely foreign to mankind in general; each person runs the risk of such a nervous irritation. But this implies that a means for calming the desire is important to everyone, both in terms of his own happiness and in terms of the possibility of actually achieving his established goal. But if we disregard here such means as relate to physical hygiene, then the inner peace which can be gained by returning to one's own 'I' plays a significant role. This peace may be gained through the altogether natural reflection, which is also independent of all dogmatics, that here it is a question of external things, which cannot have any fundamental significance for myself as such. One can also say that the consciousness of the relativity of all 'you-values', as judged from the point of view of my own self, must have significance for every man as a means for calming the nerves.

A few words should be added about the significance in this connection of certain impressions which are drawn from the contemplation of the universe. Who has not at some time experienced, when alone on a quiet, clear starry night, this feeling of peace of mind, of exaltation over all of life's struggles? He who has once found himself on a mountain peak, from which man's life and activity appear as something infinitely remote, something with which he has nothing to do, will never forget that unimpassioned stillness of soul. He will never forget how his mind was lifted up, as though it were light as a feather, above all care and all unsuccessful striving.

In this connection we should remind ourselves in particular of Spinoza's 'intellectual love of God (*amor dei intellectualis*)—the contemplative love for God, in which God signifies nothing but the inner coherence among all phenomena, determined by eternal laws, which as such are immutable and are exalted above all appetite. In the case of the peace that comes to one under the starry heavens or up in the solitariness of the mountain, it is naturally the impression of remoteness from the unrest of human life and of the stillness of the surroundings which directly produces peace of soul. To this something else may be added, however, which exerts a particularly strong influence—and indeed it *must* be taken into account because of the universal tendency of the human race to personify natural phenomena. When a hurricane blows over the ocean and raises up waves sky-high, when the atmosphere is cleft by lightning and the heavens appear like a sea of fire and there is a deafening rumble of thunder, there arises the impression of a personal power which is raging. But conversely when there is a great stillness, the same tendency to personify finds expression in the idea of a person who, spiritually regarded, reposes in himself in exalted majesty, undisturbed by the storms of appetite and passion.

In this way another element is added, which accentuates the quiescence of appetite in such an impression. One enters into the peace of soul of this person, the creature of one's own imagination, and in this way he seems to us to be given in our own feeling, at the same time with and distinct from our own 'I'. This is love for

God as an eternal repose, which Spinoza experienced, not on the basis of a chance impression but upon his turning towards the eternal coherence within the universe, lifted up above all time. He personified this eternal coherence and made it a pure 'I', reposing in itself and existing for itself, which as such is its own self without limitation and is apprehended through itself. Such an 'I' can have no purpose. It is in no way dependent on anything external of any sort at all; it has no idea of anything outside itself. It has nothing which is either past or future. For all physical nature, all time exists only with and for changing things, which themselves exist only in the eternal continuum in God. But with this God, given on the basis of an intuition of the coherence of the world—with this personification of the eternal coherence of the world—the philosopher feels himself to be one, since he participates through feeling in its eternal repose. He loves God, and this love is God's own love for himself in the philosopher. For they are both one in a mystic union (*unio mystica*).

The contemplative mood of peace which has here been described is of the same character as the mood of the Hindu sage, although in contrast to the latter it rests on an intuition of the world, not on a turning from the world. It can arise, although in a lesser degree, through the personification of stillness in the nature around us. With its independence of any other dogmatics than that which can be said to be present in a scientific view of reality, which therefore concerns itself essentially with eternal laws, it may well be a religious power of significance in any age.

The situation is somewhat different in moral religiosity as we find it in Christianity. Here a certain system of dogmatics seems to be the prerequisite for the development of the idea of a person, immediately present in our own 'I', who redeems me from moral distress and gives me power to stand against life's suffering. And certainly this religiosity presupposes a system of dogmatics, which comes into conflict with our scientific world-view, so that it can become a question whether it has sufficient vitality to withstand science. Now it is true that this dogmatics does not in any way affect the truth-value of religious experience as such. As we have already said, this experience is neither true nor false. But religious experience nevertheless seems to be a psychological prerequisite for the possibility of this system of dogmatics itself. And in this way the system of dogmatics acquires significance for the experience so that its potential conflict with science becomes significant for the survival of religion itself.

## 4. PSYCHOLOGICAL ROOTS OF THE
### TENDENCY TO OBJECTIFY THE DIVINE SPIRIT

When we attempt now to investigate the truth-value of religious dogmatics, we must first direct our attention to a peculiarity of the God who is given in religious experience. This peculiarity was touched on in an introductory way at the beginning of these lectures, but it has now for the first time received its complete elucidation. Meister Eckhart characterizes the religious person as the one who is isolated—in the sense of isolated from the world—absorbed in himself, one for whom God is one with his own 'I'. This strikes right at the heart of the matter. The religious person has his highest pleasure in a person who is given to him in his own inner 'I', who is one with it. And in this drift of feeling, he is isolated from the world. This inner life of his is the only thing that is important. But this implies that for the religious man this divine person must himself be isolated. If God himself were oriented towards the external, then pleasure in him would not isolate man from the world either.

Now as we have found earlier, this isolation does not have to signify an absolute denial of the world. Even if such a negative element is also an integral part of Christianity, there is added to this an element of overwhelming the world, an overcoming of the suffering which one's actual dependence on the world brings with it. In two respects this dependence on the world is of significance, according to the Christian belief, viz. in a moral and in a natural respect. In the first place there are unconditional duties which are involved in the external order, which are necessarily related to the preservation of one's own self. Thus failure to conform to the demand of duty becomes a spiritual suffering, from which one seeks redemption. In the second place, it is impossible to make oneself insensible to natural suffering. Now then the person who is isolated from the world is characterized by the fact that in the religious, introverted pleasure he finds the power to overcome his dependence on this suffering. But from this it follows that God himself is isolated from the world in the same sense. He is a person who preserves his inner peace in moral suffering and who resists any dependence on the natural.

But all this has *nothing* at all to do with a cosmic power, a power over the world in the external sense. It is to be noted that even Spinoza's God was essentially nothing but a being isolated from the world, since he was immediately present in the philosopher's idea of God and in his identification in feeling with him in his eternal blessedness, and since he was united with the philosopher's 'I' through a *unio mystica*. In the personification of the eternal coherence of the world, God becomes for the philosopher a pure 'I', reposing in himself, dependent on nothing external. This 'I' exists only for himself and thus also for the philosopher who is beholding him, with whom God is one. Spiritual religion in general has nothing to do with external powers.

Then whence comes the tendency in even spiritual religions to make their gods into world-powers? Only the Hindu philosophy-religion can be said to avoid slipping over into such a view. But it is also to be noticed that for this religion there is no external world and thus there is no possibility of externalizing the god, Brahman. Now of course one sees, especially in the Dionysian ecstasy, how the idea of an external power had significance for the blessedness which the knowledge of the presence of the god could bestow. For it was precisely as the eternal power to renew life against death that the presence of the god in one's own 'I', his identity with the soul, had significance in enhancing the life-feeling. Here also, therefore, it was a question, essentially if not exclusively, of a maximal heightening of the purely natural life-feeling. Therefore the Dionysian cult was also a direct outgrowth of a naturalistic magic, through which one could appropriate the natural powers in such a way as to benefit the individual. It was magic, magical power, which one could influence, as a spirit given in one's own 'I'.

We might expect that the idea of an external power would appear only where religion has significance as a heightening of the natural life-feeling, but not where religion is a pure spiritual power, un-tainted by any relation to the external world, through which, on the one hand, moral peace is restored and power is gained to withstand suffering and misery, and, on the other hand, a universal quiescence of appetite arises. Thus we might suppose that in Christianity and in the Spinozistic contemplative religion any view of God as an external power would be absent.

Perhaps it will be said that, in connection with Christianity, the matter can be understood against the background of Judaistic influences. According to the Jewish view, that is, God as the moral law-giver was also, as such, an avenger against those who broke his commandments. It is clear that as an avenger he must be an external world-power. And indeed it is also true that, according to the older Christian dogmatics, appeasing this God, and thus making moral peace possible, required the sacrifice of his only begotten Son, upon whom sins were transferred. Upon this dogmatic stony ground, one can say, the flowers of religion have grown up, and this explains the external character of the Christian God.

We might refer further to the fact that the heavenly father in Christianity always preserves a purely natural side, since he cares for his own as a natural father cares for his children. 'He who clothes the lilies of the field and feeds the birds of the heavens, will he not provide for you, you who are your heavenly father's children?' Naturally, in spite of his spiritual significance, God must have the character of an external power. We might also refer to the fact that the belief in Christ's physical resurrection is associated with the necessity of a temporal incorruptibility in eternal happiness—an entirely natural conception, although it really conflicts with the idea of the soul's repose in eternity—and to the fact that even in this supernatural power of Christ a purely natural element within Christianity thus finds expression. This natural element is related to the Greek's belief in the resurrected Dionysius as necessary for the complete life-feeling, which one experiences in the idea of the presence of the god.

But although we have indicated the connection between pure religiosity and the thought of certain external consequences, e.g. the avoidance of a certain natural evil or the achievement of a certain natural good, this explanation is not sufficient. It is to be noted, that is, that this explanation does not hold for Spinoza. For him religiosity is purely spiritual pleasure under the aspect of eternity, in which pleasure one simply rejoices in the presence of God—the pure 'I'—in one's own self. God is one with the immediately present feeling, and every thought of his significance for a palpable good or evil is absent. Thus the pleasure is merged here with pleasure in the *possession* of the complete inward blessedness, exalted above all the unrest of striving.

And yet even for Spinoza God is, theoretically regarded, a

world-power, which prevails in all things, a primordial power from which everything stems. He is not only the eternal continuum of phenomena, personified into an 'I' reposing in himself and independent of everything external. This continuum, this 'I' is also itself a power which is at work in things. Thus one must seek here for an explanation which lies deeper than the one just advanced. This explanation of the externalization of the isolated personality, which in religiosity itself is purely inward, into an external power, will prepare the way for the understanding of the peculiar character of the religious dogmatics.

## 5. SELF-CONSCIOUSNESS AND THE IDEA OF SPIRIT

We have previously sought to show that the idea of the 'I' as the idea of the purely inward, which is completely known, has itself arisen out of a connection between a world of feeling, in which we localize the content of the feeling in our own organism, and the idea of that same organism as an objective reality, existing in time. This real organism is thus apprehended as a self given in feeling. Thus the feeling itself, in which it is given, also becomes one with the apprehension of itself. It becomes the completely inward, but it is also properly given, wholly and completely, in the present apprehension of it. It becomes a spirit, which as such is characterized by being an existence only for itself, by isolation.

It is of particular interest here to observe the significance of the feeling of will. This feeling is always combined with the idea of the activity of an organism. But at the same time the organism is also regarded as given in this feeling itself, and thus it becomes one with this feeling, one with the apprehension of itself, and therefore the purely inward and spiritual. In relation to the organism as the cause, the effect—which in and for itself is always an *external* effect with which the organism is connected as the cause—is itself moved into the organism-spirit. Conversely, despite its pure inwardness, its existence only for itself, the spirit is regarded as active and therefore as standing in connection with something external as its effect. And thus there arises the idea of myself as choosing and as active in that act of choosing, although at the same time the effect is not anything external but falls entirely within myself as a will. I, as a will, determine myself, so that the effect is the same as the cause. The spirit is active within itself and thus acts upon itself, upon its own determinateness.

But now, as we have said, the idea of the 'I' has an objective element at the same time. In this idea I always conceive at the same time of a real organism, living in time. Nothing is more natural, then, than that the idea of this objectively existing organism should be influenced by the idea of the same organism as one with the apprehension of itself and thus as something completely inward. Just as the outer is internalized, so also the inner is externalized. One transfers the purely inward 'I', which is the experience of itself, to the objective organism. Just as one says, 'I exist for myself in a purely inward life, where there is no distinction between the thing and its apprehension', so one says also, 'I walk, I am in this place or that'. This latter 'I' is no longer the *purely* inward, that which is one with the apprehension of itself, the absolutely innermost. It is an external reality, which yet has an inner side at the same time. In the organism's apprehension the way goes not only from the outside inward, but also from the inside outward.

How is this possible? How can that which is inner, which is the apprehension of itself, become something outer, which is not at all the apprehension of itself but rather exists independently of the apprehension of it? We can best understand this process if we look at the matter from the point of view of the changing or constant character of the idea. Bergson says that life as such is characterized by everlasting change. Matter is only the experience, changed into something permanent, of the inward, which in its own nature is changing. Indeed, it is altogether clear that insofar as I am the completely innermost, that which is one with the experience of itself in feeling, I also change with the constantly changing stream of feelings. The 'I' of the present moment no longer exists in the next moment, because the world of feelings, in which the 'I' is given has passed away and has been succeeded by another, with the result that the 'I' also is another 'I'. Indeed, one can properly say that in the present moment I can regard myself in the past as something real, so that for this present moment the past 'I' would be a reality. For the past 'I' as such is something external to me in the present moment. But the 'I' as such is one with the experience of itself. Thus in every moment of the life of the 'I' there is for the apprehension of the 'I' only that 'I' which is one with the immediately present experience. That is to say, the past is absolutely nothing for the existing 'I'. Thus we find here an absolute flux in the proper sense, in which all that has been has absolutely vanished. In this way, the 'I' becomes the completely timeless, which lives only in the present moment, and it becomes also the completely changeable, which in an everlasting stream plunges down, as it were, into a new world.

But the situation is different in the case of our apprehension of that which is real. The real as such is something constant, which cannot be in more than one mode. No matter how much that which is real changes, the change itself as real is still always determined in a certain way. Hence also the apprehension of that which is real as such is always one and the same. Certainly one can say that even our way of apprehending reality changes through our taking in ever new experiences. Naturally the savage's world picture is different from that of the modern man of science. And even the latter's world-picture is destined to be modified with the passage of time. But this is another matter. It does not mean that reality is more than one thing. When we remove the presupposition that reality is something constant, which cannot be in more than one mode, we cut the life-nerve of thought. The very question of *what exists* becomes completely meaningless, for the question about the real is as such a question about the determinate mode, distinguished from others, in which it is found. 'Does God exist?' would then become the same question as, 'Does the devil exist?' or 'Does the cat exist?' For if reality is not only in one mode, then God is the devil and the devil is a cat.

All such scepticism is completely meaningless, because in one respect doubt always presupposes a determinate reality. What is presupposed is, as Descartes puts it, his own existence as doubting, and this existent is to be more specifically described as an investigating, studying, inquiring subject. But here Descartes has both a temporal and a spatial reality. For study is something which itself occurs in time. It signifies a continuing psychical activity. And in order to be able to distinguish this activity precisely as *his*, as contrasted with someone else's activity going on at the same time, the doubter must ascribe the activity to a certain physical organism —thus he presupposes both time and space as a certain determinate reality. And if he also issues a book about his own doubts, he pre-supposes the existence of other persons who may be disposed to share in his philosophical reflections.

The fact that the apprehension of reality itself changes with the passage of time may not be taken as proof for the proposition that reality itself may be in more than one mode. Suppose a child has the idea that the stars originated when God the Father poked holes here and there in the firmament with a stick, so that the light which lay behind could shine through. No one doubts that such an idea is definitely inferior to the view of modern astronomy. No one thinks that the same is not true of our forefathers' explanation of thunder as due to Thor's conflict with the giants, as compared with our contemporary explanation of the same phenomenon in terms of electrical power. Here it is presupposed, indeed, that one particular apprehension of the real is closer to the truth than another. And one wants to say that the present scientific understanding of the world is in one way true in the absolute sense, namely, insofar as it offers the only possible explanation of the given experiences. If new experiences are constantly modifying the world-picture, then this also presupposes two things. For one thing it presupposes the existence of a temporal and spatial reality with causal relations within itself, to which the subject who is engaged in the research himself belongs. For another thing it presupposes that this reality, however it may be more precisely characterized, must nevertheless always present a character of such kind that the experiences we have had until that time are of significance in determining it. In this it is implied that the apprehension of reality, as an apprehension of reality, is unchangeable and that the relative mutability which characterizes our world-picture does not depend upon its character of being an apprehension of *reality* (so that the very determinateness of reality could be now this, now that), but rather upon its deficiency precisely as an *apprehension* of reality. But in this it is also implied that insofar as we are really convinced that we have grasped reality, the apprehension also appears as completely unchangeable *in this character of being an apprehension of reality*.

Hence because of the inner nature of the 'I' itself, the question, 'What am I as the purely inward, the innermost?' must always be answered in different ways at every moment, so that the answer which was given at a previous moment is absolutely meaningless at a subsequent moment. The past 'I' in the inner sense does not exist in any way in the present moment, not even in such a way that it could be characterized in the present moment as *having*

K

been. But the question here is not a question about reality as such, about truth, because here only the purely subjective is involved, not that which exists whether we apprehend it or not. The question about reality itself, on the other hand, necessarily demands an answer which will hold for all time, a conception which, as an apprehension of reality, is unchangeable.

If now one proceeds from the inward to the outward, and determines the real organism through this purely inward 'I', he becomes involved in an inner self-contradiction. For this inner 'I', which in itself is absolutely changing, which exists only for itself, which is one with its own experience of an object, is to be embraced at the same time in the abstract, rigid concept of an object. That which by its own nature cannot be embraced except in an immediate, constantly changing experience, can yet be grasped, so it is thought, in an apprehension of reality, which because of the determinateness of reality is constant and unchanging and in which the thing is grasped as existing in and for itself.

Here we have, therefore, a fixation of that which by its very nature cannot be fixed, a fixation of this thing into a reality, possessed of the rigidity of the concept of reality. This fixation is understandable, indeed, from the point of view of the whole psychological situation. But it is clear that to rigidify the spiritual in this way and to make it an existing reality does not have the least cognitive value. It is not the case that I, regarded as a spirit, and therefore I as the completely innermost, either walk or sit or in general really exist. Therefore neither does the God who is given within me exist. He is neither here nor there, he has neither been nor will be. For the categories of being do not suit him.

The idea of the spiritual as an inner *reality*, which exists for itself, has its origin, therefore, in self-consciousness, as well as in the consciousness of another 'I' as immediately present within me, as one with myself. Since an objective element—the idea of a psycho-physical organism—always enters into such a consciousness, one transfers to it, in its reality, the concept of that which is inner and spiritual, that which exists for itself. In this way the spiritual comes to be regarded as something which exists independently of the apprehension of it, although as the purely inward it must be the consciousness of itself. Thus its existence becomes not an eternal existence, an existence such that it is found only in the living present, as one with the present experience. Rather the spirit exists through time. And the apprehension of the spirit, like all apprehensions of reality, becomes something which by its nature is constant and unchangeable. One says, for example, that Christ's spirit lived upon earth at a certain determinate point in time. And naturally the apprehension of this spirit of Christ as a reality, insofar as it is really a true one, is by its own nature fixed and unchangeable. It becomes dogmatics.

If one lies on one's back in the water on a beautiful summer day and allows oneself to drift with the quiet, on-flowing current, one experiences a special feeling of blissful delight. When one has come up to the shore again one may begin to reflect upon one's experience. Now it is clear that if one is of sound mind, one will say to oneself only that it is especially pleasant to be carried thus by the current. But if one explains that the pleasure exists in the current itself as an inner power within it, through which it flows on, then one is not sound in one's reflection. So it is with the spirit. When I enter into life's flowing current, I experience the spirit itself within me, as something immediately present in this moment, as one with my own feeling. Perchance I also experience the divine spirit in its eternal repose in itself, as I enter with Spinoza, perhaps, into the peace of the quiescence of desire which characterizes the coherent unity of the world, personified. Thus I identify this person with my own feeling, so that it becoms a spirit which is one with my own. Oblivious to what has been and what will be, I live in the rich world of the present and allow myself to drift with the current of life. But suppose now that I explain the matter reflectively not by saying that certain feelings and certain ideas which are connected with them present themselves, but rather by saying that there really is a spirit which persists through the different moments of my life—on the one hand, I myself, on the other hand, the divine spirit. In that case the same mistake is made as when one believes that the pleasure which one experiences in allowing oneself to be carried by the current actually exists in the current. When one reasons in this way in regard to the spirit, however, the reflection does not occur as if one were abnormal, because there is here a universal human psychological situation, which necessarily drives the reflection in this direction.

Now a distinction is to be observed here between the natural human 'I' or spirit and the divine spirit. When in immediate self-consciousness I apprehend myself as the completely innermost, as

one with my own feelings, localized in the psycho-physical
organism, then certainly this 'I', this spirit, is always isolated, in
one sense, from the world. This is so to the extent that the 'I'
exists only for itself in its own experience of feeling. But now insofar as the psycho-physical organism in its conscious life stands in
relation to the external order and perceives it, has feelings connected with it, and entertains desires directed towards it, this 'I',
this spirit, to which the conscious life of the organism is referred,
is itself situated in relation to the external order. Thus the spirit
is not isolated from the world with reference to its *content*, even
though it is isolated with reference to its *form*. Therefore it is
regarded as a real spirit, living in *time*, and only relatively independent: in spite of everything, it depends upon the external, it has
no absolute power over the external.

The situation is different in the case of the divine spirit, which is
most purely given in the feeling of blissful peace when it is introduced into an organism. This spirit is itself completely turned
away from the world, perceives nothing of the world's striving,
knows or desires nothing in the world. This spirit, the Hindu
philosopher-Braham or the Spinozistic world-coherence personified, becomes the pure 'I', reposing in itself, the 'I' which is
isolated even with reference to its content. But this holds not only
for that God which exists for the Hindu sage or for Spinoza. It
holds also, although not as simply, for the Christian God in Christ.
This is the person who experiences complete moral peace, who
overcomes all the suffering of the world through his complete
feeling of peace, the person into whom the Christian enters in his
feeling, whereby he also experiences Christ as immediately present
in his own spirit. In either instance, although more purely in the
former, a spirit is present which is isolated from the world not
only in its general formal character of spirit, but also with reference
to its whole content—the purely inward. The philosopher's
concept of the absolute, as that which exists in itself, is in its origin,
let it be observed, nothing but the divine spirit as it is in God.
It is itself the religious experience. To that extent God is nothing
but the religious person's own feeling of blessedness when he lives
in a person, is united with a person, who himself is characterized
for the religious man by a world-overcoming feeling of repose which
comes with the quiescence of desire and by moral peace. God becomes one with the feeling of complete turning from the world,

complete triumph over the world, in the religious person himself. He becomes the same pure feeling of blessedness, in relation to the world, in which he is regarded as given, and thus exists purely for himself and subsists in himself.

The absolute, as that which is isolated from everything else, that which subsists in itself, is the reality which exists only in and for itself. In order to be so, it must be a pure, complete 'I'. But the concept of the 'I' is entertained through the idea that the person himself is one with the feelings localized in him, in which the person is given. The idea of a *pure* 'I' can be entertained only by thinking of the person himself in his inner turning away from the world and overcoming of the world, and by identifying this person with the feeling associated with him, in which he is thought to be given. Thus the concept of the absolute must be, in its origin, precisely the idea of the divine spirit, as it is given in religious experience.

Note also that when Plato conceives the world of ideas as a reality subsisting in and for itself, included within itself, and independent of everything external, it is also natural for him that this world is the source of that blessedness which is independent of the external. It is complete blessedness itself, the pure good. Plato would never have come to this idea if he himself had not felt this eternal peace, which is gained when one is lost in the vision of the sunlit world of ideas, with its complete exaltation over the external order and its contradictions, its suffering, its corruptibility.

When Aristotle conceives pure thought, directed towards itself, as the absolute, which exists in and for itself, it is also for him the source of pure blessedness—it is pure blessedness itself. How should he have come to this view, if he had not experienced this eternal repose when introduced into pure thought personified, thought as such?

What is the Ur-One of Plotinus, as that which exists completely for itself, as one with blessedness or the good, if it is not a concept entertained on the basis of religious ecstasy? Has it not arisen out of the indescribable feeling of blessedness which one experiences when the consciousness of the external world and of myself in my confinement disappears completely, as the power of feeling is strained in one direction and, unrestrained by any opposition from the external and finite, stretches its wings for flight? The Ur-One is the feeling of blessedness which has arisen in this way, entirely free from the burdensome opposition of subject and object in the entire life of conception.

When like Aristotle, Hegel makes sure philosophical thought—here conceived as the overcoming of the contradiction between the finite and the infinite—the absolute, this idea has its foundation for him in religious experience, in which, as it is said, the contradiction between the finite and the infinite is eliminated in the form of imagination. That is to say, in imagination the finite spirit experiences itself as one with the God given in imagination. The subject experiences the complete *coincidentia oppositorum*, the unity, in which all opposition which belongs to the external is eliminated. This experience of the finite subject naturally presupposes the feeling of blessedness in being introduced into God's own life. Only through being identified with this feeling does God become one with my own self. The Hegelian concept of philosophical thought as the absolute is nothing but a concept gained on the basis of a philosophically influenced religious experience of eternal repose at being introduced into the self, conceived apart from the concretization of imagination, which overcomes all contradiction, the world-thought personified. In this experience the world-thought itself becomes one with the feeling which is experienced in connection with it, and thus it becomes one with the finite spirit itself.

Finally, in the case of the Swedish philosopher Boström, absolute reason, which is what it is only as a cognition of itself, is nothing but what is innermost within ourselves. It is a concept which rests on the foundation of a religious experience, in which one experiences a feeling of blissful repose in connection with the idea of pure thought, divorced from the world and personified. Thought itself regards this experience as given and is identified with it. But if the absolute is nothing but the idea of the divine spirit as it is given in religious experience, and if this spirit itself is nothing but that person, isolated from the world, who becomes one with the very experience of feeling which is associated with him, then it is clear that the absolute is in no sense essentially a world-power. The absolute is nothing but the one who is isolated from the world, regarded as one with one's own feeling of blessedness in being introduced into him.

As I said once before, in religious experience God can be the poorest beggar as well as the mightiest king. Everything depends upon the inner peace which God brings and which he who lives in and with him can experience. Thus the Christian God is also a carpenter's son from Nazareth. 'The foxes have holes, and the birds have their nests, but the Son of Man has no place where he can lay his head.' And yet Christ appears in the Christian dogmatics as one with the Creator of the world and the Ruler of the world. Out of debasement, he suddenly is exalted, and we see him sitting at the right hand of the Lord of the worlds. The change appears strange, and yet it is so natural.

## 6. THE LOGICAL ABSURDITY OF THE IDEA OF SPIRIT

We turn back now to the distinction between the human spirit and the divine spirit when objectified into a reality, which is not *one* with its own apprehension but is something independent of the apprehension. When we conceive the idea of spirit, we have said, an objective element always enters into our conception, viz. the idea of a psycho-physical organism with the character of a continuing reality. Therefore the concept of spirit is transferred to this idea of a psycho-physical organism. The organism, conceived as real, is itself a reality independent of the apprehension of it. In this organism the spirit exists. But as we have also said, the human, natural spirit—the human 'I'—is really a spirit only in form. In natural self-consciousness one inserts into this spirit a life of consciousness attached to the world, feelings and appetites determined by the external. Hence the spirit is not a spirit in its content, and therefore, as objectified in the psycho-physical organism, it has only a limited independence in relation to the external. The natural human spirit is only a relative power in the world. But the situation is different in the case of the divine spirit as it is given in religious experience. It may be that this divine spirit is given through being introduced into a determinate human person, representing the complete, world-overcoming peace. Still by its own nature, not only formally but also from the point of view of its content, it is a pure spirit, turned away from the world, reposing in itself.

How must it be, now, when this spirit is objectified into a reality in the world? It is the absolute, i.e. the pure spirit, which lives only in and for itself. Thus, if, in spite of its isolation, it is also placed in relation to the world, it becomes independent in relation to the world in such a way that the world does not exist independently of the spirit, limiting it. Rather the world itself exists wholly through the spirit, and is likewise maintained by it. The spirit becomes the world-power itself in the absolute sense.

Here then lies the heart of the business. Here lies the explanation of the double-nature of Christ as, on the one hand, God, as Creator of the world and Ruler of the world and, on the other hand, the carpenter's son, who has nothing on which to lay his head. He is isolated from the world in the supreme sense, the man who is absorbed in a pure inner life which is turned away from the world and overcomes the world. Thus for the religious experience, which rests on the foundation of one's being introduced into him, he is pure spirit, existing for himself. Placed in the world, he becomes necessarily a power *over* the world—the perfect world-power. The absolute as pure spirit has changed over into its exact opposite—an external power *sensu eminenti*.

One thing is clear however. Every interpretation of a spirit-life in the world, every idea of the spiritual in and for itself (one with its own apprehension) as a power active in the world, is false at its root, because it contains a determination of reality in a self-contradictory manner. Every attempt to base a knowledge of reality on the foundation of spiritual experience—ultimately one's own self-consciousness, but also religious experience—is by its very nature bound to be unsuccessful, although it is natural, for psychological reasons, that one should carry the spiritual over to the sphere of the objective, the non-spiritual. (The transfer is the result of the change from a thought which is essentially in flux into an apprehension of reality which by its nature is constant.) All metaphysics and religious dogmatics, which as we have found are fruits of the same tree, viz. religious experience, commit this mistake, driven by the natural tendencies which are present here.

But it is not enough to say that this is true of what are usually called metaphysics and religious dogmatics. Every stage of natural thought is infected by immediate self-consciousness, which is constantly, so to speak, throwing sand in our eyes and preventing us from seeing reality clearly. For example, what is the idea of powers, regarded as causes which produce effects out of themselves, except a transference of the inner and spiritual to the external? Naturally it is a self-contradiction to say that something can produce an effect out of itself. In that case the effect would be included within the cause, and thus it would not be other than the cause it-self. As soon as we reflect about the ordinary concept of will, however, this way of thinking becomes completely understandable. We have previously pointed out how we regard the will as an activity included within the 'I' itself, in which I determine myself, so that the effect is the same as the cause. And we have explained how this idea arises naturally out of the feeling of will, the feeling of tension, of straining, and the accompanying idea of the activity of an organism, through which certain effects are brought about. Since the organism which is active here is itself regarded as given in this feeling and as one with it, it becomes for us something spiritual, something which lives for itself. Its effects, to which it stands related, are thus also transferred into this spirit, and this again finds expression in the idea of the will as the cause of itself. But as a result the idea of a power is nothing but an abstraction, which has arisen through the transference of one's own will, re-garded in the manner indicated, over to the external—although, at least according to the general consensus, only the idea of the cause of itself remains. The will itself in the ordinary sense, as motivated by the idea of an end which belongs to it and through which it determines itself, has passed away.

Or take the ordinary proof, which appears with a kind of seduc-tive naturalness, of at least the relative independence of the soul-life in relation to the physical. It is said that consciousness, percep-tion, feeling, will are not anything which can be in space. When one observes these things one finds nothing of space there. They do not have any definite length or any definite shape, nor can they themselves be measured or weighed physically. Therefore, it is said, we have here a different kind of reality from that which is in space. But now take a quality in space, for example, a colour. This quality as such, or regarded only as a colour, is naturally not in space. Neither does it have a definite length, a definite shape, a definite weight, although the body in which it is found has these things. Therefore, one could say with equal justice, the colour does not exist in space. Or take circularity as such. It does not have any length either, nor does it *have* any shape, although it *is* a shape, nor can it be weighed. With the same justice as in the case of consciousness, one can conclude that circularity also does not exist in space. In general, it holds for qualities which are in space, consciousness included, that they themselves do not have any magnitude, whether with reference to length or to weight. But of course the concrete objects in which they are found have such magnitude. And likewise it holds of all other qualities that they are not in space if they are regarded *in abstracto*. But abstract intuition as such is incomplete.

In the case of consciousness, when one is seeking to prove its independence one presupposes that it is to be treated without any reference to the concrete organism in which it is found. This consciousness does not have length or weight, but of course this does not make it impossible that the organism in which it is found has these things. The fact that, when taken in itself, consciousness is not in space does not make it impossible that, as present in the organism, it is in space. Thus in the proof one presupposes the independence of consciousness in relation to the material. But in regard to such a consciousness it is not possible to enquire about the physical organism in which it is found. Rather the abstract intuition of consciousness in itself constitutes the real thing itself, and is not just an abstract determination of the thing.

But what has given rise to this idea, which would rule out the possibility of ever placing consciousness in any relation to the physical? If consciousness does not exist in some space, then there is no medium in which it can exist together with the physical. Well, the idea has arisen out of the fact that consciousness in general seems to us to be given in self-consciousness. But in self-consciousness the 'I' is given as one with its own apprehension and thus as existing for itself. Thus it becomes natural to regard the consciousness given within me as existing for itself. And so we have the idea.

Now, since the idea of a spirit-life in reality is a logical impossibility, it therefore seems as if materialism were the only logically possible view. It should be carefully noticed, however, that if consciousness is also in space it is not for that reason itself a physical body, nor does it have corporeal qualities itself. It is not a movement of atoms, as materialism proper taught. It is itself a specific quality of organic matter, which in itself does not have the character of matter, although it exists in matter.

The exclusion of the spirit-life from reality also brings with it the elimination of so-called agnosticism, as the view which assumes an ultimate ground of the world without regarding this ground as itself knowable. For a ground of the world cannot be conceived as part of the world, and thus neither can it be conceived as itself existing in space. But if the ground in question does not exist in space, then it is not in general *one* reality alongside another. When space is eliminated as the medium in which the ground might exist alongside another thing, the possibility of conceiving the ground as existing together with another reality is also eliminated. Under such conditions the ground of the world cannot be conceived as a reality in the same sense as that in which the world itself is real. Then it must be conceived as possessing a reality for itself, which makes it impossible to regard it as existing alongside another reality. That is to say, if the ground of the world is to be conceivable, it must be thought of as possessing that sort of reality, isolated from everything else, which characterizes the absolute. But this is the same thing as to regard it as a spirit or as something which exists only for its own consciousness. Therefore agnosticism, in so far as it generally conceives of a ground of the world, even though it is unknowable, is the same as idealism or spirit-philosophy and falls to the ground along with it.

## 7. THE POSSIBILITY OF RELIGION IN THE NATURALISTIC WORLD-VIEW

But now, if one is, so to speak, de-Christianized and dispossessed of every trace of spirituality, does not religious experience itself, the inner life itself, become an impossibility? When materialism presses to the fore, are not the roots of religiosity severed! We shall now treat this question. It is, in fact, the real religious problem of our time. For it is to be noticed that if, from the point of view of the understanding, materialism is actually the only possible world-view, then no power in the world can in the long run prevent its victorious progress. The human race cannot suppress the pursuit of knowledge, as long as it desires to live. The pursuit of knowledge has grown up out of the original struggle of the race to raise itself up over the level of beasts. It is only through his more highly developed brains and thus through his greater capacity for know-ledge that man can make himself the master of all living beings and thereby procure the conditions for the satisfaction of his needs. Therefore the pursuit of knowledge is so firmly rooted in his own nature that it is operative apart from any reference to its usefulness for other purposes. When ideas dominated by feeling triumph over the understanding, which judges objectively, the victory is a Pyrrhic victory. For every suppression of the pursuit of knowledge is a blow against the very nerve which sustains us as the masters of the world.

But how will it be if, on the other hand, religion in a certain form, namely as producing the quiescence of desire, is a necessity of life for all men? How will it be if in another form, as moral religion, the type of which is Christianity, it is a necessity of life for the introverted, moral person, who suffers because of his failure to measure up to the demand of his innermost being? Doubtless it is of the utmost importance to entertain the question of the possibility of religion for a materialistic world-view.

In fact this question has been answered already in the foregoing lectures, in a positive as well as in a negative direction. At this point we only have to draw out the consequences of this answer. First it is to be emphasized again that religious experience does not involve a reflective apprehension of reality, since in an apprehension of reality God would be given as a reality which existed independently of consciousness. Let us grant that the idea of a reality and certainly of a person as really present enters into religious experience. Still this person is never considered as existing independently of the consciousness of it, but rather he is regarded as one with the feeling in which he is given. Thus he is already differentiated from reality, considered as such.

Every person as given in a spiritual mode is differentiated from reality in just this way, that is, he is conceived as given to me in a feeling localized in relation to him—given in my identification in feeling with him—and thus as one with that feeling. But God, who is given in religious experience, is differentiated from reality in a special way, because he himself is the one who, regarded from the religious point of view, has turned away from the world and the one who overcomes the world in religious morality. Therefore he signifies pure spirituality for the religious person—pure being for and in itself. In the true sense he is the absolute, without being in any way a world-power. He may become a world-power, by virtue of the fact that his spirituality is hardened in a self-contradictory manner into a reality, which has the world alongside itself—but it is only through being the ground of the world that he can be completely independent of it and so have the world alongside himself. If he becomes a world-power in this way, however, this is only an expression of the fact that religiosity intrudes into the domain of thinking about reality and infects it.

But even though the tendency to objectify God is psychologically explicable, it does not have the least religious significance, and the repression of this tendency through a clear materialistic world-view can in no way repress the religious life itself. There is only one circumstance under which the repression of the objectifying tendency would be a real obstruction for religiosity, namely the circumstance where God acquires his significance for the religious person through the material advantages which he can bring or through being the one who realizes in the future the moral task which is defined by the moral ideal. Now concerning the former— God as a ground of material advantages—the need of such a God signifies that the religious person as such has not really turned away from the world and is not overcoming the world in his religiosity. It signifies that he does not love God as being in himself the person who has turned away from the world and overcomes the world, but rather on the ground of the external advantages which he can bestow. But neither is such a religiosity purely *spiritual* religiosity, and it is only the continuance of spiritual religiosity on a materialistic basis that is in question here.

Concerning the latter—the idea that the repression of the objectifying tendency in relation to the spiritual would also suppress the idea of God as realizing the moral ideal—the situation here is more difficult to treat. For here it is not a question of an interest which is itself foreign to the religious life, but rather a question of an interest which stands in an intimate connection with the introverted moral life, with the life which has its essential aim in being in accord with one's own innermost 'I', which is always one with God as the pure spirit. If my moral task is imposed by this 'I' and thus by God, then the interest in the possibility of its realization is necessarily bound up with the religious person's feeling of being one with God. Therefore this interest is associated in the most intimate way with the religious life itself.

But here we must draw a clear distinction, without which everything leads into confusion. The question here is: Is the idea of the possibility of the realization of the moral ideal necessarily dependent upon the idea of a real, dominant spiritual life in nature, and especially in human life? Now one ought to observe the distinction between the objective world of ideas which is the foundation of religiosity and that which proceeds from religiosity, the distinction between that which is *prius* in relation to religiosity and that which is *posterius*. For example, if we think of Spinozistic religiosity, the materialistic interpretation of an eternal continuum of nature constitutes its ground. This continuum is personified in religious experience and thus becomes the purely spiritual: the 'I' which reposes in itself and is only for itself—which is regarded as the very 'I' of the person who is contemplating the continuum of the world itself. But on the other hand, Spinoza's idea of this pure 'I' as an objective reality, independent of the observing person, which is the ground supporting the world, is determined by this religious interpretation of the continuum of nature, and thus is something *posterius*.

Now with reference to moral religiosity, we ought to distinguish in a corresponding way between the objective type of idea which constitutes the ground for this religiosity and that which is supported by it. At least as a presupposition, nothing is actually needed here except the idea of a person who by the peace of his moral religiosity overcomes the suffering that comes from without and death, and who likewise, despite all temptation, overcomes moral suffering—the suffering which comes from a failure to conform to the demand of one's own inner self. The existence of such a person is in no way an impossibility from the materialistic point of view. In point of fact it is the actual experience of spiritual religiosity itself which offers the proof of its possibility. Even if the evangelists' accounts concerning Christ should actually be false in essential respects, still at all events they are a living representation of spiritual religiosity, which possesses a profound psychological truth. In the same way a poem may be psychologically true, without for that reason being true in the objective sense, by virtue of representing a condition of soul, which we are in a position to verify in ourselves. It is with a person, represented with at least this psychological truth, that moral religiosity itself is associated. When one has this person before oneself in imagination and enters into this life of feeling, the person also acquires the required character of reality. The very question, 'Does he exist, or does he not exist?' never presents itself. For he is regarded as given in one's feelings of communion, located in him. In this way he also becomes one with one's own feeling.

Now, however, it is to be noticed that, with reference to the idea of the possibility of realizing the moral ideal, it holds in a similar way that this idea itself can be present as a foundation for moral religiosity—entirely independent of the world-picture which has been 'infected', as seen from the intellectual standpoint, by moral-religious ideas dominated by feeling. In the first place, moral ideas are endowed with such a power that the life of feeling and of will which is determined by them appears as unavoidable, so that for the person who is generally introverted it becomes an expression for his innermost self—notwithstanding the fact that moral ideas have nothing at all to do with truth and reality itself. The existence of moral ideas endowed with this power shows that it is a question here of powers which lie behind conscious life, which are called instincts, which take their course in such a way.

Furthermore one must consider that these ideas are by and large in accord with the demands of social life. That is to say, the mode of action which is promoted in them is what is advantageous for society as a whole, advantageous with reference to the general happiness and culture. As has often been pointed out in the history of morals, one can definitely observe a development towards universality in moral ideas. That is, that mode of action is good which is demanded by the well-being of the whole race. If one thinks of the Christian idea as mutual love among all people, then its significance for the welfare of the race is obvious, since under all circumstances mercy and considerateness are continually needed for the happiness of the race. This is true not only because of the direct possibility of happiness for other people and for the person who gives, but also because such modes of action counter-act the anti-social forces which destroy community and solidarity. But it is only through community and solidarity that the race generally can achieve happiness and culture. Therefore one must assume that the instincts which underlie moral ideas are the social, true instincts, which generally sustain society and without which the race could not continue as the master of nature, making use of it for its service. But from this it follows that in the instincts which underlie moral ideas one must seek for the strongest powers in the race.

In spite of all the powers which would destroy society, human society persists and has developed in the course of time to such an extent that the various powers of man have been placed more and more in the service of the construction and development of society.

And in such a time as the present the human race generally continues, despite all contrary forces, to be the lord over nature. This circumstance shows that the instincts which underlie our moral ideas are the strongest.

From what has been said it follows that the faith that the moral task will be realized more and more is a faith in the power of the social instincts in the race. Nevertheless this faith is not at all an objectively groundless idea. Now here we have a foundation for the possibility of moral religiosity, which may be reconciled very well with a materialistic world-view. The morally religious person, whether fictitious or real, with whom moral religiosity is united, himself appears in religious experience as an expression of the strongest power in the race—the social instinct—the instinct which serves the happiness and culture of the race. This instinct is thus personified in this person and, in virtue of the religious person's spiritual communion with him, acquires a spiritual character itself. It is clear that the faith in the relative actualization of the moral ideal in the future, which is so intimately associated with moral religiosity, does not at all need to be contradicted by a materialistic world-view, at the expense of that religiosity. The very objective foundation for religious experience involves such a conviction, which is completely reasonable from the standpoint of science, without in any way presupposing the reality of spirit as such.

Now one can ask, however, 'Is it possible for man to lead a spiritual life on the basis of belief in a reality which is completely pure from all spirituality, a reality which is ruled only by physical or psychical forces, and thus also on the basis of the belief that he himself is only a moment in the universal continuum of nature, without any freedom or existence for himself?' To this it may be replied that his own feeling and will still belong to this 'spiritually dead' reality.   Consequently man has in his hands the possibility, without thereby falsifying the truth, of living in the consciousness of himself as a spirit—not in the objective sense, but as being one with the feeling in which the spirit is given as the purely inward which does not exist independently of his experience of it. In the same way man has the possibility of regarding himself as standing in spiritual communion with other persons—not as existing outside him, but as having existence in his own feeling of identification with them. In truth one can say to mankind: 'If the darkness in the world causes you to suffer, this is simply due to the fact that you have not ignited the torch which alone can make the world light. You are waiting for the light to come from without, presenting itself to you. But such a light can only be an illusion. Ignite the light yourself, and it will burn with an undiminished flame.'

# APPENDICES

# METAPHYSICS IN THE SPECIAL SCIENCES[1]

And now to turn from philosophy to the special sciences. First it may be pointed out that certain 'concepts' in the ordinary consciousness— the 'concepts' of thing, motion, and power—reappear in modern natural science. But these are nothing but words whose character has not been carefully considered.

First, the 'concept' of a *thing* with properties. Take the case of a particular object of thought, which is designated as a thing. If one disregards the properties, then there is nothing remaining—and still there is supposed to be a thing there which *supports* these properties. However one understands what it is a question of here when one considers that properties must *exist* only in the thing. Thus the *thing* must be their reality. But this reality must remain as itself real. At this point the whole dissolves into words without thought. The psychological ground of this sort of characterization cannot be treated here.

Then the 'concept' of motion. In this 'concept' the *thing, which is identified with itself and which 'persists'*, changes its condition. Now it is obvious that the condition belongs as much to the thing, as *this* thing, as do its so-called properties. If the condition is changed, then the thing is another thing. And this can be said with real meaning only in the sense that in both of the objects, one of which follows the other in time, there are common determinations. Thus according to the ordinary consciousness the persisting thing which moves has determinations in relation to its condition which are inconsistent with one another. Perhaps it is said that one determination may stand together with every other because of the fact that these determinations do not exist *at the same time*. But the contradiction is by no means adjusted in this way, since the thing which exists at the different points in time must be the *same* thing. In any case the same thing would have to acquire determinations of its situation which mutually exclude one another.

Obviously the ordinary view of motion belongs together with the conception of a thing. One reasons that the determinateness of condition is something *external* and *incidental* to the reality of the thing. Determinations of the state of the thing which are mutually exclusive therefore do not affect the thing as such. Or expressed very simply, determinations

[1] From an earlier version of the *Selbstdarstellung* (Autobiographical Statement), written in Swedish in 1927 but never published. (Hagërström manuscript No. K 6 II, pp. 69-78). See above p. 47, n.l.)

of condition lack reality in themselves. The thing alone has reality in itself! If one likewise says that the mutually exclusive determinations stand together with one another only if they occur at different times, one assumes that if the actual, perceptible change from one spatial location to another, which has an actually unambiguous determinateness, did not appear before consciousness, then *meaninglessness* would immediately come into play. One thinks that one can avoid the contradiction by making reference to the fact of motion, but this is completely different from what is represented in the word.

Finally, as concerns the 'concept' of power, its scholastic character already famous.

The dependence of science upon these concepts in the ordinary consciousness has left its mark in striking metaphysical constructions. Mention must first be made of atomism, *insofar* as it is a theory of matter as consisting of quality-less atoms. (It ought to be noticed here that it does not matter whether one says that they certainly have qualities, although not conceived by us, or whether one says that they are quality-less. For in the former assertion it is by no means the case that any qualities whatsoever are thought of.) However where does such a view lead to? What distinguishes the atoms, which are only quantitatively determinate, from empty space? Their impenetrability? But impenetrability presupposes motion. Nothing external to the atom can enter into it through motion. But indeed motion presupposes something more than empty space. If now the atom is to be the only real thing in space, motion and thus impenetrability as well presuppose the atom. Then perhaps the atom is to be determined as a centre of power in space? To say nothing of the fact that 'power' itself is a word, not a real concept; still the word may well lose all foundation apart from the assumption of motion. But in motion the atom is presupposed. How ridiculous it sounds then: the atom is distinguished from empty space through being the *real* which exists in space.

Even today people are occupied with the metaphysics of Democritus: the atom is *being*, empty space is *not-being*. What significance the atomic theory still has as a hypothesis in natural science, it has, certainly, not as an idea of quality-less bodies. For such an idea has no foundation whatsoever. Secretly, although not in words, one ascribes to the atom a quality which can be conceived through which alone it becomes possible, to think of the atom as distinguished from empty space. *What* quality it is may be left unexamined here. But it is certain that it is only through this quality that atomism acquires scientific significance. In common usage this quality is suppressed, although it is conceived in any case. But the simple explanation of that fact is that the atom has immediate significance as an element in the explanation of physical and chemical processes only as a corporeal *magnitude* and thus is to be counted as the ultimate unity. In any case the quality has mediating significance as the foundation for forming the concept of simple, corporeal magnitude.

However the atomic theory, which is metaphysical and meaningless, leads to speculations which are ultimately meaningless—a weaving of words. This it does through all kinds of thought-transitions, which are occasioned by the concepts associated with the words being used. If the simple body alone is 'substance' or 'thing', then also space, in which the body is located, is not anything substantial, not anything real. This word leads thought to mere subjective existence. For just as simple 'being' is an expression for a feeling of certainty, so on the other hand the word 'not-being' awakens the feeling of renunciation which is attached to an assumption which we realize has only subjective significance. This feeling brings with it the conception of mere subjective existence. Thus one reaches the explanation of space (which, indeed, may not be anything real in the proper sense) as something which is merely subjective. On the other hand, what becomes now of the atom, the corporeally substantial unity? A body, which is not a body—it becomes a mathematical point. And so it becomes reality itself, if one disregards the psychic biphenomenon—a mass of points, which yet cannot be found alongside one another in space but are supposed to stand in a numerical relation to one another.

Space does not permit me to enter more fully into mathematical metaphysics, e.g. into the assumption of a space with more dimensions than those which are given to us. In any case this much is clear, that without scruples one assumes at least the possibility of that which is completely inconceivable and therefore determines something as possibly real without there being anything before one which one so determines. Further, it is clear that the other spaces cannot be thought to persist together with that space which is given to us, because there is no inclusive context in which they are both included. For example, if a six-dimensional space is assumed, it must be the only objective space. Our space then has only subjective existence. But then one would not only have to deny the possibility of representing oneself as objectively existing alongside other conscious beings, but one would also have to deny the very objectivity of number, even though it is only numerical relations which have led to the assumption of a space with more dimensions than are given to us. That is, number, as a sum of unities, of whch *the one is not distinguished from the other*, presupposes the possibility of conceiving a relation of separation without any actual difference between the things which are separated from one another. But without the perception of space it is impossible to possess a conception of such a separation. The concept of number is therefore nothing but a concept of parts of space as separate from one another, independent of all actual difference. It is clear that if it is always possible to think in this connection of a greater or a lesser, then it is also possible to think of a series of numbers in which each number is greater or less, respectively, than the one standing next to it in the series. That number depends upon space appears clearly in the fact that units of time (e.g. in successive notes or movements of a pendulum) are *counted* only through conceptions of their following one another, like a line with sections. Thus time itself leads over to space. Therefore to explain that the perception of space has only subjective reality and to replace the space which is given to us by another space as the objective one, is the same as to deny the objectivity of the foundation upon which objective space is built. However the theory in question would receive its complete elucidation only through the exhibition of the transition of thought which obtains in the aforementioned proof of the possibility of a space with more dimensions than the given. But such an investigation cannot be furnished here.

# THE PHILOSOPHY OF
# AXEL HÄGERSTRÖM[1]

(Born 1868 in Vireda parish, province of Jönköping; became student in Uppsala 1886, doctor of philosophy and docent there in 1893. From 1911–33 had tenure as professor of practical philosophy in Uppsala. Died 1939. For this work Hägerström has furnished the following statement concerning his philosophy.)

## I. THEORY OF KNOWLEDGE

In my books the *Principle of Science I, Reality* (*Das Prinzip der Wissenschaft I, Die Realität*, 1907) and *The Botanist and the Philosopher* (*Botanisten och filosofen*, 1910), which take their departure both positively and negatively from Kant, I have maintained the following basic ideas, although I have not carried them through.

1. The general presupposition for philosophy in modern times (even for Kant), viz. that the only thing which is immediately given to us is our own ideas, is false. In knowledge of my own ideas, the reality given in space and time is presupposed. In this spatio-temporal reality I locate myself and my ideas as real.

2. In every judgment the *reality* of that concerning which one makes a judgment is presupposed. (This is not to say that the existence of that thing is presupposed, but more concerning this directly.) What reality is cannot be determined through anything else. For in its being determined through something else, the *reality* of the thing itself is presupposed. The truth of the judgment is the reality of the thing. But how can one know anything concerning the thing? Reality means the same thing as *determinateness* ('self-identity'). One cannot conceive anything as real unless that thing is *determinate* in a certain way. To conceive a circle and a square as together real, without regarding the one as lying outside the other in space, is impossible. If such a conception were possible, the relation between the two would become indeterminate. The two would coincide. But it is impossible to conceive a circle as a square. This is expressed in the law of contradiction: A cannot be not-A. The law signifies that A and that which is excluded from A cannot be conceived as together real, unless A is determined as falling outside not-

[1] From *Filosofiskt lexikon*, edited by Alf Ahlberg, Stockholm, Natur och Kultur, 1933. The article was written by Hägerström himself.

A in time or space. Or it means also that it is impossible to conceive two realities as existing together, in the first of which A exists *along with* the idea of A, while in the second A exists only as conceived, without placing them in *such* a relation to one another that the first exists only as the content of an idea belonging to the other. The determinateness of reality is presupposed in every conclusion. The necessity of the conclusion signifies that its denial —i.e. more properly, the supposition that its content exists only as conceived—is impossible if one supposes that the content of the premises possesses reality *along with* the idea of those premises. If anyone 'apprehends' that the premises are true while the conclusion is false, he only apparently grasps the objective reality of the premises *along with* the content of the conclusion as something merely conceived. That is, he 'grasps' the indeterminate as real—and thereby contradicts himself. Since the determinateness of reality is itself what is necessary in every proof, naturally *it* itself cannot be derived from something else. But it can be proved that *we presuppose* it in every proof. Now if reality cannot be determined more precisely through anything else, then determinateness, insofar as it belongs to reality, must *be the same* as reality itself.

But this means that the truth of the judgment is the same as the determinateness of the content or its non-contradictoriness. Since in a contradictory 'judgment' it is actually only apparent that something is grasped as real, the judgment as such is true. But what is meant by the statement that it is false that Gustaf Adolph II died in 1633 and true that he died in 1632? There is nothing contradictory or meaningless in either of these judgments. It simply means that the one content of consciousness cannot be apprehended consistently as real unless it is apprehended as conceived, while the other cannot be apprehended consistently except as real *along with* the idea of it. That which is determined as real, on the basis of the particular conditions of experience, cannot be apprehended consistently as real in any other way than as existing along with the idea. For no one can without contradiction conceive himself as something merely conceived. But when one conceives of one's own existence as something alongside the idea of it, then the world of time and space, in which one places oneself, is presupposed as something which has reality along with the idea of it. This is what is called *existence*, which certainly involves reality but also implies in the thing which is real a certain peculiarity in relation to the idea of the thing. When a mistake is corrected through a wider experience, this implies tht something which is conceived as real along with the idea of it, cannot be regarded without contradiction as real, unless it is determined as existing only as the content of that idea in which it has been apprehended in the incorrect way. In this way the content of the idea is determined only more precisely, but it is not for that reason revealed as nothing.

In summary, knowledge is only a non-contradictory apprehension of something as real or as determinate.

3. The sensible relation of exclusion in time and space has nothing to do with logical contradiction. The reality of A is not incompatible with the reality of not-A. The reality of A is itself not limited to the time and the space in which it exists. The very reality of something cannot be limited. The sensible is therefore not self-contradictory on account of the mutual relation of exclusion which belongs to it.

4. But 'reality in itself,' absolute reality, is a self-contradictory idea. Here some particular real thing is supposed to be identical with the concept of reality. Everything else suffers from a lack of reality. But the unreal cannot be real. In all metaphysics—idealistic or materialistic —the problem is incorrectly posed.

## 2. MORAL PHILOSOPHY

My major works are *Critical Points in the Psychology of Value* ('Kritiska punkter i värdepsykologien' in *Festskrift tillägnad E. O. Burman*, 1910); *On the Truth of Moral Propositions* (*Om moraliska föreställningars sanning*, 1911); and *On the Question of the Concept of Objective Law* (*Till frågan om den objektiva rättens begrepp, I. Viljeteorien*, 1917).

Knowledge of value is impossible. For all knowledge is a determination of what is real. But value cannot be a reality alongside the theoretical. For the relation between them would be indeterminate. Thus that which is determined as real, when one regards value and the world of experience as *together* real, lacks determinateness. That is, the apprehension is self-contradictory. The same thing is evident from the fact that good or bad as predicates of objects or actions have meaning for us only insofar as we feel desire or aversion towards or are interested in the thing. But a feeling or an interest cannot possibly be a cognition. The 'value-judgment' is in reality only an expression in the indicative form of a feeling or an interest in connection with the idea of something. This indicative utterance makes it appear that we have before us a real apprehension of a quality of value in the object or the action. Or the 'value-judgment' is an apprehension of an expression of feeling or of will as belonging to the object or the action, which has the significance that it evokes in us a corresponding feeling or will. If this effect does not ensue, it is impossible to conceive such a thing. A moral law, for example, which characterizes certain actions as actions which ought to be done, is nothing but an apprehension of an expression of command (e.g. 'Thou shalt'. 'It is right to', etc.) as belonging to the action. The apprehension of this expression of command operates upon the will by way of suggestion in the direction of performing the action.

## 3. PHILOSOPHY OF LAW

My major works are *Is Objective Law an Expression of Will?* ('Är gällande rätt uttryck av vilja? in *Festskrift tillägnad Vitalis Norström,* 1916); *On the Question of the Concept of Objective Law* (*Till frågan om den objektiva rättens begrepp, I. Viljeteorien,* 1917); *Natural Law in the Science of the Law of Punishment?* ('Naturrätt i straffrättsvetenskapen?' in *Svensk juridisk tidskrift,* 1920); *The Roman Concept of Obligation I* (*Der römische Obligationsbegriff I,* 1927).

Positive law is not a declaration of will from the side of the state, which itself has no will, nor is it an authoritative prescription of each person's rights and duties. It is only a system of rules for the so-called organs of the state—themselves defined in the rules—a system of rules which is actually carried through. The idea of rights in another sense than the advantages which the individual is granted through the system of rules, is an idea of super-sensible powers. And since the super-sensible cannot be conceived without contradiction alongside the sensible, every such idea is false.

The explanation of legal propositions from the consciousness of law is false. For this consciousness is itself controlled by the interest in society or the interest in a class, which are thus ultimately determinative for it.

For the rest see V. Lundstedt '*Scandinavian Theories of Compensation*' ('Nordiska skådestandstheorier' in *Tidskrift for Retsvidenskab,* 1923).

# BIBLIOGRAPHY OF THE PUBLISHED WRITINGS
## OF HÄGERSTRÖM

*Aristoteles etiska grundtankar och deras teoretiska förutsättningar*, Uppsala. Akademiska boktryckeriet, E. Berling, 1893.

'Axel Hägerström', *Filosofiskt lexikon*, ed. Alf Ahlberg, Natur och Kultur, Third edition, 1951.

'Begreppet viljeförklaring på privaträttens område', *Theoria*, Vol. 1, 1935, pp. 32 ff., 121 ff.

*Botanisten och filosofen. Om kunskapsfilosofiens nödvändighet*, Stockholm, Bonnier, 1910.

'Erkenntnistheoretische Voraussetzungen der speziellen Relativitetstheorie Einsteins', *Theoria*, Vol. 12, 1946, pp. 1–68.

*Filosofi och vetenskap*, ed. Martin Fries, Stockholm, Ehlins, 1957.

*Inquiries into the Nature of Law and Morals*, tr. C. D. Broad, Uppsala, Almqvist and Wiksell, 1953.

*Kants Ethik im Verhältnis zu seinen erkenntnistheoretischen Grundgedanken*, Uppsala, Almqvist and Wiksell, 1902.

'Kritiska punkter i värdepsykologien', *Festskrift tillägnad E. O. Burman*, Uppsala, K. W. Appelbergs boktryckeri, 1910, pp. 16–75.

'Lectures on So-called Spiritual Religion', tr. C. D. Broad, *Theoria*, Vol. 14, 1948, pp. 28–67.

*Moralpsykologi*, ed. Martin Fries, Stockholm, Natur och Kultur, 1952.

*Om den moraliska känslan och driften såsom förnuftig i den moderna rationalismens huvudformer*, Uppsala, 1895.

*Om filosofiens betydelse för människan*, Uppsala, Almqvist and Wiksell, 1898.

*Om moraliska föreställningars sanning*, Stockholm, Bonnier, 1911.

*Das Prinzip der Wissenschaft. Eine logisch-erkenntnistheoretische Untersuchung. I. Die Realität*, Uppsala, Almqvist and Wiksell, 1908.

*Rechtsanschauung*, Uppsala, Almqvist and Wiksell, 1942.

*Religionsfilosofi*, ed. Martin Fries, Stockholm, Natur och Kultur, 1949.

*Der römische Obligationsbegriff im Lichte der allgemeinen römische Rechtsanschauung*, Uppsala, Almqvist and Wiksell; Part I, 1927; Part II, 1939.

*Selbstdarstellung* in *Die Philosophie der Gegenwart in Selbstdarstellung*, Vol. 7, Leipzig, Felix Meiner, 1929.

*Socialfilosofiska uppsatser*, ed. Martin Fries, Stockholm, Bonnier, 1939.

*De socialistiska idéernas historia*, ed. Martin Fries, Stockholm, Natur och Kultur, 1946.

*Socialteleologi i Marxismen*, Uppsala, Akademiska boktryckeriet, E. Berling, 1909.

*Stat och rätt. En rättsfilosofisk undersökning*, Uppsala, Almqvist and Wiksell, 1904.

*Till analysen av det empiriska självmedvetandet. En psykologisk och filosofisk undersökning*, Uppsala, E. Berling, 1910.

*Till frågan om den gällande rättens begrepp. I. Viljeteorien*, Uppsala, Almqvist and Wiksell, 1917.

'Über die Gleichungen der speziellen Relativitätstheorie', *Adolf Phalén in Memoriam*, Uppsala, Almqvist and Wiksell, 1937.

'Vergleich zwischen den Kraftvorstellungen der primitiven und der modernen Kulturvölker', *Festskrift tillägnad Arvi Grotenfelt*, Helsingfors, 1933.

# INDEX